SEABROOK'S COMPLETE BATTLE BOOK

⁌ THE LOCHLAINN SEABROOK COLLECTION ⁍

AMERICAN CIVIL WAR
Abraham Lincoln Was a Liberal, Jefferson Davis Was a Conservative: The Missing Key to Understanding the American Civil War
Confederacy 101: Amazing Facts You Never Knew About America's Oldest Political Tradition
Confederate Blood and Treasure: An Interview With Lochlainn Seabrook
Everything You Were Taught About African-Americans and the Civil War is Wrong, Ask a Southerner!
Everything You Were Taught About the Civil War is Wrong, Ask a Southerner!
Give This Book to a Yankee! A Southern Guide to the Civil War For Northerners
Heroes of the Southern Confederacy: The Illustrated Book of Confederate Officials, Soldiers, and Civilians
Lincoln's War: The Real Cause, the Real Winner, the Real Loser
Seabrook's Complete Battle Book: War Between the States, 1861-1865
The Great Yankee Coverup: What the North Doesn't Want You to Know About Lincoln's War!
The Ultimate Civil War Quiz Book: How Much Do You Really Know About America's Most Misunderstood Conflict?
Women in Gray: A Tribute to the Ladies Who Supported the Southern Confederacy

CONFEDERATE MONUMENTS
Confederate Monuments: Why Every American Should Honor Confederate Soldiers and Their Memorials

CONFEDERATE FLAG
Confederate Flag Facts: What Every American Should Know About Dixie's Southern Cross
What the Confederate Flag Means to Me: Americans Speak Out in Defense of Southern Honor, Heritage, and History

SECESSION
All We Ask Is To Be Let Alone: The Southern Secession Fact Book

RECONSTRUCTION
Twelve Years in Hell: Victorian Southerners Debunk the Myth of Reconstruction, 1865-1877

SLAVERY
Everything You Were Taught About American Slavery is Wrong, Ask a Southerner!
Slavery 101: Amazing Facts You Never Knew About America's "Peculiar Institution"
The Bittersweet Bond: Race Relations in the Old South as Described by White and Black Southerners

NATHAN BEDFORD FORREST
A Rebel Born: A Defense of Nathan Bedford Forrest - Confederate General, American Legend (winner of the 2011 Jefferson Davis Historical Gold Medal)
A Rebel Born: The Screenplay (film about N. B. Forrest)
Forrest! 99 Reasons to Love Nathan Bedford Forrest
Give 'Em Hell Boys! The Complete Military Correspondence of Nathan Bedford Forrest
I Rode With Forrest! Confederate Soldiers Who Served With the World's Greatest Cavalry Leader
Nathan Bedford Forrest and African-Americans: Yankee Myth, Confederate Fact
Nathan Bedford Forrest and the Battle of Fort Pillow: Yankee Myth, Confederate Fact
Nathan Bedford Forrest and the Ku Klux Klan: Yankee Myth, Confederate Fact
Nathan Bedford Forrest: Southern Hero, American Patriot - Honoring a Confederate Icon and the Old South
Saddle, Sword, and Gun: A Biography of Nathan Bedford Forrest For Teens
The God of War: Nathan Bedford Forrest As He Was Seen By His Contemporaries
The Quotable Nathan Bedford Forrest: Selections From the Writings and Speeches of the Confederacy's Most Brilliant Cavalryman

QUOTABLE SERIES
The Alexander H. Stephens Reader: Excerpts From the Works of a Confederate Founding Father
The Quotable Alexander H. Stephens: Selections From the Writings and Speeches of the Confederacy's First Vice President
The Quotable Jefferson Davis: Selections From the Writings and Speeches of the Confederacy's First President
The Quotable Nathan Bedford Forrest: Selections From the Writings and Speeches of the Confederacy's Most Brilliant Cavalryman
The Quotable Robert E. Lee: Selections From the Writings and Speeches of the South's Most Beloved Civil War General
The Quotable Stonewall Jackson: Selections From the Writings and Speeches of the South's Most Famous General
The Unquotable Abraham Lincoln: The President's Quotes They Don't Want You To Know!

CIVIL WAR BATTLES
Encyclopedia of the Battle of Franklin - A Comprehensive Guide to the Conflict that Changed the Civil War
Nathan Bedford Forrest and the Battle of Fort Pillow: Yankee Myth, Confederate Fact
Seabrook's Complete Battle Book: War Between the States, 1861-1865
The Battle of Franklin: Recollections of Confederate and Union Soldiers
The Battle of Nashville: Recollections of Confederate and Union Soldiers
The Battle of Spring Hill: Recollections of Confederate and Union Soldiers

CONSTITUTIONAL HISTORY
America's Three Constitutions: Complete Texts of the Articles of Confederation, Constitution of the United States of America, and Constitution of the Confederate States of America
The Articles of Confederation Explained: A Clause-by-Clause Study of America's First Constitution
The Constitution of the Confederate States of America Explained: A Clause-by-Clause Study of the South's Magna Carta

CHILDREN
Honest Jeff and Dishonest Abe: A Southern Children's Guide to the Civil War
Saddle, Sword, and Gun: A Biography of Nathan Bedford Forrest For Teens

VICTORIAN CONFEDERATE LITERATURE
I, Confederate: Why Dixie Seceded and Fought in the Words of Southern Soldiers
Rise Up and Call Them Blessed: Victorian Tributes to the Confederate Soldier, 1861-1901
Support Your Local Confederate: Wit and Humor in the Southern Confederacy
The Bittersweet Bond: Race Relations in the Old South as Described by White and Black Southerners
The God of War: Nathan Bedford Forrest As He Was Seen By His Contemporaries
The Old Rebel: Robert E. Lee As He Was Seen By His Contemporaries
Victorian Confederate Poetry: The Southern Cause in Verse, 1861-1901

ABRAHAM LINCOLN
Abraham Lincoln: The Southern View - Demythologizing America's Sixteenth President
Lincolnology: The Real Abraham Lincoln Revealed in His Own Words - A Study of Lincoln's Suppressed, Misinterpreted, and Forgotten Writings and Speeches
Lincoln's War: The Real Cause, the Real Winner, the Real Loser
The Great Impersonator! 99 Reasons to Dislike Abraham Lincoln
The Unholy Crusade: Lincoln's Legacy of Destruction in the American South
The Unquotable Abraham Lincoln: The President's Quotes They Don't Want You To Know!

NATURAL HISTORY
North America's Amazing Mammals: An Encyclopedia for the Whole Family
The Concise Book of Owls: A Guide to Nature's Most Mysterious Birds
The Concise Book of Tigers: A Guide to Nature's Most Remarkable Cats

PARANORMAL
Carnton Plantation Ghost Stories: True Tales of the Unexplained from Tennessee's Most Haunted Civil War House!
UFOs and Aliens: The Complete Guidebook

FAMILY HISTORIES
The Blakeneys: An Etymological, Ethnological, and Genealogical Study - Uncovering the Mysterious Origins of the Blakeney Family and Name
The Caudills: An Etymological, Ethnological, and Genealogical Study - Exploring the Name and National Origins of a European-American Family
The McGavocks of Carnton Plantation: A Southern History - Celebrating One of Dixie's Most Noble Confederate Families and Their Tennessee Home

MIND, BODY, SPIRIT
Autobiography of a Non-Yogi: A Scientist's Journey From Hinduism to Christianity (Dr. Amitava Dasgupta, with Lochlainn Seabrook)
Britannia Rules: Goddess-Worship in Ancient Anglo-Celtic Society - An Academic Look at the United Kingdom's Matricentric Spiritual Past
Christ Is All and In All: Rediscovering Your Divine Nature and the Kingdom Within
Christmas Before Christianity: How the Birthday of the "Sun" Became the Birthday of the "Son"
Jesus and the Gospel of Q: Christ's Pre-Christian Teachings As Recorded in the New Testament
Jesus and the Law of Attraction: The Bible-Based Guide to Creating Perfect Health, Wealth, and Happiness Following Christ's Simple Formula
Seabrook's Bible Dictionary of Traditional and Mystical Christian Doctrines
Sea Raven Press Blank Page Journal: For Reflections, Notes, and Sketches
The Bible and the Law of Attraction: 99 Teachings of Jesus, the Apostles, and the Prophets
The Book of Kelle: An Introduction to Goddess-Worship and the Great Celtic Mother-Goddess Kelle, Original Blessed Lady of Ireland
The Goddess Dictionary of Words and Phrases: Introducing a New Core Vocabulary for the Women's Spirituality Movement
The Martian Anomalies: A Photographic Search for Intelligent Life on Mars
Victorian Hernia Cures: Nonsurgical Self-Treatment of Inguinal Hernia
Vintage Southern Cookbook: 2,000 Delicious Dishes From Dixie

WOMEN
Aphrodite's Trade: The Hidden History of Prostitution Unveiled
Princess Diana: Modern Day Moon-Goddess - A Psychoanalytical and Mythological Look at Diana Spencer's Life, Marriage, and Death (with Dr. Jane Goldberg)
Women in Gray: A Tribute to the Ladies Who Supported the Southern Confederacy

REPRINTS
A Short History of the Confederate States of America (author Jefferson Davis; editor Lochlainn Seabrook)
Prison Life of Jefferson Davis (author John J. Craven; editor Lochlainn Seabrook)
Life of Beethoven (author Ludwig Nohl; editor Lochlainn Seabrook)
The New Revelation (author Arthur Conan Doyle; editor Lochlainn Seabrook)
The Rise and Fall of the Confederate Government (author Jefferson Davis; editor Lochlainn Seabrook)

Lochlainn Seabrook does not author books for fame and glory, but for the love of writing and sharing his knowledge.

SeaRavenPress.com

SEABROOK'S COMPLETE BATTLE BOOK

War Between the States, 1861-1865

CONCEIVED, COLLECTED, EDITED, ARRANGED, & DESIGNED WITH AN INTRODUCTION BY
"THE VOICE OF THE TRADITIONAL SOUTH," HISTORIAN COLONEL

LOCHLAINN SEABROOK

SCV MEMBER AND JEFFERSON DAVIS HISTORICAL GOLD MEDAL WINNER

Diligently Researched and Generously Illustrated
by the Author for the Elucidation of the Reader

2023

Sea Raven Press, Park County, Wyoming, USA

SEABROOK'S COMPLETE BATTLE BOOK

Published by
Sea Raven Press, Cassidy Ravensdale, President
Park County, Wyoming, USA
SeaRavenPress.com

Copyright © all text and illustrations Lochlainn Seabrook 2023
in accordance with U.S. and international copyright laws and regulations, as stated and protected under the Berne Union for the Protection of Literary and Artistic Property (Berne Convention), and the Universal Copyright Convention (the UCC). All rights reserved under the Pan-American and International Copyright Conventions.

PRINTING HISTORY
1st SRP paperback edition, 1st printing, September 2023 • ISBN: 978-1-955351-30-0
1st SRP hardcover edition, 1st printing, September 2023 • ISBN: 978-1-955351-31-7

ISBN: 978-1-955351-30-0 (paperback)
Library of Congress Control Number: 2023945166

This work is the copyrighted intellectual property of Lochlainn Seabrook and has been registered with the Copyright Office at the Library of Congress in Washington, D.C., USA. No part of this work (including text, covers, drawings, photos, illustrations, maps, images, diagrams, etc.), in whole or in part, may be used, reproduced, stored in a retrieval system, or transmitted, in any form or by any means now known or hereafter invented, without written permission from the publisher. The sale, duplication, hire, lending, copying, digitalization, or reproduction of this material, in any manner or form whatsoever, is also prohibited, and is a violation of federal, civil, and digital copyright law, which provides severe civil and criminal penalties for any violations.

Seabrook's Complete Battle Book: War Between the States, 1861-1865, by Lochlainn Seabrook. Includes an introduction, illustrations, artwork, index, endnotes, and bibliography.

ARTWORK
Front and back cover design and art, book design, layout, font selection, and interior art by Lochlainn Seabrook.
All images, image captions, graphic design, and graphic art copyright © Lochlainn Seabrook.
All images selected, placed, manipulated, cleaned, colored, tinted, and/or created by Lochlainn Seabrook.
Cover design by Lochlainn Seabrook copyright © 2023
Cover image: Third Battle of Winchester, Sept. 19, 1864, lithograph by Louis Kurz and Alexander Allison, 1893

All persons who approve of the authority and principles of Colonel Lochlainn Seabrook's literary work, and realize its benefits as a means of reeducating the world about facts left out of mainstream books, are hereby requested to avidly recommend his titles to others and to vigorously cooperate in extending their reach, scope, and influence around the globe.

The views documented in this book concerning the War for Southern Independence are those of the publisher.
WRITTEN, DESIGNED, PUBLISHED, PRINTED, & MANUFACTURED IN THE UNITED STATES OF AMERICA

Dedication

To the Southern Victorian scribblers, note-takers, secretaries, bookkeepers, reporters, journalists, clerks, registrars, administrators, copyists, amanuenses, aids-de-camp, soldiers, officers, archivists, historians, and scholars who helped record and preserve the often dull but all-important statistics of the War Between the States for future generations.

Epigraph

THE MEN WHO COMPOSED THE CONFEDERATE ARMIES

Our artillery, though inferior in guns, ammunition and equipment, was always a match for that to which it was opposed; the men who rode with Turner Ashby, Wade Hampton and Fitz Lee, or "followed the feather" of "Jeb" Stuart, though greatly inferior in mount and equipment to the Federal cavalry, were masters of the situation on any fair field; and the army of Northern Virginia as a whole, was, in gallant dash, steady resistance, patient endurance, heroic courage, and all other qualities which go to make up the best soldiers, not only unrivaled by the army of the Potomac, but the equals of any other army that ever marched under any flag, or fought for any cause.

And I give equal honor to the other armies of the Confederacy. The men who defended Fort Sumter and Charleston and Savannah and Mobile and Fort Fisher; who fought under Albert Sidney Johnston, Beauregard, Bragg, Joseph E. Johnston, Hood, Stephen D. Lee, Pemberton, Van Dorn, Price, Dick Taylor, Kirby Smith, Forrest, Joe Wheeler, John Morgan, and others, were the peers of those who followed Lee and Stonewall Jackson and deserve equal praise.

The world never saw better soldiers than those who composed the Confederate armies. The world never saw an army composed of more superb material, intellectually, physically and morally—in all that constitutes what we call morale in an army—than the armies of the Confederate States of America.

J. William Jones, D.D., 1899

CONTENTS

Notes to the Reader, by Lochlainn Seabrook ❧ page 13
Introduction, by Lochlainn Seabrook ❧ page 21

CHRONOLOGICAL LIST OF ENGAGEMENTS
- BY STATE, COUNTRY, & TERRITORY -

CHAPTER 1: ALABAMA ❧ page 33
CHAPTER 2: ARIZONA ❧ page 39
CHAPTER 3: ARKANSAS ❧ page 41
CHAPTER 4: COLORADO ❧ page 51
CHAPTER 5: COLORADO TERRITORY ❧ page 53
CHAPTER 6: DAKOTA ❧ page 55
CHAPTER 7: DAKOTA TERRITORY ❧ page 57
CHAPTER 8: FLORIDA ❧ page 59
CHAPTER 9: GEORGIA ❧ page 63
CHAPTER 10: IDAHO ❧ page 71
CHAPTER 11: IDAHO TERRITORY ❧ page 73
CHAPTER 12: ILLINOIS ❧ page 75
CHAPTER 13: INDIANA ❧ page 77
CHAPTER 14: INDIAN TERRITORY ❧ page 79
CHAPTER 15: IOWA ❧ page 81
CHAPTER 16: KANSAS ❧ page 83
CHAPTER 17: KENTUCKY ❧ page 85
CHAPTER 18: LOUISIANA ❧ page 95
CHAPTER 19: MAINE ❧ page 105
CHAPTER 20: MARYLAND ❧ page 107

CHAPTER 21: MEXICO ❧ page 111
CHAPTER 22: MINNESOTA ❧ page 113
CHAPTER 23: MISSISSIPPI ❧ page 115
CHAPTER 24: MISSOURI ❧ page 127
CHAPTER 25: MONTANA TERRITORY ❧ page 143
CHAPTER 26: NEBRASKA ❧ page 145
CHAPTER 27: NEBRASKA TERRITORY ❧ page 147
CHAPTER 28: NEW MEXICO ❧ page 149
CHAPTER 29: NORTH CAROLINA ❧ page 151
CHAPTER 30: OHIO ❧ page 157
CHAPTER 31: PENNSYLVANIA ❧ page 159
CHAPTER 32: SOUTH CAROLINA ❧ page 161
CHAPTER 33: TENNESSEE ❧ page 167
CHAPTER 34: TEXAS ❧ page 187
CHAPTER 35: VERMONT ❧ page 189
CHAPTER 36: VIRGINIA ❧ page 191
CHAPTER 37: WASHINGTON, D.C. ❧ page 219
CHAPTER 38: WEST VIRGINIA ❧ page 221
CHAPTER 39: MISCELLANEOUS ❧ page 231

Notes ❧ page 233
Bibliography ❧ page 235
Index ❧ page 241
Meet the Author ❧ page 299
Learn More ❧ page 301

"Books invite all; they constrain none."
Hartley Burr Alexander (1873-1939)

NOTES TO THE READER

"NOTHING IN THE PAST IS DEAD TO THE MAN WHO WOULD
LEARN HOW THE PRESENT CAME TO BE WHAT IT IS."

WILLIAM STUBBS, VICTORIAN ENGLISH HISTORIAN

THE TWO MAIN POLITICAL PARTIES IN 1860

☞ In any study of America's antebellum, bellum, and postbellum periods, it is vitally important to understand that in 1860 the two major political parties—the Democrats and the newly formed Republicans—were the opposite of what they are today. In other words, the Democrats of the mid 19th Century (founded by what we now call "right-wingers" or "traditionalists")[1] were Conservatives, akin to the Republican Party of today, while the Republicans of the mid 19th Century (founded by what we now call "left-wingers" or "progressives")[2] were Liberals, akin to the Democratic Party of today.[3]

The author's cousin, Confederate Vice President and Democrat Alexander H. Stephens: a Southern Conservative.

Thus the Confederacy's Democratic president, Jefferson Davis, was a Conservative (with libertarian leanings); the Union's Republican president, Abraham Lincoln, was a Liberal (with socialistic leanings).[4] This is why, in the mid 1800s, the conservative wing of the Democratic Party was known as "the States' Rights Party,"[5] as opposed to the Republican Party, which was widely known to have been created in 1854 by "progressive elements."[6] Indeed, the party's first candidate was radical (that is, socialist), and later Union general, John C. Frémont. As socialist Eugene V. Debs asserted: "Lincoln would not join today's Republican Party any more than Thomas Jefferson would become a member of today's Democratic Party,"[7] correctly adding: "The Republican Party was once Red."[8]

Hence, the Democrats of the Civil War period referred to themselves as "conservatives," "confederates," "anti-centralists," or "constitutionalists" (the latter because they favored strict adherence to the original Constitution—which tacitly guaranteed states' rights—as created by the Founding Fathers). The Civil War Republicans, on the other hand, called themselves "liberals," "nationalists," "centralists," or "consolidationists" (the latter three because their goal was to nationalize the central government and consolidate political power in Washington, D.C.).[9]

More evidence comes from a common phrase used at the time, "states' rights Democrats," a term that could have only applied to Conservatives, since then, as today, Liberals are squarely against states' rights (unless, in hypocritical fashion, they find that states' rights benefit their agenda in some way).[10]

In 1889 Right-wing Democrat President Davis himself, who referred to the 1860 Democrats as "the conservative power of the country,"[11] described the political situation at the time in the following manner:

> . . . the names adopted by political parties in the United States have not always been strictly significant of their principles. In general terms it may be said that the old Federal party (Liberal) inclined to nationalism (then a term for big government), or consolidation (that is, consolidation of power in the Federal government), and that the Whig party (liberalistic), which succeeded it, although not identical with it, was favorable, in the main, to a strong Central Government (liberalism, socialism, communism). On the other hand, its opponent, the Republican (Conservative), afterward known as the Democratic party, was dominated by the idea of the sovereignty of the States and the federal or confederate character of the Union (Americanism, traditionalism, conservatism). Although other elements have entered into its organization at different periods, this has been its vital, cardinal, and abiding principle.[12]

We will note here that, while Davis would not live to witness the transition, a mere six years after he penned these words, during the 1896 U.S. presidential election, the two major parties would reverse positions, the Democratic Party adopting a Left-wing platform, the Republican Party adopting a Right-wing platform—the status they hold to this day.

The War for Southern Independence pitted Northern Liberals (then the Republican Party) against Southern Conservatives (then the Democratic Party).

Since this idea is new to most of my readers, let us further demystify it by viewing it from the perspective of the American Revolutionary War. If Davis and his Conservative Southern constituents (the Democrats of 1861) had been alive in 1775, they would have sided with George Washington and his followers, the independence-loving American colonists (known as "patriots" or "rebels")—who sought to secede from the tyrannical government of Great Britain; if Lincoln and his Liberal Northern constituents (the Republicans of 1861) had been alive at that time, they would have sided with King George III and the English monarchy, who sought to maintain the American colonies as possessions of the British Empire. It is due to this very comparison that we Southerners often refer to our secession from the U.S. as the Second Declaration of Independence, and the "Civil War" as the Second American Revolutionary War.

Without a basic understanding of these facts, the American "Civil War" will forever remain incomprehensible. For a full discussion of this all-important topic see my book, *Abraham Lincoln Was a Liberal, Jefferson Davis Was a Conservative: The Missing Key to Understanding the American Civil War*.

THE TERM "CIVIL WAR"
☛ As I heartily dislike the phrase "Civil War," its use throughout this book (as well as in my other works) is worthy of explanation.

Our entire modern literary system refers to the conflict of 1861 using the Northern term the "Civil War," whether we in the South like it or not. Of course, this is purposeful, for America's book industry, which determines everything

The American "Civil War" was not a true civil war as Webster defines it: "A conflict between opposing groups of citizens of the *same* country." It was a fight between two individual countries; or to be more specific, two separate and constitutionally formed confederacies: the C.S.A. and the U.S.A.

from how books are categorized and designed to how they are marketed and sold, is almost solely controlled by Liberals, socialists, globalists, collectivists, and communists, individuals who will do anything to prevent the truth about Lincoln's War from coming out. An important aspect of this wholesale revisionism of American history is the use of the phrase "Civil War," which

Confederate General Nathan Bedford Forrest, just one of many Southern officials who referred to the conflict of 1861 as the "Civil War."

Yankee Liberals thrust into the public forum even as big government Leftwinger Lincoln was diabolically tricking the Conservative South into firing the first shot at the First Battle of Fort Sumter in April 1861.[13]

The progressives' blatant American "Civil War" coverup continues to this day, one of the more overt results which pertains to how books are coded, indexed, and identified.[14] Thus, as all book searches by readers, libraries, and retail outlets are now performed online, and as all bookstores categorize works from or about this period under the heading "Civil War," honest book publishers and authors who deal with this particular topic have little choice but to use this deceptive term. If I were to refuse to use it, as some of my Southern colleagues have suggested, few people would ever find or read my books.

Add to this the fact that scarcely any non-Southerners have ever heard of the names we in the South use for the conflict, such as "the War for Southern Independence," "the War Against Northern Aggression," "Lincoln's War," or my personal preference, because it is the most accurate: "the War for the Constitution." It only makes sense then to use the term "Civil War" in most commercial situations, historically inaccurate though it is.

We should also bear in mind that while today educated persons, particularly educated Southerners, all share an abhorrence for the phrase "Civil War," it was not always so. Confederates who lived through and even fought in the conflict regularly used the term throughout the 1860s, and even long after. Among them were Confederate generals such as Nathan Bedford Forrest, Richard Taylor, and Joseph E. Johnston, not to mention the Confederacy's vice president, Alexander H. Stephens.

In 1895 Confederate General James Longstreet wrote about his military experiences in a work subtitled, *Memoirs of the Civil War in America*, while in 1903 Confederate General John Brown Gordon, the first commander-in-chief of the United Confederate Veterans, entitled his autobiography, *Reminiscences of the Civil War*. Even the Confederacy's highest leader, President Jefferson Davis, used the term "Civil War,"[15] and in one case at least, as late as 1881—the year he wrote his brilliant exposition, *The Rise and Fall of the Confederate Government* (see the Sea Raven Press reprint of this book, of which I am the editor, collector, technician, and designer).[16]

Authors writing for *Confederate Veteran* magazine sometimes used the phrase well into the early 1900s,[17] and in 1898, at the Eighth Annual Meeting and Reunion of the United Confederate Veterans (the forerunner of today's Sons of Confederate Veterans), the following resolution was proposed: that from then on the Great War of 1861 was to be designated "the Civil War Between the States."[18]

A WORD ON EARLY AMERICAN MATERIAL

☛ In order to preserve the authentic historicity of the antebellum, bellum, and postbellum periods, I have retained the original spellings, formatting, and punctuation of the early Americans I quote. These include such items as British-English spellings, long-running paragraphs, obsolete words, and various literary devices peculiar to the time. However, I have corrected misspelled names to prevent confusion, and also *where possible*, inaccurate dates and locations (the inevitable result of aging faulty memories). Bracketed words are my additions and clarifications (added mainly for my new, foreign, and young readers), while italicized words are (where indicated) my emphasis.

Union General August von Willich: Typically labeled a "radical" in mainstream history books, Willich was actually a card-carrying communist who led a revolutionary workers' party, studiously followed the teachings of Karl Marx, and participated in the failed European socialist revolution of 1848—all before joining Lincoln's army in 1861.

19TH-CENTURY CODE WORDS

☛ An early American *Southern* abolitionist was someone who simply desired the end of slavery. *Northern* abolitionists, however, were something quite different altogether: they identified themselves with socialism and communism—the modern forms which were developed in the 1840s by German revolutionary Karl Marx. Also, as noted above, our modern political party names have different meanings than those of the mid 1800s. Hence, one must bear the following in mind when reading 19th-Century literature:

1. "Abolitionist" (Northern): A 19th-Century Left-wing euphemism for a socialist or communist.
2. "Radical" (Northern): Also a 19th-Century Left-wing euphemism for a socialist or communist.
3. "Republican": Between 1854 and 1896 the Republicans were the major Left-wing or Liberal party of that era.
4. "Democrat": Between 1828 and 1896, the Democrats were the major Right-wing or Conservative party of that era.

For more information on items 1 and 2 above, see my introduction in my book *The Bittersweet Bond: Race Relations in the Old South As Described by White and Black Southerners.*

For more information on items 3 and 4 above, see my books *Abraham Lincoln Was a Liberal, Jefferson Davis Was a Conservative: The Missing Key to Understanding the American Civil War,* and *Lincoln's War: The Real Cause, the Real Winner, the Real Loser.*

PRESENTISM

☛ As a historian I view *presentism* (judging the past according to present day mores and customs) as the enemy of authentic history. And this is precisely why the Left employs it in its ongoing war against traditional American, conservative, and Christian values. By looking at history through the lens of modern day beliefs—and, just as heinous, fabricating obviously fake history based on emotion, opinion, and political ideology—they are able to distort, revise, and reshape the past into a false narrative that fits their ideological agenda: the liberalization *and* Northernization of America, the enlargement and further centralization of the national government, and total control of American political, economic, educational, and social power, the same plan that Lincoln championed.[19]

Judging our ancestors by our own standards is dishonest, unfair, unjust, misleading, and unethical.

This book rejects presentism and replaces it with what I call *historicalism*: judging our ancestors based on the values of their own time.

To get the most from this work the reader is invited to reject presentism as well. In this way—along with casting aside preconceived notions and the fake history churned out by our Left-wing education system—the truth in this work will be most readily ascertained and absorbed; truth that has been rigorously researched and forensically uncovered by myself using the scientific method. In 1901 Confederate Colonel Bennett H. Young noted:

> History is valuable only as it is true. Opinions concerning acts are not history; acts themselves alone are historic.[20]

CONTINUE YOUR SOUTHERN HISTORY EDUCATION

☛ Lincoln's War on the Constitution and the American people can never be fully understood without a thorough knowledge of the South's perspective. As this book is only meant to be a brief introductory guide to these topics, one cannot hope to learn the complete story here. For those who are interested in additional material from Dixie's viewpoint, please see my comprehensive histories listed on pages 2 and 3. You are either for or against the Truth. There is not and can never be true neutrality on this subject, which is why there is no such thing as a purely "neutral" book on the War Between the States—despite the claims of many pro-North partisans. Thus in the year 1900, former Confederate General John Brown Gordon wrote:

> Neutrality has no place in masterful minds nor in heroic hearts. Neutrality has never yet developed a great character nor characterized a great people nor written one sparkling page in human history.[21]

FINAL THOUGHTS: HOW TO HONOR BOTH OUR SOUTHERN & OUR AMERICAN HERITAGE

☛ To all Americans: It is time to resurrect the South's true history. It is time to allow the authentic chronicle of past events to be told accurately and honestly. It is time to disseminate this knowledge far and wide, guilelessly and decisively. It is time to shine the Light of Truth into the dark corners of ignorance, malice, divisiveness, and deceit fomented by the gaslighting enemies of the South.[22] Then and only then do we truly honor our gallant Confederate ancestors, do justice to their names, military service, and memories, and confer upon them the respect and reverence so they richly deserve as American patriots.

LOCHLAINN SEABROOK

Keep Your Body, Mind, & Spirit Vibrating at Their Highest Level

YOU CAN DO SO BY READING THE BOOKS OF

SEA RAVEN PRESS

There is nothing that will so perfectly keep your body, mind, and spirit in a healthy condition as to think wisely and positively. Hence you should not only read this book, but also the other books that we offer. They will quicken your physical, mental, and spiritual vibrations, enabling you to maintain a position in society as a healthy erudite person.

KEEP YOURSELF WELL-INFORMED!

The well-informed person is always at the head of the procession, while the ignorant, the lazy, and the unthoughtful hang onto the rear. If you are a Spiritual man or woman, do yourself a great favor: read Sea Raven Press books and stay well posted on the Truth. It is almost criminal for one to remain in ignorance while the opportunity to gain knowledge is open to all at a nominal price.

We invite you to visit our Webstore for a wide selection of wholesome, family-friendly, well-researched, educational books for all ages. You will be glad you did!

Unique Books & Gifts for the Whole Family!

SeaRavenPress.com

LochlainnSeabrook.com
TheBestCivilWarBookEver.com
AmbianceGoneWild.com

INTRODUCTION

DEFINING MY BOOK

THIS BOOK IS A COLLECTION of the military conflicts that occurred during the War for the Constitution, more generally known as the War Between the States, or by Northern propagandists as the "Civil War." In other words, this is an in-depth catalog of statistics, one that includes a complete list of the engagements that took place between the C.S.A. and the U.S.A. in the years 1861, 1862, 1863, 1864, and 1865.

Note that I use the word "complete" here, and in my title, reservedly, as no list could ever include every single conflict for the simple fact that not every one is known, nor was every conflict recorded. We also have the problem of memories, which are subjective and imperfect. Add to this mixture the art of writing, which is just that, and which is thus an inherently flawed method of chronicling history.

What this all means, in essence, is that no two lists will ever agree on all points: my list will include engagements missing from other lists, while other lists will include engagements that are missing from mine. Some of my names and dates will also differ from others.

First Battle of Manassas.

The unknowable truth will always lie somewhere in between. This is simply a fact of history, for true history is seldom a single black and white scene (as the fact-hating political Left paints it), but rather a highly nuanced panorama of varying shades of gray that cover a wide spectrum of knowledge, facts, recollections, and opinions.

IMPORTANT PERSPECTIVE
Being a 17th-generation Southerner, a proud descendant of Confederate soldiers, and a devout member of the Sons of Confederate Veterans, naturally *this work is written from the Southern point of view*, and more specifically from a Confederate outlook.

Thus, when the description of an engagement reads, for example: "Skirmish with Indians at," it actually means "Confederate forces skirmish with Indians at." When a description reads "action on the road to" it actually means "Confederate forces met up with Union forces on the road to." When a description reads "combat at" it actually means "Confederate forces engaged in combat with Yankee forces at."

In every case, in every entry, in every statement, in every summary listed in this book, I am always referring to the event from the Southern or Confederate perspective.

PRIMARY SOURCES
The scaffolding for my battle catalog was the 12-volume work *Confederate Military History*, penned by "distinguished men of the South," and edited by Confederate General Clement A. Evans. As such, the individual or individuals behind the specific material I used from the CMH are unknown and thus not identifiable by name. I can credit only the tome itself. I also depended heavily on the U.S. government's massive 158-volume compilation popularly known as the "Official Records," which is indispensable in establishing the truth that lies buried beneath approved "Civil War" histories (see ORA and ORN in my bibliography).

Battle of Frayser's Farm.

An important secondary source was the U.S. National Park Service, which though pro-Union—and thus, in my opinion, not always factually reliable (especially when it comes to biographical and political "Civil War" material)—I have found to be fairly accurate when it comes to the science of battle statistics. I also tapped into my extensive personal library, a majority of volumes which are related to both Lincoln's War and American history. From this resource alone I was able to uncover thousands of salient facts related to the topic of this book.

Battle of Leesburg.

Lastly, I must make mention of one other vital source: my own books (*A Rebel Born* was particularly helpful). My literary works are the products of decades of study, thousands of hours of research, countless personal experiences, and extensive travels across the U.S., not to mention my time as a "Civil War" docent at a historic Confederate plantation house in the Volunteer State. Thus to this source list must be added firsthand knowledge, for I have not only visited, but have actually lived in or near many of the cities, towns, and natural features mentioned in this book; places quite familiar to me, as I have studied, explored, discussed, lectured on, written about, and photographed them in minute detail over the years.

VICTORIAN MILITARY TERMINOLOGY, ERRORS, & CORRECTIONS

Our Confederate ancestors used many different words to describe their violent military encounters with Yankees, such as battle, siege, engagement, skirmish, affair, action, combat, demonstration, and attack. As these words are somewhat subjective, it is not always clear what the originally intended meaning was. Even a casual perusal of the material in this book reveals that the manner in which Confederate veterans and officials viewed their own military experiences can and often do differ from how we view them today.

For example, while we now list the conflict that took place in Baldwin County, Alabama, between March 27 and April 8, 1865, as the Battle of Spanish Fort, those who fought in it described it as the "siege of Spanish Fort." What we now call the Battle of Lexington, they labeled a "skirmish." What we now call the Battle of Fort Pillow they referred to as the "capture of Fort Pillow." What we now know as the Battle of Spring Hill was originally called an "engagement at Spring Hill." The major conflicts we today recognize as the Battle of Brice's Cross-Roads, the Battle of Galveston, and the Battle of Spotsylvania Court House were not even mentioned in the 19-Century Confederate works I studied, and so on, *ad infinitum.*

Moreover, a number of conflicts have two different names (sometimes as many as five, six, or even more), namely Southern or Confederate names and Northern or Yankee names, not to mention local and colloquial names that were unknown one town over. (Note that Southerners tended to emphasize and choose battle names related to terrain, while Northerners were inclined to emphasize and choose battle names related to water.) This maddingly perplexing myriad of battle names often comes tied up with a multitude of curious and sometimes incongruous nicknames that have accumulated over the years, only adding to the disorder, with some separate and unrelated battles (which took place in different states) sharing the same name *and* a host of various spellings of the same words.

Battle of Mechanicsville.

Adding to this lingual chaos is the curious if not bizarre fact that the "distinguished men of the South" who compiled many of the conflicts I cite, often used *Yankee* battle names instead of *Confederate* battle names—the latter which would have been expected. (I have corrected this eccentricity whenever possible.)

To avoid confounding my readers with these wild discrepancies and oddities, I have included familiar modern battle names and both Confederate and Union battle names, along with spelling variations, when known. In addition, on some occasions, when the historical disarray was so great as to be unresolvable, I found it necessary to create my own battle names—if for no other reason than to maintain order for myself and render the data intelligible to my readers.

Finally, due to the sectional confusion over battle names, dates, and locations that already existed during and shortly after the War (when much of the war history was written), errors were copied from book to book by both early Southern and Northern historians.

Inevitably, despite my best efforts to track them down, some of these mistakes will have crept into my book. *Caveat lector.*

To make my modern book, which is comprised mainly of 150 year old stats, more understandable, let us take a brief look at the customary military definitions of the words used by Victorian Southerners when describing military actions (alphabetized):

- Action: An initial effort meant to bring about a result.
- Affair: A somewhat casual encounter, with little or no bloodshed.
- Attack: An aggressive action using physical force.
- Battle: A usually large and important encounter between armies.
- Combat: Active fighting between military groups.
- Demonstration: A show of armed force intended to intimidate.
- Engagement: A hostile encounter between armies.
- Siege: A blockade or persistent attack meant to force surrender.
- Skirmish: A minor, light, or brief fight.

VICTORIAN BATTLE DATES
Along with differences in military terms, the dates used by 19th-Century Southern historians also sometimes conflict with ours. For instance, today we date the Battle of Stone's River from December 31, 1862, to January 2, 1863. However, Confederates dated it from December 31, 1862, to January 3, 1863, a difference of one day—quite significant when it comes to establishing historical facts. Also, instead of viewing the Battle of Stone's River and the Battle of Murfreesboro as one and the same, as we now do, Victorian Southerners considered them separate conflicts, listing the former as occurring singly on December 31, 1862. Endless such examples could be given.

Battle of Belmont.

BATTLE DESIGNATIONS
While on this topic, we 21st-century historians divide the major conflicts at Murfreesboro into two battles: the First Battle of Murfreesboro, July 13, 1862, and the Second Battle of

Battle of Fort Jackson and Fort St. Philip.

Murfreesboro, December 31, 1862, to January 2, 1863. Confederate veterans, however, did not consider the former engagement a battle, but merely described it as "action at Murfreesboro." Another example: What we call the Battle of Fort Pulaski (April 10-11, 1862) was not even mentioned by 19th-Century Southerners. Again, dozens if not hundreds of such illustrations could be provided.

These problems, along with a host of other incongruities and deviations between 19th-Century and 21st-Century customs, views, and descriptions, mean that one must always err on the conservative side when approaching this subject.

BATTLES BY THE NUMBERS
Two stats of particular interest:

- The first or earliest engagement in my battle catalog occurred on April 12-14, 1861: the First Battle of Fort Sumter, South Carolina.
- The last or latest engagement in my battle catalog took place on September 5 and 8, 1865, at the Powder River, Montana.

Besides the fact that "top ten" lists are amusing, they can also provide serious value when it comes to research. Since this is indeed a reference work, below I have compiled a cursory list of the states, countries, and territories itemized in this book by the (very roughly) estimated number of engagements that took place within their borders—from the highest number to the lowest.

1: Virginia—approximately 1,200 engagements.
2: Tennessee—approximately 900 engagements.
3: Missouri—approximately 625 engagements.
4: Arkansas—approximately 460 engagements.
5: Mississippi—approximately 400 engagements.
6: West Virginia—approximately 340 engagements.

7: Louisiana—approximately 325 engagements.
8: Kentucky—approximately 320 engagements.
9: Alabama—approximately 260 engagements.
10: Georgia—approximately 250 engagements.
11: North Carolina—approximately 225 engagements.
12: South Carolina—approximately 200 engagements.
13: Maryland—approximately 140 engagements.
14: Florida—approximately 75 engagements.
15: Kansas—approximately 40 engagements.
16: Texas—approximately 40 engagements.
17: New Mexico—approximately 35 engagements.
18: Indian Territory—approximately 30 engagements.
19: Pennsylvania—approximately 30 engagements.
20: Colorado Territory—approximately 18 engagements.
21: Dakota Territory—approximately 17 engagements.
22: Ohio—approximately 15 engagements.
23: Dakota—approximately 8 engagements.
24: Minnesota—approximately 8 engagements.
25: Nebraska Territory—approximately 5 engagements.
26: Colorado—approximately 4 engagements.
27: Arizona—approximately 3 engagements.
28: Indiana—approximately 3 engagements.
29: Nebraska—approximately 3 engagements.
30: Mexico—approximately 2 engagements.
31: Montana Territory—approximately 2 engagements.
32: Washington, D.C.—approximately 1 engagement.
33. Iowa—approximately 1 engagement.
34. Maine—approximately 1 engagement.
35. Vermont—approximately 1 engagement.
36: Idaho—approximately 1 engagement.
37: Idaho Territory—approximately 1 engagement.
38: Illinois—approximately 1 engagement.[23]
Total: approximately 6,000 known and identified engagements.

MAINSTREAM HISTORY IS FAKE HISTORY
Let us note here that nearly all of the states in the first half of this list, that is, those with the most engagements, are Southern states. Nearly all of those in the second half, those with the least amount of engagements, are from states, countries, and territories outside the South.

Thus, these numbers, like this book itself, bear explicit testimony to who the real initiator, offender, and aggressor was, a fact that clearly contradicts and destroys the false view put forth by conventional historians that "the South started and maintained the War."

Because it exists mainly for the purpose of propagandizing, confusing, and misleading, as well as to justify unconstitutional acts and conceal war crimes, nearly all *mainstream "Civil War" history is fake history*. And nowhere is this fact more abundantly demonstrated than in the battle number statistics found within the following pages.

HOW TO USE THIS BOOK
The Index I created is quite comprehensive: it lists not only the proper names of battles, but also both their nicknames and their alternate names (including Confederate and Yankee names). I have also listed towns, cities, states, names of businesses and homes, general locations, and affiliated natural features (both geological and hydrological), as well as topics, people, keywords, spelling variations, and key phrases that are associated with any and all known "Civil War" engagements—the purpose being to make it as easy as possible to find what you are looking for.

First Battle of Fort Sumter.

Thus, if you know the name of the battle or engagement you are interested in, simply turn to the index at the back of the book, where you will find an exhaustive alphabetized list. If you do not know the name of the conflict you are interested in, but know the state it occurred in, check the Table of Contents at the front of the book for that particular state. If you do not know the name of your battle, but know the name of the town or natural feature connected with it, use the Index to look up either name.

USES FOR THIS BOOK
As a reference work *Seabrook's Complete Battle Book* will be of use to historians, scholars, academicians, educators, writers, and lecturers, as well as students of American history and, more particularly, of the War for the Constitution.

Additionally, "Civil War" heritage organizations, such as the

SCV or Sons of Confederate Veterans (to which I belong), the UDC or United Daughters of the Confederacy, the MOSB or Military Order of Stars and Bars, and the OCR or Order of Confederate Rose, will find my book useful for planning the locations of war-related events, such as

Battle of New Bern.

rallies, trade shows, conventions, and re-enactments. And while my book is written from a Confederate perspective, it will also be of use to members of the SUV or Sons of Union Veterans for the same purposes.

Casual readers will find my book helpful in determining what, if any, military engagements took place in or around their home or work place; it can also be used to decide where to seek the remains of, artifacts from, or signs of little known battles and skirmishes; conflicts that are seldom discussed or have never been officially recognized or publicly marked. (The book is filled with these.)

A use that is not as obvious as those above concerns "Civil War" monuments. I encourage my readers to use the war data I have collected here to ascertain where to erect new (or replace missing, defaced, or demolished) statues, shrines, sculptures, gravestones, tablets, obelisks, cairns, markers, memorials, or any other type of stone commemorative dedicated to our courageous ancestors: the veterans of the War Between the States. In this group I include family members as well, for it was they who supported their grandfathers, fathers, uncles, husbands, sweethearts, brothers, sons, nephews, and male friends and neighbors who went off to War, likewise suffering (for sixteen long years, 1861-1877) in the attempt to retain their constitutional rights as laid down by the American Founding Fathers. Any one who knows the true history of the South will understand when I say that *we can never have too many Confederate memorials.*

In closing: Blessings to all, and may this book provide you and your heirs with many years of utility, education, and enjoyment.

LOCHLAINN SEABROOK
Park County, Wyoming USA
September 2023
In Nobis Regnat Christus

Confederate Gen. Robert E. Lee at the First Battle of Fredericksburg, Dec. 13, 1862.

SEABROOK'S
COMPLETE BATTLE BOOK

CHAPTER ONE
ALABAMA

1862

Jan. 20—*Andracita*, British schooner, contest over, on coast of Alabama.
April 23-27—Bridgeport, skirmishes at.
April 24-25—Tuscumbia, skirmishes at.
April 28—Bolivar, skirmish at.
April 28—Paint Rock Bridge, skirmish at.
April 29—West Bridge, action at, near Bridgeport.
May 1-2—Athens, operations in vicinity of.
May 8—Athens, skirmish at.
May 10-14—Lamb's Ferry, skirmishes at.
May 29—Whitesburg, skirmish at.
June 4-5—Huntsville, skirmishes at.
July 2—Huntsville, skirmish at.
July 3—Russellville, skirmish near.
July 12—Davis Gap, skirmish near.
July 26—Jonesboro, action near.
July 26—Spangler's Mill, action near.
July 28—Guntersville, skirmish at.
July 28—Law's Landing, skirmish at.
July 28—Stevenson, skirmish at.
July 29—Old Deposit Ferry, skirmish at
Aug. 4—Woodville, attack on Union pickets near.
Aug. 5—New Market, skirmish near.
Aug. 7—Decatur, attack on convalescent train near.
Aug. 22—Trinity, skirmish at.
Aug. 23—Trinity, affair near.

Aug. 27—Bridgeport, skirmish at.
Aug. 30—Larkinsville, skirmish near.
Aug. 31—Stevenson, skirmish at.
Sept. 1—Huntsville, skirmish at.
Dec. 12—Cherokee Station, skirmish at
Dec. 12—Little Bear Creek, skirmish at.

1863

Feb. 22—Tuscumbia, attack on.
March 25—Florence, affair with Union gunboats near.
April 6, 27—Town Creek, skirmishes at.
April 17—Barton Station, skirmish at.
April 17—Cherokee Station, skirmish at.
April 17—Great Bear Creek, skirmish at.
April 17—Lundy's Lane, skirmish at.
April 19, 23—Dickson Station, skirmishes at.
April 22—Rock Cut, action at.
April 23—Florence, skirmish at.
April 23—Leighton, skirmish at.
April 23—Tuscumbia, skirmish at.
April 23—Town Creek, action at.
April 30—Crooked Creek, action at.
April 30—Battle of Day's Gap, also known as the Battle of Sand Mountain.
April 30—Hoe Mountain, action at
May 1—Blountsville, skirmish at.
May 1—East Branch of the Big Warrior River, skirmish at.
May 2—Black Creek, skirmish at
May 2—Blount's Plantation, action at.
May 2—Centre, skirmish near.
May 2—Gadsden, skirmish near.
May 3—Cedar Bluff, skirmish and surrender near.
May 28—Florence, skirmish at.
June 11—Burnsville, skirmish at.
July 27—Paint Rock, steamer, attack on.
July 29—Bridgeport, skirmish near.
Aug. 21—Maysville, skirmish at.
Aug. 24—Gunter's Landing, near Port Deposit, skirmish at.
Aug. 29—Caperton's Ferry, skirmish at.
Aug. 31—Will's Valley, skirmish in.

Sept. 1—Davis' Gap, skirmish at.
Sept. 1, 17—Neal's Gap, skirmishes at.
Sept. 1—Tap's Gap, skirmish at.
Sept. 5—Lebanon, skirmish at.
Sept. 7—Stevenson, skirmish at.
Sept. 8—Winston's Gap, skirmish at.
Sept. 26—Larkinsville, skirmish at Hunt's Mill, near.
Oct. 12—New Market, skirmish at Buckhorn Tavern, near.
Oct. 20—Cane Creek, skirmish at.
Oct. 20—Dickson's Station, skirmish at.
Oct. 21—Cherokee Station, action at.
Oct. 24-25—Tuscumbia, skirmishes at.
Oct. 26—Cane Creek, and at Barton's Station, skirmishes near.
Oct. 27—Little Bear Creek, skirmish at.
Oct. 29—Cherokee Station, skirmish at.
Oct. 31—Barton's Station, skirmish at.
Nov. 4—Maysville, skirmish at.
Dec. 20—Sand Mountain, skirmish at.

1864

Jan. 14—Shoal Creek, skirmish at.
Jan. 26—Battle of Athens.
March 7—Decatur, skirmish at.
March 8—Courtland and Moulton, affairs at.
March 14—Claysville, skirmish at.
March 21—Moulton, skirmish near.
March 29—Caperton's Ferry, affair at.
April 7—Woodall's Bridge, skirmish at.
April 8—Paint Rock Bridge, skirmish at.
April 11—Kelly's Plantation, Sulphur Springs Road, affair near.
April 11—Sulphur Springs road, affair on.
April 12—Florence, skirmish near.
April 17—Flint River, affair at.
April 21—Harrison's Gap, affair at.
April 30—Decatur, skirmish at.
May 7—Florence, skirmish near.
May 8—Decatur, skirmish at.
May 12—Jackson's Ferry (Hallowell's Landing), skirmish at.
May 15—Center Star, skirmish at.
May 17—Madison Station, affair at.

May 18—Fletcher's Ferry, skirmish at.
May 27—Pond Springs, skirmish at.
May 29—Moulton, action at.
June 24—Curtis' Wells, skirmish at.
June 27—Big Cove Valley, skirmish in.
June 29—Pond Springs, affair at.
July 8—Vienna, skirmish near.
July 13—Coosa River, skirmish near.
July 14—Greenpoint, skirmish near.
July 14—Ten Island Ford, skirmish at.
July 18—Auburn, skirmish near.
July 18—Chehaw, skirmish near.
July 25—Courtland, affair at.
July 28—Danville Road, near Decatur, affair on the.
July 28—Decatur, affair near.
July 30—Paint Rock Station, skirmish at.
July 31—Watkins' Plantation, affair near.
Aug. 2-23—Battle of Mobile Bay.
Aug. 6—Decatur, affair near.
Aug. 6—Somerville Road near Decatur, affair on the.
Aug. 8—Fort Gaines, surrender of.
Aug. 9-22—Fort Morgan, siege of.
Aug. 18-19—Antioch Church, skirmish near.
Sept. 20—Morgan's Ferry, skirmish at.
Sept. 23—Athens, skirmish at.
Sept. 24—Athens, action at and surrender of.
Sept. 25—Battle of Sulphur Branch Trestle, at Elkmont; surrender of.
Oct. 1, 18—Huntsville, skirmishes near.
Oct. 1-2—Athens, skirmish at.
Oct. 6-7—Florence, skirmishes at.
Oct. 9—Mobile Bay, attack on U.S.S. *Sebago* in.
Oct. 9—*Sebago*, U.S.S., attack on, in Mobile Bay.
Oct. 20—Blue Pond, skirmish at.
Oct. 20—Little River, skirmish at.
Oct. 21—Leesburg, skirmish at.
Oct. 25—Gadsden Road, skirmish on.
Oct. 25—Round Mountain, skirmish near.
Oct. 25—Turkeytown, skirmish at.
Oct. 26-29—Battle of Decatur; demonstration against.
Oct. 28—Goshen, skirmish at.
Oct. 28—Ladiga, skirmish at.
Oct. 30—Florence, skirmish near.

Oct. 31—Shoal Creek, skirmish near.
Nov. 5-6, 9, 11—Shoal Creek, skirmishes at.
Nov. 16-20—Shoal Creek, skirmishes on the line of.
Nov. 17—Maysville, skirmish near.
Nov. 17—New Market, skirmish near.
Nov. 19—Duckett's Plantation, near Paint Rock River, skirmish at.
Nov. 19—Paint Rock River, skirmish at Duckett's Plantation, near. (See Duckett's Plantation.)
Dec. 7—Paint Rock Bridge, skirmish near.
Dec. 13-19—Pollard, expedition from Barrancas, Fla., to, and skirmishes.
Dec. 27, 28—Decatur, skirmishes at and near.
Dec. 29—Hillsboro, skirmish at.
Dec. 29—Pond Spring, skirmish at.
Dec. 30—Leighton, skirmish near.
Dec. 31—Paint Rock Bridge, affair at.
Dec. 31—Russellville, skirmish at.

1865

Jan. 4—Thorn Hill, skirmish near.
Jan. 26—Paint Rock, skirmish at.
Jan. 27—Elrod's Tan-yard, De Kalb County, skirmish at.
Jan. 28—Mobile Bay, attack on U.S.S. *Octorara* in.
Feb. 3-4—Ladd's House, Hog Jaw Valley, skirmish at.
Feb. 12—Waterloo, skirmish at.
Feb. 16—Gurley's Tank, skirmish near.
Feb. 20—Tuscumbia, skirmishes near.
March 3—Decatur, skirmish at.
March 7—Elyton, skirmish at.
March 10—Boyd's Station, skirmish near.
March 15-18—Boyd's Station and Stevenson's Gap, skirmishes at.
March 18-22—Fowl River Narrows, expedition from Dauphin Island to, and skirmishes.
March 23-24—Dannelly's Mills, skirmishes near.
March 24—Dannelly's Mills, affair near.
March 24—Evergreen, affair near.
March 23—Deer Park Road, skirmishes on the.
March 26—Muddy Creek, skirmish at.
March 26—Spanish Fort, skirmish near.

March 27-April 8—Battle of Spanish Fort; siege and capture of.
March 28—Elyton, skirmish near.
March 30—Montevallo, skirmish at.
March 31—Montevallo, action near.
March 31—Six-Mile Creek, action at.
April 1—Blakely, skirmish near.
April 1—Maplesville, skirmish at.
April 1—Plantersville, skirmish at.
April 1—Randolph, skirmish near.
April 1—Trion, skirmish at.
April 1, 2—Centerville, skirmishes at and near.
April 2-9—Battle of Fort Blakely; siege and capture of.
April 2—Scottsville, skirmish near.
April 2—Battle of Selma.
April 2—Summerfield, skirmish at.
April 3—Northport, near Tuscaloosa, action at.
April 3—Tuscaloosa, action at Northport, near.
April 4—Battle of Tuscaloosa.
April 6—King's Store, skirmish at.
April 6—Lanier's Mills, Sipsey Creek, skirmish near.
April 7—Cahawba River, skirmish on, at Fike's Ferry.
April 9-11—Batteries Huger and Tracy, bombardment and capture of.
April 10—Benton, skirmish near.
April 10—Lowndesboro, skirmish at.
April 11—Mount Pleasant, skirmish near.
April 12, 14—Columbus Road, skirmishes on.
April 12—Montgomery, skirmish on the Columbus Road near.
April 13—Wetumpka, skirmish at.
April 13—Whistler or Eight-Mile Creek Bridge, skirmish at.
April 14—Tuskegee, skirmish on the Columbus Road, near.
April 16—Crawford, skirmish at.
April 16—Girard, skirmish at.
April 16—Opelika, skirmish near.
April 20—Montpelier Springs, skirmish at.
April 23—Munford's Station, action at.
May 4—Citronelle, surrender of the Confederate forces in the Department of Alabama, Mississippi, and East Louisiana at.
May 4—Wetumpka, skirmish at.
May 25—Mobile, explosion of Ordnance Depot at.

CHAPTER TWO
ARIZONA

1864

Feb. 27—Pinos Altos, skirmish at.
Dec. 15—Hassayampa Creek, skirmish on.

1865

Jan. 1—Sycamore Springs, skirmish at.

Battle of Five Forks.

Confederate soldiers and brothers. Left: James McHenry Howard (1838-1916), First Maryland Infantry, C.S.A. Right: Private David Ridgely Howard (1844-1927), Second Maryland Infantry, C.S.A. Photo taken in 1864, at the height of the War; from my book *I, Confederate: Why Dixie Seceded and Fought in the Words of Southern Soldiers*.

CHAPTER THREE
ARKANSAS

1862

Feb. 16—Potts' Hill, Sugar Creek, action at.
Feb. 17—Sugar Creek, action at.
Feb. 18—Bentonville, action of.
Feb. 28—Osago Springs, affair at.
March 6-8—Battle of Elkhorn Tavern (Yankee name: Battle of Pea Ridge).
March 13—Spring River, action at
April 19—Talbot's Ferry, skirmish at.
April 21—Pocahontas, skirmish at.
May 2—Litchfield, skirmish at.
May 3—Batesville, skirmish at.
May 14—Cotton Plant, skirmish at.
May 15—Chalk Bluff, skirmish at.
May 17—Little Red River, skirmish on.
May 19—Searcy Landing, skirmish at.
May 21—Village Creek, skirmish at.
May 26—Calico Rock, skirmish at.
May 27—Big Indian Creek, skirmish at.
May 28—Cache River Bridge, skirmish at.
May 29—Kickapoo Bottom, near Sylamore, skirmish at.
May 29—Sylamore, skirmish near.
June 2—Galloway's Farm, affair at.
June 2—Jacksonport, affair near.
June 5-7—Little Red River, skirmishes on.
June 7—Fairview, skirmish at.
June 12—Jacksonport, skirmish near.

June 12—Village Creek, skirmish at.
June 12—Waddell's Farm, near Village Creek, skirmish at.
June 17—Battle of Saint Charles.
June 17—Smithville, skirmish near.
June 19—Blue Mountains, expedition to, including skirmish near Knight's Cove.
June 19—Knight's Cove, skirmish near.
June 25—Yellville, skirmish at.
June 27—Stewart's Plantation, skirmish at.
June 30—Adams' Bluff, skirmish at.
July 6—Cache Bayou, skirmish at.
July 6—Devall's Bluff, skirmish near.
July 6—Grand Prairie, skirmish at.
July 7—De View Bayou, skirmish at.
July 7—Battle of Hill's Plantation, also known as the Battle of Cotton Plant; Cache River, action at.
July 7—Round Hill, skirmish at.
July 14—Batesville, skirmish near.
July 14—Helena, skirmish near.
July 15—Fayetteville, action near.
July 20—Gaines' Landing, skirmish at.
Aug. 2—Jonesboro, skirmish at.
Aug. 3—Jackson, skirmish at.
Aug. 3—L'Anguille Ferry, skirmish at.
Aug. 3—Scatterville, skirmish at.
Aug. 11—Helena, skirmish near.
Aug. 15—Clarendon, skirmish at.
Sept. 6—La Grange, skirmish at.
Sept. 19-20—Helena, skirmishes near.
Sept. 23—McGuire's Ferry, skirmish at.
Oct. 11-18—Helena, skirmishes near.
Oct. 14—Trenton, skirmish at.
Oct 16—Elkhorn Tavern, skirmish at.
Oct. 17—Mountain Home, skirmish at.
Oct. 17—Sugar Creek, skirmish, at.
Oct. 18—Cross Hollow, skirmish at.
Oct. 20, 22, 25—Helena, skirmishes near.
Oct. 22—Huntsville, skirmish at.
Oct. 24, 27—Fayetteville, skirmishes at and near.
Oct. 27—Pitman's Ferry, skirmish at.
Oct. 28—McGuire's, action at.
Oct. 28—Oxford Bend, White River, action at.
Nov. 1-8—La Grange, skirmishes at.

Nov. 7—Boonsboro, skirmish at.
Nov. 7—Rhea's Mill, skirmish at.
Nov. 8—Cove Creek, skirmish at.
Nov. 8—Marianna, skirmish at.
Nov. 9—Boston Mountains, skirmish at.
Nov. 9—Cane Hill and Fayetteville, skirmish between.
Nov. 9—Fayetteville and Cane Hill, skirmish between.
Nov 25—Cane Hill, skirmish near.
Nov. 28—Battle of Cane Hill.
Dec. 6—Reed's Mountain, skirmish at.
Dec. 7—Battle of Prairie Grove.
Dec. 14—Helena, affair near.
Dec. 23—Saint Francis Road, near Helena, skirmish on the.
Dec. 28—Dripping Springs, skirmish at.

1863

Jan. 1—Helena, affair near.
Jan. 2—White Springs, skirmish at.
Jan. 9-11—Battle of Arkansas Post, also known as the Battle of Fort Hindman.
Jan. 12—Lick Creek, near Helena, skirmish at.
Feb. 2—Vine Prairie, skirmish at.
Feb. 3—Mulberry River, skirmish near mouth of.
Feb. 4—Batesville, skirmish at.
Feb. 10—Van Buren, skirmish near.
Feb. 15—Arkadelphia, skirmish near.
Feb. 19—Cypress Bend, skirmish at.
March 19—Frog Bayou, skirmish on.
March 22—White River, skirmish near the head of.
March 31—Clapper's Saw-Mill, Crooked Creek, skirmish at.
April 18—Fayetteville, action at.
May 1—La Grange, skirmish at.
May 1-2—Battle of Chalk Bluff.
May 11—Crowley's Ridge, skirmish at.
May 11—Taylor's Creek, skirmish at.
May 22—Bentonville, skirmish at.
May 25—Polk's Plantation, near Helena, skirmish at.
June 28—Gaines' Landing, skirmish near.
July 4—Battle of Helena.
July 30—Elm Springs, skirmishes near.

Aug. 14—West Point, engagement at.
Aug. 16—Harrison's Landing, skirmish at.
Aug. 23—Fayetteville, skirmish at.
Aug. 25—Battle of Brownsville.
Aug. 26—Meto Bayou, skirmish near.
Aug. 27—Meto Bayou, action at.
Aug. 27—Reed's Bridge, action at.
Aug. 30—Shallow Ford, Bayou Meto, skirmish at.
Sept. 1—Battle of Backbone Mountain (Yankee name: Battle of Devil's Backbone).
Sept. 1—Jenny Lind, skirmish at.
Sept. 2—Shallow Ford, Bayou Meto, skirmish near.
Sept. 5—Maysville, skirmish near.
Sept. 7—Ashley's Mills, skirmish at.
Sept. 7—Ferry Landing, skirmish at.
Sept. 10—Fourche Bayou, engagement at.
Sept. 12—Dardanelle, skirmish at.
Sept. 27—Moffat's Station, Franklin County, skirmish at.
Oct. 11-14—Fayetteville, demonstration against.
Oct. 24—Buffalo Mountains, skirmish at.
Oct. 25—Battle of Pine Bluff.
Oct. 26—Johnson County, skirmish in.
Nov. 7-13—Frog Bayou, skirmishes.
Nov. 9—Huntsville, skirmish near.
Nov. 10—Kingston, skirmish near.
Nov. 11—Caddo Gap, skirmish at.
Nov. 13—Mount Ida, skirmish at.
Nov. 19—Green's Farm, near Lawrenceville, skirmish at.
Nov. 21—Jacksonport, affair at.
Nov. 28—Boston Mountains, engagement at.
Dec. 1—Benton, skirmish near.
Dec. 1—Devall's Bluff, skirmish near.
Dec. 8—Princeton, skirmish at.
Dec. 14—Caddo Mill, skirmish at.
Dec. 23—Stroud's Store, skirmish at.
Dec. 25—Buffalo River, skirmish on.
Dec. 29—Waldron, attack on.

Fort Pulaski.

1864

Jan. 7—Martin's Creek, skirmish at.
Jan, 10—King's River, skirmish at.
Jan. 17—Lewisburg, skirmish at.
Jan. 19—Branchville, skirmish at.
Jan. 21-25—Baker's Springs, skirmish at.
Jan. 22—Clear Creek and Tomahawk, skirmishes at.
Jan. 23—Burrowsville, skirmishes near.
Jan. 23—Rolling Prairie, skirmish on.
Jan. 25—Sulphur Springs, skirmish at.
Jan. 25—Sylamore, skirmish at.
Jan. 26—Caddo Gap, skirmish at.
Jan. 28—Dallas, skirmish at.
Feb. 1—Waldron, skirmish at.
Feb. 4—Hot Springs, skirmish at.
Feb. 4—Mountain Fork, skirmish at.
Feb. 4—Rolling Prairie, skirmish at.
Feb. 5—Crooked Creek, skirmish on.
Feb. 9—Morgan's Mill, Spring River, skirmish at.
Feb. 9—Tomahawk Gap, skirmish at.
Feb. 9—White County, skirmish in.
Feb. 10—Lake Village, skirmish at.
Feb. 12, 16—Caddo Gap, skirmishes at.
Feb. 14—Ross Landing, skirmish at.
Feb. 14—Washita Cove, skirmish at.
Feb. 15—Saline River, skirmish at.
Feb. 16—Indian Bay, skirmish at.
Feb. 17—Black's Mill, skirmish at.
Feb. 17—Horse Head Creek, skirmish at.
Feb. 22—Luna Landing, skirmish at.
March 1—Buffalo City, skirmish at.
March 1—Cedar Glade, skirmish at.
March 2—Bennett's Bayou, skirmish at.
March 6—Flint Creek, skirmish at.
March 13—Carrollton, skirmish at.
March 14—Hopefield, skirmish at.
March 15—Clarendon, skirmish at.
March 18—Monticello, skirmish at.
March 18—Spring Creek, affair on.
March 20-29, 31—Arkadelphia, skirmishes at and near.
March 20—Roseville Creek, skirmish at.

March 23-24—Benton Road, skirmishes on the.
March 24, 27—Oil Trough Bottom, skirmishes at.
March 25—Dover, skirmish at.
March 25—Rockport, skirmish at.
March 25—Van Buren County, skirmish in.
March 25—White River, skirmish near.
March 26—Clarendon, skirmish near.
March 26—Quitman, skirmish near.
March 27—Branchville, affair at.
March 27—Brooks' Mill, skirmish at.
March 28—Danville, skirmish at.
March 28—Mount Elba, skirmish at.
March 29—Long View, skirmish at.
March 29—Roseville, skirmish at.
March 30—Mount Elba, action at.
April 1—Augusta, action at Fitzhugh's Woods, near.
April 2—Antoine, or Terre Noir Creek, and on Wolf Creek.
April 2-3—Okolona, skirmishes at.
April 2-4—Battle of Elkin's Ferry; Little Missouri River.
April 3—Clarksville, affair near.
April 4—Charlestown, skirmish at.
April 4, 5, 15—Roseville, skirmishes at.
April 5—Marks' Mills, skirmish at.
April 5—Whiteley's Mills, skirmish at.
April 5-9—Little River, near Osceola, skirmish in the swamps of.
April 5-9—Pemiscot Bayou, skirmish on.
April 6—Little Missouri River, skirmish at the.
April 6—Piney Mountain, skirmish at.
April 6-7—Prairie Grove, skirmish near.
April 7—Rhea's Mills, skirmish at.
April 9-13—Battle of Prairie D'Ane.
April 11, 13-14—Richland Creek, skirmishes at and near.
April 12—Van Buren, skirmish at.
April 13—Indian Bay, skirmish at.
April 13—Moscow, action at.
April 13—Smithville, skirmish on Spring River, near.
April 14—Dutch Mills, skirmish at.
April 14—White Oak Creek, skirmish at.
April 15, 16-18—Camden, skirmishes at and about.
April 16—Liberty Post-Office, skirmish at.
April 16—Osage Branch of King's River, affair on the.
April 17—Limestone Valley, skirmish in.
April 17—Red Mound, skirmish at.

April 18—Battle of Poison Spring.
April 19—King's River, skirmish at.
April 20, 24—Camden, skirmishes near.
April 20—Jacksonport, attack on.
April 21, 22—Cotton Plant, Cache River, affairs at.
April 21—Camden, Confederate demonstration on.
April 23—Swan Lake, affair at.
April 25—Little Rock, skirmish near.
April 25—Battle of Marks' Mills.
April 25-26—Moro Bottom, skirmishes in.
April 28—Princeton, skirmish near.
April 29—Ouachita River, skirmish at the.
April 29—Saline Bottom, skirmish near.
April 30—Battle of Jenkins' Ferry.
April 30—Whitmore's Mill, skirmish at.
May 1—Lee's Creek, skirmish at.
May 1, 21—Pine Bluff, skirmishes at.
May 3, 5—Richland Creek, skirmishes near mouth of.
May 8—Cherokee Bay, skirmish at.
May 8—Maysville, skirmish near.
May 9—Eudora Church, skirmish at.
May 10, 15—Dardanelle, skirmishes at and near.
May 13—Cypress Creek, Perry County, skirmish at.
May 13—Spavinaw, skirmish at.
May 17—Dardanelle, capture of.
May 18—Clarksville, skirmish at.
May 18—Searcy, affair near.
May 19—Fayetteville, skirmish at.
May 19—Norristown, skirmish near.
May 20—Stony Point, skirmish at.
May 22—Devall's Bluff, affair near.
May 24, 28—Little Rock, skirmishes near.
May 25—Buck Horn, skirmish at.
May 25—*Curlew*, U.S.S., engagement with.
May 25, 30—*Lebanon* and *Clara Eames*, steamers, capture of.
May 28—Washington, skirmish at.
June 1—*Exchange*, U.S.S., engagement with.
June 2—*Adams* and *Monarch*, U.S. steamers, engagement with.
June 3—Searcy, skirmish at.
June 5—Worthington's Landing, skirmish at.
June 6—Bealer's Ferry, on Little Red River, skirmish at.
June 6—Battle of Old River Lake, also known as the Battle of Lake Chicot.

June 7—Sunnyside Landing, skirmish at.
June 10—Lewisburg, skirmish at.
June 16—West Point, skirmish at.
June 17—Pine Bluff, skirmish on the Monticello Road, near.
June 19—Hahn's Farm, near Waldron, skirmish at.
June 22—White River Station, skirmish at.
June 24—Fayetteville, affair near.
June 24-25—*Naumkeag* and *Tyler*, U.S.S., engagement with.
June 29—Meffleton Lodge, affair at.
July 4—Searcy County, skirmish in.
July 6—Benton, skirmish near.
July 7—Van Buren, skirmish at.
July 8—Huntersville, skirmish near.
July 10, 19—Little Rock, skirmishes near.
July 10—Petit Jean, skirmish near.
July 13, 30—Brownsville, skirmishes near.
July 14—Bayou des Arc, action at.
July 19—Benton Road, skirmish on.
July 20—Maysville, skirmish near.
July 22, 30—Pine Bluff, skirmishes near.
July 24—*Clara Bell*, steamer, attack on.
July 25—Benton, affair at.
July 26—Wallace's Ferry, Big Creek, action at.
July 27, 31—Fort Smith, actions near.
July 27—Massard Prairie, near Fort Smith, action at.
July 28—Scatterville, skirmish at.
July 30—Hay Station No. 3, skirmish at.
Aug. 1—Lamb's Plantation, skirmish at, near Helena.
Aug. 2—Osceola, skirmish at.
Aug. 5—Redmount Camp, skirmish near.
Aug. 7—Bull Bayou, skirmish at.
Aug. 7—Hickory Plains, skirmish at.
Aug. 9—Hatch's Ferry, skirmish at,
Aug. 10—Augusta, skirmish near.
Aug. 11—White Oak Creek, skirmish on.
Aug. 12—Van Buren, skirmish at.
Aug. 13—Searcy, skirmish near.
Aug. 15—Carrollton, skirmish at.
Aug. 16—Richland Creek, skirmish at.
Aug. 18—Benton, skirmish at.
Aug. 18—Pine Bluff, skirmish near.
Aug. 24—Ashley's and Jones' Stations, near Devall's Bluff, action at.

Aug. 24—Gerald Mountain, skirmish at.
Aug. 24—Mud Town, skirmish at.
Aug. 27-28—Fayetteville, skirmishes at.
Aug. 30—Dardanelle, skirmish near.
Sept. 1—Beatty's Mill, skirmish near.
Sept. 1—Fort Smith, skirmish at.
Sept. 2—Little Rock, skirmish near.
Sept. 2—Quitman, skirmish near.
Sept. 3—Kendal's Grist-Mill, affair at.
Sept. 4—Brownsville, skirmish at.
Sept. 4—Gregory's Landing, attack on steamers *Celeste* and *Commercial* at.
Sept. 6—Norristown, skirmish at.
Sept. 6—Richland, skirmish at.
Sept. 6—Searcy, skirmish at.
Sept. 8—Glass Village, skirmish near.
Sept. 9—*J. D. Perry*, steamer, attack on, at Clarendon.
Sept. 10—Monticello, skirmish near.
Sept. 11—Brewer's Lane, skirmish at.
Sept. 11—Fort Smith, skirmish near.
Sept. 13—Searcy, skirmish near.
Sept. 14—White River, skirmish at Rodgers' Crossing of.
Sept. 23—Fort Smith, affair near.
Sept. 26—Vache Grass, skirmish at.
Sept. 28—Clarksville, skirmish at.
Sept. 29—White Oak Creek, skirmish at.
Oct. 9—Clarksville, skirmish at.
Oct. 11—White River, attack on steamer *Resolute*, on.
Oct. 14—Fort Smith, skirmish near.
Oct. 20—Benton County, skirmish in.
Oct. 22—Saint Charles, attack on Union transports near.
Nov. 2—Hazen's Farm, affair at, near Devall's Bluff.
Nov. 6—Cane Hill, skirmish at.
Nov. 6—Cincinnati, skirmishes near.
Nov. 11-12—Huntsville and Yellville, scout from Springfield, Mo.
Nov. 20—Buckskull, Randolph County, skirmish at.
Nov. 29—Dardanelle, attack on steamer *Alamo* near.
Dec. 1—Cypress Creek, Perry County, skirmish near.
Dec. 3—Perry County, skirmish in.
Dec. 5, 6—Lewisburg, skirmishes.
Dec. 12—*Resolute*, C.S.S., capture of.
Dec. 13—Devall's Bluff, affair near.
Dec. 19—Rector's Farm, skirmish at.

Dec. 24—Fort Smith, skirmish near.
Dec. 24—Richland, skirmish near.

1865

Jan. 1—Bentonville, skirmish at.
Jan. 6—Huntsville, skirmish at.
Jan. 7—Johnson County, skirmish in.
Jan. 8—Ivey's Ford, skirmish near.
Jan. 9—Pine Bluff, skirmish.
Jan. 12—Sugar Loaf Prairie, affair near.
Jan. 15—Madison County, skirmish in.
Jan. 17—Ivey's Ford, action at.
Jan. 18—Clarksville, skirmish at.
Jan. 22—Little Rock, skirmish on the Benton Road, near.
Jan. 24—Boggs' Mills, skirmish at.
Jan. 24—Fayetteville, skirmish at.
Feb. 9-10—Devall's Bluff, scout from Pine Bluff to.
Feb. 11—Clear Creek, skirmish at.
Feb. 11—Pine Bluff, skirmish near.
Feb. 12—Lewisburg, skirmish near.
Feb. 12—Madison, skirmish near.
Feb. 17—Washington County, skirmish.
Feb. 21—Battle of Douglas Landing.
Feb. 23—Voche's, Mrs., skirmish at.
March 4—Pine Bluff, affair near.
March 11—Clear Lake, skirmish at.
March 11—Washington, skirmish at.
March 20—Talbot's Ferry, skirmish at.
April 2—Hickory Station, skirmish near.
April 2—Van Buren, skirmish near.
April 11—Saint Charles, skirmish at.
April 23—Snake Creek, skirmish on.
May 16—Monticello Road, skirmish or.
May 24—Monticello, skirmish at.

CHAPTER FOUR
COLORADO

1863

April 11—Squirrel Creek Crossing, skirmish near.

1864

April 12—Fremont's Orchard, skirmish near.
May 3—Cedar Bluffs, skirmish at.

1865

June 8-14—Overland Stage Road, attack by Indians on, in Kansas and Colorado, with skirmishes, etc.

Fort Arbuckle, Indian Territory.

Photo of the staff of the First U.S. Volunteer Regiment, the "Rough Riders," in Tampa, Florida, around 1899. Front row of three, from left to right: Confederate General Joseph Wheeler (holding hat in left hand), future twenty-sixth U.S. president Theodore Roosevelt, and Leonard Wood. Back row of three, from left to right: Major George Dunn, Major Alexander Oswald Brodie, and Chaplain Henry A. Brown.

CHAPTER FIVE
COLORADO TERRITORY

1864

Aug. 7—Fort Lyon (CO), affair near.
Aug. 11—Sand Creek, Col. Ter. (Colorado Territory), skirmish near.
Oct. 10—Valley Station (CO), skirmish near.
Nov. 6-16—Fort Lyon (CO), affairs at.
Nov. 29—Sand Creek, Col. Ter., engagement with Indians on.

1865

Jan. 7—Valley Station and Julesburg, Col. Ter. (Colorado Territory), skirmishes with Indians at.
Jan. 14—Godfrey's Ranch, Col. Ter. (Colorado Territory), skirmish with Indians at.
Jan. 15—Morrison's or American Ranch, Col. Ter. (Colorado Territory), skirmish with Indians at.

Jan. 15 and 28—Valley Station, Col. Ter. (Colorado Territory), skirmishes with Indians near.
Jan. 15—Wisconsin Ranch, Col. Ter. (Colorado Territory), skirmish with Indians at.
Jan. 25—Gittrell's Ranch, Col. Ter. (Colorado Territory), skirmish with Indians at.
Jan. 26—Moore's Ranch, Col. Ter. (Colorado Territory), skirmish with Indians at.
Jan. 27—Lillian Springs Ranch, Col. Ter. (Colorado Territory), skirmish with Indians at.
Feb. 2—Julesburg, Col. Ter. (Colorado Territory), attack on the Overland Stage Station at.
April 1—Fort Garland (CO), affair near.
May 13—Julesburg, Col. Ter. (Colorado Territory), skirmish with Indians at Dan Smith's Ranch near.
June 4-10—Fort Collins, Col. Ter. (Colorado Territory), operations against Indians near.
June 8—Sage Creek (CO), skirmish at.

American statesman, Southern hero, Jefferson Davis.

CHAPTER SIX
DAKOTA

1862

Sept 3-23—Fort Abercrombie (ND), actions at.
Sept. 6, 26—Fort Abercrombie (ND), skirmishes at.

1863

Feb. 20—Fort Halleck (WY), skirmish near.
July 24—Big Mound (MO), action at the.
July 26—Dead Buffalo Lake (ND), action at.
July 28—Stony Lake (ND), action at.
Sept. 3—White Stone Hill (ND), action near.
Sept. 5—White Stone Hill (ND), skirmish near.

Battle of the ironclads at Hampton Roads.

Confederate Lieutenant John Grimball of the C.S.S. cruiser *Shenandoah*, in C.S. navy uniform; photo circa 1864.

CHAPTER SEVEN
DAKOTA TERRITORY

1864

July 28—Battle of Tahkahokuty Mountain (ND), or Battle of Killdeer Mountain.

1865

April 26—Fort Rice (ND), affair near.
May 20—Deer Creek, skirmishes on.
May 26, 28—Sweetwater Station, Dak. Ter. (Dakota Territory), skirmishes with Indians at.
May 27—Saint Mary's Station, Dak. Ter. (Dakota Territory), skirmish with Indians at.
June 1—Sweetwater Station, Dak. Ter. (Dakota Territory), skirmish with Indians at.
June 2—Fort Rice (ND), operations about,
June 3—Dry Creek, Dak. Ter. (Dakota Territory), skirmish with

Indians at.
June 3—Platte Bridge, Dak. Ter. (Dakota Territory), skirmish with Indians at.
June 14—Horse Creek, Dak. Ter. (Dakota Territory), action with Indians at.
June 17—Dead Man's Fork, skirmish on.
June 30—Rock Creek, Dak. Ter. (Dakota Territory), skirmish with Indians at.
July 26—Platte Bridge, Dak. Ter. (Dakota Territory), skirmish with Indians at.
Aug. 1—Big Laramie and Little Laramie, affairs at.
Aug. 13—Powder River, skirmish near.
Aug. 16—Powder River, skirmish at.
Aug. 28—Tongue River, action at.

Confederate soldier, name unknown, Staunton, VA, circa 1862.

CHAPTER EIGHT
FLORIDA

1861

Oct. 9—Battle of Santa Rosa Island.
Nov. 22-23—Pensacola, bombardment of Confederate lines about.

1862

Jan. 1—Fort McRee, bombardment of.
March 21—Smyrna, affair at.
April 7—Saint Andrew's Bay, affair at.
April 10—Fernandina, skirmish near.
May 20—Crooked River, affair on.
June 15—Saint Mark's, naval descent upon.
June 25—Pensacola, skirmish near.
June 30-July 1—Battle of Tampa; bombardment of.
Sept. 11, 17—Saint John's Bluff, engagements at.
Oct. 1-3—Battle of Saint John's Bluff.
Oct. 2—Mayport Mills and Saint John's Bluff, skirmishes.

1863

Jan. 26—Township, skirmish at.
March 9—Saint Augustine, skirmish near.
March 20—Saint Andrew's Bay, affair in.

March 24—Ocklocknee Bay, affair in.
March 25, 29—Jacksonville, skirmishes at and near.
March 27—Palatka, skirmish at.
Aug. 19—Saint John's Mill, capture of signal station at.
Oct. 16-18—Battle of Fort Brooke.
Dec. 25—Fort Brooke, engagement at.
Dec. 30—Saint Augustine, skirmish near.

1864

Feb. 8—Ten-Mile Run, near Camp Finegan, skirmish at.
Feb. 9—Point Washington, skirmish near.
Feb. 10—Barber's Ford, skirmish at.
Feb. 10—Camp Cooper, capture of.
Feb. 10—Lake City, skirmish at.
Feb. 13, 20—Pease Creek, skirmishes at.
Feb. 14—Gainesville, skirmish at.
Feb. 20—Battle of Olustee (Yankee name: Battle of Ocean Pond).
March 1—Cedar and McGirt's Creeks, skirmishes at.
March 16—Palatka, skirmish near.
March 31—Palatka, skirmish at.
April 2—Cedar Creek, skirmish on.
April 2—Cow Ford Creek, near Pensacola, skirmish at.
May 6—Tampa, affair at.
May 19—Saunders, affair at.
May 19—Welaka, affair at.
May 25—Camp Finegan, skirmish near.
May 25—Jackson's Bridge, near Pensacola, affair at.
May 28—Jacksonville, skirmish near.
July 15—Trout Creek, skirmish at.
July 22—Camp Gonzales, skirmish at.
July 24—Whitesville, skirmish at.
July 27—Whiteside, Black Creek, skirmish at.
Aug. 10-12—Baldwin, skirmishes at.
Aug. 13—Palatka, skirmish at.
Aug. 17—Gainesville, action at.
Aug. 29—Milton, skirmish at.
Sept. 21—Euchee Anna Court House, affair at.
Sept. 24—Magnolia, skirmish at.
Sept. 27—Marianna, skirmish at.
Oct. 18—Milton, skirmish near.

Oct. 21—Bryant's Plantation, skirmish at.
Oct. 24—Magnolia, skirmish near.
Oct. 26—Milton, skirmish at.

1865

Feb. 2—Saint John's River, skirmish on.
Feb. 5—Welaka, action at Braddock's Farm, near.
Feb. 13—Station Four, action at.
Feb. 16—Cedar Keys, skirmish near.
Feb. 20—Fort Myers, attack on.
Feb. 22-25—Milton, expedition from Barrancas to, and skirmishes.
March 4-5—East River Bridge, skirmishes at.
March 5-6—Newport Bridge, skirmishes at.
March 6—Battle of Natural Bridge.
March 19—Welaka and Saunders, skirmishes at.
March 25—Canoe Creek, or Bluff Springs, action at.
March 25—Cotton Creek, skirmish at.
March 25—Escambia River, skirmish at.

Battle of Atlanta.

Black Confederate soldier, Private Steve Perry, of Rome, Georgia, one of the 1 million African-Americans who voluntarily, and often eagerly, served in the Confederate military as cooks, nurses, servants, hostlers, drivers, musicians, and trained soldiers, among other occupations (note: the precise number will never be known because black military service was not officially recognized until near the end of the War). The mere existence of men like Perry—who went by the name "Uncle" Steve Everhart or simply Eberhart—completely eviscerates the Left-wing myths concerning the "racist South" and the "total absence of blacks in the Confederate army and navy," as well as the fabrication that the South fought to "preserve slavery." The C.S. government, in fact, was ironing out the details of complete emancipation and official black enlistment months before the War ended. In fact, the War delayed Southern abolition. As for black Confederates, Stonewall Jackson alone enlisted some 3,000 armed African-American soldiers in his army—as a concerned Frederick Douglass once affirmed. The photo above was taken around 1937, when Perry was 102 years old. According to the loyal Confederate veteran at the time: "I seldom miss a Confederate Reunion, having been a servant of a Confederate officer." An attendee of countless Confederate veteran reunions, where he was always enthusiastically welcomed, Perry proudly wore his Confederate badges on his jacket, including a 1932 U.C.V. (United Confederate Veterans) Richmond reunion badge, as well as stylish feathers on his hat.

CHAPTER NINE
GEORGIA

1862

Feb. 15—Venus Point, action at.
March 30-31—Whitemarsh and Wilmington Islands, affairs on.
April 10-11—Battle of Fort Pulaski; bombardment and capture of.
April 16—Whitemarsh Island, skirmish on.
May 3—Watkins' Ferry, skirmish at.
Nov. 7—Spaulding's, skirmish at.
Nov. 13-18—Doboy River, expedition to and skirmish.

1863

Jan. 27—Fort McAllister, naval attack on.
Feb. 1—Fort McAllister, naval attack on.
Feb. 28—Fort McAllister, naval attack on.
March 3—Fort McAllister, naval attack on.
March 5—First Battle of Fort McAllister.
March 9—Fort McAllister, affair at.
June 8—Brunswick, affair near.
June 11—Darien, attack on.
Sept. 3, 5—Alpine, skirmishes near.
Sept. 6, 18—Stevens' Gap, skirmishes at.
Sept. 6-7—Summerville, skirmishes at.
Sept. 8, 12—Alpine, skirmishes at.
Sept. 9—Lookout Mountain, skirmish at.
Sept. 10—Pea Vine Creek, skirmishes at and near Graysville.
Sept. 10-11—Battle of Davis' Cross Roads.

Sept. 10, 15—Summerville, skirmishes at.
Sept. 11—Blue Bird Gap, skirmish near.
Sept. 11—Davis' House, skirmish at.
Sept. 11—Dug Gap, skirmish near.
Sept. 11—Ringgold, skirmish at Tunnel Hill, near.
Sept. 11—Tunnel Hill, skirmish at, near Ringgold.
Sept. 11-13—Lee and Gordon's Mills, skirmishes near.
Sept. 12—Dirt Town, skirmish at.
Sept. 12—La Fayette Road, skirmish on the, near Chattanooga River.
Sept. 12—Leet's Tan-yard, or Rock Spring, skirmish near.
Sept. 13—La Fayette, reconnoissance from Leo and Gordon's Mills toward, and skirmish.
Sept. 13—La Fayette, reconnoissance from Henderson's Gap to, and skirmish.
Sept. 13—Summerville, skirmish near.
Sept. 14—La Fayette, skirmish near.
Sept. 15, 18—Catlett's Gap, Pigeon Mountain, skirmishes at.
Sept. 15—Trion Factory, skirmish at.
Sept. 16-18—Lee and Gordon's Mills, skirmishes near.
Sept. 17—Owens' Ford, West Chickamauga Creek, skirmish at.
Sept. 17—Ringgold, skirmish at.
Sept. 18—Pea Vine Ridge, Alexander's and Reed's Bridges, Dyer's Ford, Spring Creek, and near Stevens' Gap, skirmishes at.
Sept. 18-20—Battle of Chickamauga.
Sept. 21—Rossville, Lookout Church and Dry Valley, skirmishes at.
Nov. 18—Trenton, skirmish at.
Nov. 26—Graysville, skirmish near.
Nov. 27—Taylor's Ridge, engagement at.
Nov. 27—Battle of Ringgold Gap.
Dec. 12—La Fayette, skirmish at.

1864

Jan. 6—Dalton, skirmish at.
Jan. 22—Subligna, affair at.
Jan. 30—Chickamauga Creek, skirmish at.
Feb. 8, 18—Ringgold, skirmishes at.
Feb. 22-27—First Battle of Dalton.
Feb. 22—Whitemarsh Island, skirmish at.

Feb. 22—Tunnel Hill, skirmish at.
Feb. 24-25—Buzzard Roost, skirmish at.
Feb. 24-25—Rocky Face Ridge (or Crow's Valley), skirmish at.
Feb. 27—Stone Church, near Catoosa Platform, skirmish at the.
March 5—Leet's Tan-yard, skirmish at.
March 9—Nickajack Gap, skirmish near.
April 3—Ducktown Road, skirmish on.
April 14—Taylor's Ridge, skirmish at.
April 23—Nickajack Trace, attack on Union pickets at.
April 27—Taylor's Ridge, near Ringgold, attack on Union pickets on.
May 1—Stone Church, skirmish at.
May 2—Lee's Cross-Roads, near Tunnel Hill, skirmish at.
May 2—Ringgold Gap, skirmish near.
May 2, 5—Tunnel Hill, skirmishes near.
May 3—Catoosa Springs, skirmish at.
May 3—Chickamauga Creek, skirmish at.
May 3—Red Clay, skirmish at.
May 4—Varnell's Station Road, skirmish on the.
May 6-7—Tunnel Hill, skirmishes at.
May 7—Nickajack Gap, skirmish near.
May 7—Varnell's Station, skirmish at.
May 7-13—Battle of Rocky Face Ridge.
May 9—Snake Creek Gap, combat at.
May 9, 12—Varnell's Station, combats near.
May 9-13—Dalton, demonstration against.
May 12—Sugar Valley, combat at.
May 13—Dalton, combat at.
May 13—Tilton, skirmish at.
May 13-15—Battle of Resaca.
May 15—Armuchee Creek, skirmish at.
May 15—Rome, skirmish near.
May 16—Calhoun, skirmish near.
May 16—Floyd's Spring, skirmish at.
May 16—Parker's Cross-Roads, action at.
May 17—Battle of Adairsville.
May 17—Rome, action at.
May 18—Pine Log Creek, skirmish at.
May 18-19—Cassville, combats near.
May 18-19—Kingston, combats near.
May 20—Etowah River, near Cartersville, skirmish at.
May 23—Stilesboro, action at.
May 24—Burnt Hickory, or Huntsville, skirmish at.

May 24—Cass Station and Cassville, skirmishes at.
May 24—Dallas, skirmish near.
May 24—Huntsville, skirmish at.
May 25-26—Battle of New Hope Church.
May 26-June 4—Battle of Dallas.
May 27—Battle of Pickett's Mill.
June 6-July 3—Battle of Marietta; and operations about.
June 9—Big Shanty and Stilesboro, skirmishes near.
June 9—Stilesboro, skirmish near.
June 10—Calhoun, skirmish at.
June 11-15—Lost Mountain, combats at.
June 12—McAfee's Cross-Roads, combat at.
June 14—Pine Hill, combat at.
June 15-16—Gilgal Church, combat at.
June 17—Nose's Creek, action at.
June 18—Noyes' Creek, combat at.
June 20—Noonday Creek, combat at.
June 20—Powder Springs, combat at.
June 22—Battle of Kolb's Farm.
June 24—La Fayette, action at.
June 27—Olley's Creek, combat at.
June 27—Battle of Kennesaw Mountain.
July 2-5—Nickajack Creek, combat at.
July 4—Neal Dow Station, skirmish at.
July 4—Rottenwood Creek, skirmish at.
July 4—Ruff's Mill, Neal Dow Station, and Rottenwood Creek, skirmishes at.
July 5-17—Chattahoochee River, operations on the line of.
July 18—Buck Head, skirmish at.
July 19—Peachtree Creek, skirmishes on.
July 20—Battle of Peachtree Creek.
July 21—Bald (or Leggett's) Hill, engagement at.
July 22—Battle of Atlanta.
July 24—Cartersville, skirmish near.
July 27—Snapfinger Creek, skirmish at.
July 28—Battle of Ezra Church; near Atlanta.
July 28—Campbellton, skirmish near.
July 28—Flat Rock Bridge, skirmish at.
July 28—Lithonia, skirmish at.
July 29—Lovejoy's Station, skirmish near.
July 30—Clear Creek, skirmish at.
July 30—Clinton, combat at.
July 30—Macon, combat at.

July 30—Newnan, action near.
July 30, 31—Hillsboro, combats at.
Aug. 3—Jug Tavern, combat at.
Aug. 3—Mulberry Creek, combat at.
Aug. 5-7—Battle of Utoy Creek; Federal assault.
Aug. 14-15—Second Battle of Dalton.
Aug. 15—Fairburn, skirmish at.
Aug. 15—Sandtown, skirmish at.
Aug. 17—South Newport, skirmish at.
Aug. 18—Camp Creek, combat at.
Aug. 19—Flint River, combat at.
Aug. 19—Red Oak, combat at.
Aug. 20—Battle of Lovejoy's Station.
Aug. 29—Red Oak, skirmish near.
Aug. 30—East Point, skirmish near.
Aug. 30—Flint River Bridge, action at.
Aug. 31—Rough and Ready Station, skirmish near.
Aug. 31-Sept. 1—Battle of Jonesboro; sometimes spelled Battle of Jonesborough.
Sept. 2-5—Lovejoy's Station, actions at.
Sept. 10—Campbellton, affair at.
Sept. 15—Lumpkin County, skirmish in.
Sept. 15—Snake Creek Gap, skirmish at.
Sept. 20—Cartersville, skirmish at.
Sept. 26—Roswell, skirmish near.
Sept. 28—Decatur, skirmish near.
Sept. 30—Camp Creek, skirmish at.
Oct. 1—Salt Springs, skirmish at.
Oct. 2—Fairburn, skirmishes near.
Oct. 2—Flat Rock and McDonough Roads, skirmish at the crossing of.
Oct. 2—Sand Mountain, skirmish near.
Oct. 2—Westbrook's, skirmish at.
Oct. 2-3—Powder Springs, skirmishes near.
Oct. 3—Big Shanty, skirmish at.
Oct. 3—Kenesaw Water Tank, skirmish at.
Oct. 4—Acworth, skirmish at.
Oct. 4—Moon's Station, skirmish at.
Oct. 4-7—Lost Mountain, skirmishes near.
Oct. 5—Battle of Allatoona.
Oct. 5—New Hope Church, skirmish near.
Oct. 7—Dallas, skirmish at.
Oct. 9-10—Van Wert, skirmishes near.

Oct. 10-11-12-13—Rome, skirmishes near.
Oct. 11-14—Flat Creek, expedition from Atlanta to and skirmishes.
Oct. 12—La Fayette, skirmish at.
Oct. 12-13—Coosaville Road, near Rome, skirmishes on.
Oct. 12-13—Resaca, skirmishes at.
Oct. 13-14—Buzzard Roost Gap, combat at.
Oct. 15—Snake Creek Gap, skirmish at.
Oct. 16—Ship's Gap, skirmish at.
Oct. 18—Summerville, skirmish near.
Oct. 19—Ruff's Station, skirmish at.
Oct. 19—Turner's and Howell's Ferries, skirmishes near.
Oct. 24—South River, skirmish near
Oct. 27—Lawrenceville, skirmish near.
Nov. 6—McDonough Road, near Atlanta, skirmish on.
Nov. 6, 9—Atlanta, skirmishes near.
Nov. 15—East Point, skirmish near.
Nov. 15—Jonesboro, skirmish at.
Nov. 15—Rough and Ready and Stockbridge, skirmishes near.
Nov. 16—Bear Creek Station, skirmish at.
Nov. 16—Cotton River Bridge, skirmish at.
Nov. 16—Lovejoy's Station, action at.
Nov. 17—Towaliga Bridge, affair at.
Nov. 19—Buck Head Station, skirmish at.
Nov. 20—East Macon, skirmish at.
Nov. 20—Walnut Creek, skirmish at.
Nov. 20, 21—Griswoldville, skirmishes at.
Nov. 20, 21-23—Clinton, skirmishes.
Nov. 21—Eatonton, skirmish near.
Nov. 21—Gordon, skirmish at.
Nov. 21—Macon, skirmish near.
Nov. 22—Battle of Griswoldville.
Nov. 23-25—Ball's Ferry and the Georgia Central Railroad Bridge, Oconee River, skirmishes at.
Nov. 25, 26—Sandersville, skirmishes.
Nov. 27—Sylvan Grove, skirmish at.
Nov. 27, 28—Waynesboro, action at.
Nov. 28—Battle of Buck Head Creek.
Nov. 28—Buck Head Church, skirmish at.
Nov. 28—Davisboro, skirmish near.
Nov. 28—Waynesboro, skirmish near.
Nov. 29, 30—Louisville, skirmishes.
Nov. 30—Dalton, skirmish near

Dec. 1—Millen's (or Shady) Grove, skirmish at.
Dec. 2—Buck Head Creek, skirmish at.
Dec. 2—Rocky Creek Church, skirmish at.
Dec. 3—Thomas' Station, skirmish at.
Dec. 4—Lumpkin's Station, skirmish near
Dec. 4—Statesboro, skirmish near.
Dec. 4—Station No. 5, Georgia Central Railroad, skirmish at.
Dec. 4—Battle of Waynesboro.
Dec. 4, 5—Little Ogeechee River, skirmishes at.
Dec. 5—Dalton, skirmish near.
Dec. 7—Buck Creek, skirmish at.
Dec. 7—Cypress Swamp, near Sister's Ferry, skirmish at.
Dec. 7—Jenks' Bridge, Ogeechee River, skirmish at.
Dec. 8—Bryan Court House, skirmish near.
Dec. 8—Ebenezer Creek, skirmish at.
Dec. 9—Cuyler's Plantation, skirmish at.
Dec. 9—Eden and Pooler Stations, skirmish between.
Dec, 9—Monteith Swamp, skirmish at.
Dec. 9—Ogeechee Canal, skirmish at.
Dec. 10—*Ida*, C.S.S., capture of.
Dec. 10—Savannah, skirmish near.
Dec. 10—Springfield, skirmish near.
Dec. 13—Second Battle of Fort McAllister.
Dec. 14-21—Fort Rosedew and Fort Beaulieu, Vernon River, naval attack on.
Dec. 16—Hinesville, skirmish at.

1865

Feb. 10—Johnson's Crook, skirmish in.
Feb. 27—Spring Place, skirmish at.
March 1—Holly Creek, skirmish at.
March 3—Tunnel Hill, skirmish near.
March 13—Dalton, affair near.
March 14—Dalton, skirmish near.
March 20—Ringgold, skirmish at.
April 1-4—Spring Place and Coosawattee River, expedition from Dalton to, with skirmishes.
April 16—Battle of Columbus.
April 16—Battle of West Point (Fort Tyler).
April 17—Columbus, destruction of C.S. gunboat *Muscogee* or

Jackson at.
April 18—Flint River, skirmishes at Double Bridges over.
April 18—Pleasant Hill, skirmish at.
April 10—Barnesville, skirmish near.
April 20—Macon, skirmish at Rocky Creek Bridge, near.
April 20—Spring Hill, skirmish near.
April 20—Tobesolkee Creek, skirmish at Mimm's Mills on.
April 22—Buzzard Roost, skirmish near.
May 5—Summerville, skirmish at.

Confederate General John Clifford Pemberton.

CHAPTER TEN
IDAHO

1863

July 7—Grand Pass, skirmish with Indians at.

Confederate officer, name unknown, circa 1861.

Confederate General John Sappington Marmaduke, circa 1862.

CHAPTER ELEVEN
IDAHO TERRITORY

1865

March 8—Poison Creek, skirmish at.

U.S. President Abraham Lincoln on the Battlefield of Sharpsburg, Oct. 1862.

Confederate General William Nelson Rector Beall, circa 1864.

CHAPTER TWELVE
ILLINOIS

1864

April 6—Prairie Du Rocher, affair at.

Confederate surgeon Dr. William Gibbs McNeill Whistler, circa 1864. From my book *I, Confederate: Why Dixie Seceded and Fought in the Words of Southern Soldiers*.

Confederate officer, name unknown, Richmond, VA, circa 1863.

CHAPTER THIRTEEN
INDIANA

1863

July 9—Battle of Corydon.
July 10—Salem, skirmish at.
July 11—Pekin, skirmish at.

The Confederate Cabinet at Montgomery, AL. Front row (seated), left to right: Attorney General Judah P. Benjamin, Secretary of the Navy Stephen R. Mallory, Vice President Alexander Hamilton Stephens, President Jefferson Davis, Postmaster John H. Reagan, and Secretary of State Robert A. Toombs. Back row (standing), from left to right: Secretary of the Treasury Christopher S. Memminger and Secretary of War Leroy Pope Walker.

Confederate Acting Master's Mate William McBlair, Jr., C.S. navy, circa 1864. From my book *I, Confederate: Why Dixie Seceded and Fought in the Words of Southern Soldiers*.

CHAPTER FOURTEEN
INDIAN TERRITORY

1861

Nov. 19—Battle of Round Mountain.
Dec. 9—Battle of Chusto-Talasah.
Dec. 26—Battle of Chustenahlah.

1862

June 5—Round Grove, skirmish at.
June 6—Grand River, skirmish at.
July 3—Locust Grove, skirmish at.
July 27—Bernard Bayou, skirmish at.
Oct. 15—Fort Gibson, skirmish at.
Oct. 22—Beattie's Prairie, action at.
Oct. 22—Battle of Old Fort Wayne (OK).

1863

April 25—Webber's Falls, skirmish at.
May 8 (?)—Martin's House, skirmish at.
May 20—Fort Gibson, action near (OK).
May 28—Fort Gibson, skirmish near (OK).
June 16—Greenleaf Prairie, skirmish on.
July 1-2—Battle of Cabin Creek (OK).
July 17—Battle of Elk Creek, also known as the Battle of Honey Springs (OK).
Aug. 26—Perryville, skirmish at.
Aug. 30-31—Scullyville, skirmishes at and near.
Dec. 16—Fort Gibson, demonstration on (OK).
Dec. 18—Sheldon's Place, Barren Fork, skirmish near.

1864

Feb. 13—Battle of Middle Boggy Depot (OK).
April 3—Fort Gibson, skirmish near (OK).
June 4—Hudson's Crossing, Neosho River, affair at.
June 15-16—San Bois Creek, skirmish at.
June 19—Iron Bridge, skirmish at.
Aug. 24—Gunter's Prairie, skirmish on.
Sept. 16—Fort Gibson, action near (OK).
Sept. 16—Hay Station, action at.
Sept. 19—Pryor's Creek, action at.

1865

April 24—Boggy Depot, skirmish near.

Fort Lancaster, Sheffield, TX.

CHAPTER FIFTEEN
IOWA

1861

Aug. 5—Battle of Croton, also known as the Battle of Athens.

Southern woman in mourning dress, wearing brooch with photo of her husband, a Confederate soldier; her child is wearing a Confederate kepi; circa 1864. From my book *Heroes of the Southern Confederacy: The Illustrated Book of Confederate Officials, Soldiers, and Civilians.*

Confederate Soldier Monument, Confederate Stockade Cemetery, Johnson's Island, Sandusky, OH.

CHAPTER SIXTEEN
KANSAS

1861

Sept. 1—Fort Scott, skirmish at.

1862

March 12—Aubrey, skirmish near.
Nov. 6-11—Fort Scott, expedition from, and skirmishes.
Nov. 8—Cato, skirmish near.

1863

June 8—Fort Scott, affair near.
Aug. 21—Brooklyn, skirmish near.
Aug. 21—Lawrence, burning of.
Aug. 21—Paola, skirmish near.
Sept. 6—Fort Scott, attack on train between Carthage, Mo., and.
Oct. 6—Battle of Baxter Springs, also known as the Battle of Fort Blair.

Jefferson City, MO, 1861.

1864

May 16—Big Bushes, near Smoky Hill, action at.
Aug. 1—Baxter Springs, scout to, with skirmish.
Aug. 16—Smoky Hill Crossing, Kan., skirmish near, with Indians.
Sept. 21—Council Grove, affair near.
Sept. 25—Walnut Creek, skirmish at.
Sept. 26—Osage Mission, skirmish at.
Oct. 25—Fort Lincoln, skirmish at.
Oct. 25—Battle of Little Osage River, also known as the Battle of Mine Creek.
Oct. 25—Battle of Marais des Cygnes.
Oct. 25—Mound City and Fort Lincoln, skirmishes at.
Nov. 13—Ash Creek, Kan., skirmish with Indians at, near Fort Larned.
Nov. 20—Fort Zarah, Kan., skirmishes with Indians near.
Nov. 28—Cow Creek, skirmish on.
Dec. 4—Cow Creek, skirmish on.
Dec. 4—Fort Zarah, Kan., skirmish with Indians near.

1868

Jan. 20—Point of Rocks or Nine-Mile Ridge, skirmish at.
Jan. 20—Fort Larned, Kan., skirmish near.
Jan. 31—Oxford, skirmish near.
Feb. 1—Fort Zarah, skirmish at.
Feb. 12-20—Fort Riley and Fort Larned, operations about.
March 7—Fort Larned, Kan., skirmish with Indians eighty west of.
April 23—Fort Zarah, affair near.
May 20—Pawnee Rock, affair near.
June 8, 12—Fort Dodge, Kan., skirmishes at.
June 8-14—Overland Stage Road, attack by Indians on, in Kansas and Colorado, with skirmishes, etc.
June 9—Chavis Creek, skirmish at, near Cow Creek Station.
June 12—Pawnee Rock, skirmish near.
June 12—Plum Butte, skirmish near.
June 29—Fort Dodge, Kan., skirmish with Indians near.

CHAPTER SEVENTEEN
KENTUCKY

1861

Aug. 22—*Samuel Orr*, steamboat, capture of.
Aug. 22—*W. B. Terry*, steamboat, capture of.
Sept. 4—Columbus, engagement at.
Sept. 4—Hickman, engagement at.
Sept. 19—Battle of Barbourville.
Sept. 21-22—Mayfield Creek, skirmish at.
Sept. 23 (?)—Albany, affair at.
Sept. 26—Muddy River, destruction of lock at mouth of.
Sept. 29—Hopkinsville, skirmish at.
Oct. 12—Upton's Hill, skirmish near.
Oct. 21—Battle of Wild Cat, or Battle of Camp Wildcat.
Oct. 21—Rockcastle Hills, action at.
Oct. 24—Camp Joe Underwood, attack on.
Oct. 26—Saratoga, skirmish at.
Oct. 29—Woodbury, skirmishes at and near.
Oct. 31—Morgantown, skirmish near.
Nov. 7—Columbus, demonstration upon, from Paducah.
Nov. 8—Battle of Ivy Mountain.
Nov. 9—Piketon, skirmish at.
Nov. 20—Brownsville, skirmish at.
Dec. 1—Fort Holt, demonstration on, by gunboats.
Dec. 1—Whippoorwill Creek, skirmish at.
Dec. 1-2—Camp Goggin, skirmishes near.
Dec. 8—Fishing Creek, skirmish at.
Dec. 12—Gradyville, skirmish at.
Dec. 17—Battle of Rowlett's Station; Green River.
Dec. 28—Grider's Ferry, Cumberland River, skirmish at.
Dec. 28—Battle of Sacramento.

1862

Jan. 7—Jennie's Creek, skirmish at.
Jan. 8—Fishing Creek, skirmish at.
Jan. 10—Battle of Middle Creek, near Prestonburg.
Jan. 19—Battle of Mill Springs (Yankee name: Battle of Logan's Cross-Roads).
Feb. 13—Fort Heiman, skirmish near.
March 16—Pound Gap, action at.
May 11—Cave City, affair at.
June 6—Tompkinsville, skirmish near.
June 11—Monterey, skirmish near.
June 20—Lusby's Mill, skirmish near.
June 20-23—Owen County, affairs in.
July 12—Lebanon, skirmish near and capture of.
July 14—Mackville, skirmish near.
July 17—First Battle of Cynthiana.
July 19—Paris, skirmish near.
July 29—Russellville, skirmish at.
Aug. 3—Morganfield, skirmish at.
Aug. 17—Flat Lick, skirmish at.
Aug. 17—London, action at.
Aug. 17—Mammoth Cave, skirmish near.
Aug. 23—Big Hill, action at.
Aug. 25—Madisonville, skirmish at.
Aug. 25—Red Bird Creek, skirmish at.
Aug. 29—Big Hill and Richmond, skirmish between.
Aug. 30—Mount Zion Church, engagement at.
Aug. 30—Battle of Richmond.
Aug. 30—White's Farm, engagement at.
Aug. 31—Kentucky River, skirmish on the.
Sept. 1—Morganfield, skirmish near.
Sept. 1—Tait's Ferry, skirmish at.
Sept. 1—Uniontown, skirmish at.
Sept. 3—Geiger's Lake, skirmish at.
Sept. 4—Shelbyville, skirmish at.
Sept. 5—Madisonville, skirmish near.
Sept. 8—Barboursville, skirmish at.
Sept. 8—Kentucky Line, affair at.
Sept. 9—Franklin Road, skirmish on the.
Sept. 9—Scottsville Road, skirmish on the.
Sept. 10—Covington, skirmish near.

Sept. 10—Log Church, skirmish at.
Sept. 10—Fort Mitchel, skirmish at.
Sept. 10, 12—Woodburn, skirmishes at and near.
Sept. 11—Smith's, skirmish at.
Sept. 12—Brandenburg, skirmish at.
Sept. 14-17—Battle of Munfordville.
Sept. 14-17—Battle of Woodsonville.
Sept. 16—Oakland Station, skirmish near.
Sept. 17—Bowling Green Road, skirmish on the.
Sept. 17—Falmouth, skirmish near.
Sept. 17—Merry Oaks, skirmish at.
Sept. 18—Cave City, skirmish near.
Sept. 18—Florence, skirmish near.
Sept. 18—Glasgow, affair at.
Sept. 18—Owensboro, skirmish at.
Sept. 19—Bear Wallow, skirmish at.
Sept. 19—Horse Cave, skirmish at.
Sept. 19—Southerland's Farm, skirmish at.
Sept. 20-21—Munfordville, actions near.
Sept. 22—Vinegar Hill, skirmish at.
Sept. 25—Ashbysburg, skirmish at.
Sept. 25—Snow's Pond, skirmish near.
Sept. 26—West Liberty, action at.
Sept. 27—Augusta, skirmish at.
Sept. 28—Brookville, skirmish at.
Sept. 28—Lebanon Junction, skirmish near.
Sept. 29—Elizabethtown Road, skirmish on the.
Sept. 30—Glasgow, skirmish at.
Sept. 30—Louisville, skirmish near.
Sept. 30—Russellville and Glasgow, skirmishes at.
Oct. 1—Bardstown Pike, skirmish on the.
Oct. 1—Fern Creek, skirmish on.
Oct. 1—Frankfort and Louisville Road, skirmish on the.
Oct. 1—Mount Washington, skirmish near.
Oct. 2—Shepherdsville Road, skirmish on the.
Oct. 3—Cedar Church, skirmish at.
Oct. 3—Shepherdsville, skirmish near.
Oct. 4, 19—Bardstown, skirmishes at and near.
Oct. 4—Bardstown Pike, action on the.
Oct. 4—Clay Village, skirmish near.
Oct. 6—Beach Fork, skirmish at.
Oct. 6—Burnt Cross-Roads, skirmish at.
Oct. 6—Fair Grounds, skirmish at.

Oct. 6—Grassy Mound, skirmish at.
Oct. 6—Springfield, skirmish at.
Oct. 7—Brown Hill, skirmish at.
Oct. 7—Perryville, skirmish at.
Oct. 8, 11, 25—Lawrenceburg, skirmishes at.
Oct. 8—Battle of Perryville (Yankee name: Battle of Chaplin Hills).
Oct. 9—Bardstown Road, skirmish on the.
Oct. 9—Chesser's Store, action at.
Oct. 9—Mackville Pike, skirmish on.
Oct. 10—Danville Cross-Roads, skirmish at.
Oct. 10—Danville, skirmishes at.
Oct. 11—Dick's Ford, skirmish at.
Oct. 13—Lancaster Road, skirmish on the.
Oct. 14—Crab Orchard Road, skirmish on the.
Oct. 14—Lancaster, skirmish at.
Oct. 14—Manchester, skirmish at.
Oct. 14—Stanford, skirmish at.
Oct. 14-16—Mountain Gap, skirmishes near.
Oct. 15—Barren Mound, skirmish at.
Oct. 16 (15?)—Crab Orchard, skirmish near.
Oct. 16—Big Rock Castle Creek, skirmish at.
Oct. 16—Mount Vernon, skirmish near.
Oct. 17—Wild Cat Mountain, skirmish at.
Oct. 17—Rocky Hill, skirmish at.
Oct. 17—Valley Woods, skirmish at.
Oct. 17—Wild Cat Camp, skirmishes about.
Oct. 18—Big Hill, skirmish at.
Oct. 18—Bloomfield, skirmish at.
Oct. 18—Cross-Roads, skirmish at.
Oct. 18—Lexington, action at.
Oct. 18—Little Rockcastle River, skirmish at.
Oct. 18—Mountain Side, skirmish at.
Oct. 18—Nelson's Cross-Roads, skirmish at.
Oct. 18—Rockcastle River, skirmish at.
Oct. 19-21—Pitman's Cross-Roads, skirmishes at.
Oct. 19-20—Wild Cat (Camp or Mountain?), skirmishes at and near.
Nov. 1—Henderson County, skirmish in.
Nov. 5—Piketon, affair near.
Nov. 6—Garrettsburg, skirmish at.
Nov. 8—Burkesville, skirmish at.
Nov. 19—Tunnel Hill, skirmish at.

Nov. 19, 24—Tompkinsville, skirmishes near.
Nov. 25—Calhoun, skirmish at.
Dec. 4—Floyd County, skirmish in.
Dec. 4-5—Prestonburg, capture of transports and skirmishes near.
Dec. 24—Glasgow, skirmish at.
Dec. 25—Bear Wallow, skirmish at.
Dec. 25—Burkesville Road, skirmish on the.
Dec. 25—Green's Chapel, skirmish near.
Dec. 26—Bacon Creek, skirmish at.
Dec. 26—Munfordville, skirmish near.
Dec. 26—Nolin, capture of stockade at.
Dec. 27—Elizabethtown, capture of Union forces at.
Dec. 28—Muldraugh's Hill, skirmish at.
Dec. 29—Boston, capture of stockade at.
Dec. 29—Hamilton's Ford, skirmish at.
Dec. 29—Johnson's Ferry, skirmish near.
Dec. 30—New Haven, skirmish at.
Dec. 30—Springfield, affair at.
Dec. 31—Muldraugh's Hill, affair at.
Dec. 31—New Market, affair near.

1863

Feb. 22—Coombs' Ferry, skirmish at.
Feb. 23—Athens, affair at.
Feb. 24—Stoner Bridge, skirmish at.
March 2, 19—Mount Sterling, skirmishes at and near.
March 2—Slate Creek, skirmish at.
March 9, 19—Hazle Green, skirmish at.
March 11—Paris, affair near.
March 12, 25, 26—Louisa, skirmishes at and near.
March 24, 26, 28—Danville, skirmishes at.
March 28—Hickman's Bridge, skirmish at.
March 30—Dutton's Hill, action at.
March 30—Somerset, action near.
April 15—Piketon, skirmish at.
April 16—Paris, skirmish at.
April 19—Celina, skirmish at.
April 19—Creelsboro, skirmish at.
April 27—Barboursville, skirmish at.
April 27—Negro Head Cut, skirmish at.

April 27—Woodburn, skirmish.
April 28—Monticello, skirmish near.
May 2—Monticello, skirmish near.
May 3—South Union, skirmish near.
May 6—Waitsboro, accident at.
May 9—Alcorn's Distillery, near Monticello, skirmish at.
May 10—Horseshoe Bottom, Cumberland River, action at.
May 10—Phillips' Fork, Red Bird Creek, skirmish at.
May 13—Woodburn, skirmish near.
May 29—Mill Springs, skirmishes at and near.
June 2—Jamestown, skirmish at.
June 6—Waitsboro, skirmish at.
June 7—Edmonton, skirmish near.
June 9—Kettle Creek, skirmish at.
June 9—Monticello and Rocky Gap, affairs at.
June 11—Scottsville, affair at.
June 13—Howard's Mills, skirmish at.
June 13—Mud Lick Springs, Bath County, skirmish near.
June 16—Fox Springs, skirmish at.
June 16—Maysville, skirmish at.
June 16—Mount Carmel, skirmish at.
June 16—Triplett's Bridge, Rowan County, action at.
June 28—Russellville, skirmish at.
June 29—Columbia and Creelsboro, skirmishes at.
July 1—Christiansburg, affair at.
July 2—Coal Run, Pike County, skirmish at mouth of.
July 2—Marrowbone, skirmish at.
July 3—Columbia, skirmish at.
July 4—Green River Bridge, engagement at.
July 5—Bardstown, skirmish at.
July 5—Franklin, skirmish at.
July 5—Battle of Lebanon.
July 5—Woodburn, skirmish near.
July 6—Pond Creek, skirmish on.
July 7—Cumming's Ferry, skirmish near.
July 7—Shepherdsville, skirmish at.
July 8—Cumming's Ferry, skirmish at.
July 9—Brandenburg, skirmish at.
July 10—Martin Creek, skirmish on.
July 25—New Hope Station, skirmish near.
July 25—Williamsburg, skirmish at.
July 26—London, skirmish at.
July 27—Rogersville, skirmish near.

July 28—Richmond, action at.
July 29—Paris, skirmish at.
July 29—Winchester, skirmish near.
July 30—Irvine, skirmish at.
July 31—Lancaster, skirmish at.
July 31—Paint Lick Bridge, skirmish at.
July 31—Stanford, skirmish at.
Aug. 1—Smith's Shoals, Cumberland River, skirmish at.
Aug. 18—Albany, skirmish near.
Aug. 18—Crab Orchard, skirmish near.
Aug. 27—Carter County, skirmish in.
Aug. 27—Clark's Neck, Lawrence County, skirmish at.
Sept. 10—Brimstone Creek, skirmish at.
Sept. 11—Greenville, skirmish near.
Sept. 22—Marrowbone Creek, skirmish at.
Oct. 6—Glasgow, skirmish at.
Oct. 6—Morgan County, skirmish in
Oct. 10—Sawyerville, skirmish at.
Oct. 12—West Liberty, skirmish at.
Oct. 22—Volley, skirmish near.
Oct. 30—Sawyerville, skirmish at.
Nov. 27—La Fayette, skirmish at.
Nov. 27—Monticello, skirmish at.
Nov. 30—Sawyerville, skirmish at.
Dec. 1—Salyersville, skirmish at.
Dec. 1-10—Mount Sterling and Jackson, affairs at.
Dec. 3—Greenville, skirmish at.
Dec. 8—Scottsville, skirmish at and near.

1864

Jan. 9—Terman's Ferry, skirmish at.
Jan. 12—Marshall, skirmish at.
Jan. 13—Ragland Mills, Bath County, skirmish at.
Feb. 8—Barboursville, skirmish at.
March 6—Columbus, attack on Union pickets at.
March 6—Island No. 10, Mississippi River, affair near.
March 22—Fancy Farms, affair at.
March 25—Battle of Paducah.
March 27—Columbus, skirmish at.
March 28—New Hope, affair at.

March 31—Forks of Beaver, skirmish at.
April 5—Quicksand Creek, skirmish on.
April 7—Bushy Creek, skirmish on.
April 11, 13—Columbus, skirmishes at.
April 13—Paintsville, skirmish at.
April 14—Booneville, affair near.
April 14—Half Mountain, on Licking River, action at.
April 14—Paducah, skirmish at.
April 16—Salyersville, skirmish at.
April 27—Troublesome Creek, skirmish on.
May 6—Morganfield, skirmish near.
May 9—Pound Gap, skirmish near.
May 16—Pond Creek, Pike County, skirmish at.
May 16, 18—Pike County, skirmishes in.
May 18—Wolf River, skirmish at.
May 20—Mayfield, skirmish near.
June 1—Pound Gap, skirmish near.
June 8—Mount Sterling, capture of.
June 9—Mount Sterling, action at.
June 9—Pleasureville, affair near.
June 10—Benson's Bridge, affair near.
June 10—Lexington, capture of.
June 10-12—Frankfort, demonstration on.
June 11-12—Second Battle of Cynthiana; capture of.
June 11—Keller's Bridge, near Cynthiana, action at.
June 25—Morganfield, skirmish at.
June 25—Morganfield, skirmish at.
June 27—Crittenden, affair at.
July 10—Clinton, skirmish at.
July 13—Bell Mines, skirmish at.
July 14—Morganfield, skirmish at.
July 15—Geiger's Lake, skirmish at.
Aug. 1—Bardstown, skirmish near.
Aug. 2—New Haven, skirmish near.
Aug. 8—Salem, skirmish at.
Aug. 17—White Oak Springs, skirmish at.
Aug. 18—Geiger's Lake, skirmish at.
Aug. 19—Smith's Mills, skirmish at.
Aug. 21—Grubb's Cross-Roads, skirmish at.
Aug. 22—Canton and Roaring Spring, skirmishes at.
Aug. 27—Owensboro, skirmish at.
Aug. 29—Ghent, skirmish near.
Sept. 2—Union City, skirmishes at and near.

Sept. 3—Sibley County, skirmish in.
Sept. 14—Weston, affair near.
Sept. 20—McCormick's Gap, skirmish at.
Sept. 25—Henderson, skirmish near.
Oct. 17—Eddyville, skirmish at.
Oct. 21—Harrodsburg, skirmish at.
Oct. 29—Vanceburg, attack on.
Oct. 30—Fort Heiman, capture of gunboat *Undine*, No. 55 and transports near.
Nov. 5—Bloomfield, skirmish at.
Nov. 5-6—Big Pigeon River, skirmishes at.
Dec. 31—Sharpsburg, skirmish at.

1865

Jan. 25—Simpsonville, Shelby County, skirmish near.
Jan. 29—Danville, affair at.
Jan. 29—Harrodsburg, skirmish near.
Jan. 30—Chaplintown, skirmish near.
Feb. 8-9—New Market, Bradfordsville and Hustonville, affairs at.
Feb. 18—Fort Jones, near Colesburg, attack on.
Feb. 25—Piketon, skirmish at.
March 9—Howard's Mills, skirmish at.
March 25—Glasgow, skirmish near.
March 26—Bath County, skirmish in.
March 29—Blackwater River, skirmish at.
April 18—Taylorsville, skirmish near.
April 29—Lyon County, skirmish in.

Arsenal at Fayetteville, NC.

Confederate General Richard Taylor, circa 1860s.

CHAPTER EIGHTEEN
LOUISIANA

1861

Oct. 12—Mississippi River, affair at Southwest Pass.

1862

Jan. 1—Fort Barrancas, bombardment of.
April 12-13—Fort Bisland, engagement at.
April 16-28—Battle of Fort Jackson and Fort St. Philip; bombardment of.
April 25-May 1—New Orleans, siege and capture of.
April 27—Fort Livingston, recapture of, by Union forces.
May 1—Fort Jackson, capture of.
June 17—Pass Manchac, skirmish at.
June 20-22—Des Allemands Bayou, skirmishes at.
July 24—Amite River, skirmish on the.
July 27—Covington, skirmish at.
July 27—Madisonville, skirmish at.
Aug. 5—Battle of Baton Rouge.
Aug. 9—First Battle of Donaldsonville; bombardment of.
Aug. 10, 23—Bayou Sara, affairs at.
Aug. 18—*Fair Play*, steamer, capture of the.
Aug. 18—Milliken's Bend, affair at.
Aug. 19—Tallulah, skirmish at.
Aug. 20-21—Baton Rouge, skirmish at.
Aug. 29—Port Hudson, engagements between batteries at, and Anglo-American U.S.S.

Aug. 29—Saint Charles Court House, skirmish near.
Sept. 4—Des Allemands Bayou, affair at.
Sept. 5—Boutte Station, affair at.
Sept. 7-8—Saint Charles Court House, skirmish.
Sept. 13-15—Pass Manchac, expedition to, and skirmish.
Sept. 13-15—Ponchatoula, expeditions to, and skirmishes.
Sept. 21-25—Donaldsonville, expedition to, and skirmish.
Oct. 19—Bonnet Carré, skirmish at.
Oct. 27—Battle of Georgia Landing.
Nov. 1-6—Berwick Bay, naval operations on.
Nov. 21—Bonfouca, Bayou, skirmish at.
Nov. 21-22—Petite Anse Island, affairs at.
Dec. 10—Desert Station, skirmish at.

1863

Jan. 14—Teche Bayou, engagement on.
Jan. 28—Indian Village, skirmish at.
Jan. 29—Richmond, skirmish near.
Feb. 10—Old River, skirmish at.
March 14-15—Port Hudson, demonstration on land front against.
March 21, 30—Ponchatoula, skirmishes at.
March 31—Richmond, skirmish at.
April 4—Richmond, skirmish at.
April 5—New Carthage, skirmish near.
April 6-8—James' Plantation, near New Carthage, skirmishes at.
April 7, 15—Dunbar's Plantation, Bayou Vidal, skirmishes near.
April 11—Pattersonville, skirmish near.
April 12—Amite River, affair on the.
April 12-13—Centreville, engagement near.
April 12-13—Teche Bayou, engagement on.
April 13—Indian Bend, skirmish at.
April 13—Porter's and McWilliams' Plantations, skirmish at.
April 14—Irish Bend, engagement at.
April 14—Jeanerette, skirmish at.
April 16—Newtown, skirmish at.
April 17—Amite River, skirmish on the.
April 17—Vermillion Bayou, action at.
April 18—Plaquemine, affairs at and near.
April 22—Boeuf Bayou, skirmish at.
April 22—Washington, skirmish at.

April 25-29—Hard Times Landing, expedition to, with skirmishes.
April 26—Clark's Bayou, skirmish at.
April 26—Phelps' Bayou, skirmish at.
April 28—Choctaw Bayou, or Lake Bruin, skirmish at.
May 1—Greensburg, skirmish near.
May 1—Walls Bridge, Tickfaw River, skirmish at.
May 1—Washington, skirmish near.
May 1—Williams' Bridge, skirmish at.
May 2—Comite River, skirmish at Roberts' Ford, on the.
May 4—Fort De Russy, Red River, engagement at.
May 5—Black River, skirmish near.
May 9—Bayou Tensas, near Lake Providence, skirmish at.
May 10—Fort Beauregard, attack on.
May 10—Caledonia and Pin Hook, skirmishes at.
May 10—Macon Bayou, skirmish at.
May 13—Ponchatoula, skirmish at.
May 14—Boyce's Bridge, Cotile Bayou, skirmish at.
May 15—Independence Station, skirmish at.
May 16—Tickfaw Bridge, skirmish at.
May 21—Battle of Plains Store, also known as the Battle of Plains Store Road, and the Battle of Springfield Road.
May 21-July 9—Battle of Port Hudson.
May 22—Barre's Landing, Steamer *Louisiana Belle* attacked near.
May 22—Bayou Courtableau, skirmish at.
May 23—Springfield and Plains Store Roads, skirmishes on the.
May 24, 27—Lake Providence, skirmishes near.
May 25—Centreville, skirmish at.
May 25—*Starlight* and *Red Chief*, capture of the Confederate Steamers.
May 25—Thompson's Creek, skirmish at.
May 27—Port Hudson, assault on.
June 1—Berwick, skirmish at.
June 3—Simsport, engagement near.
June 4—Atchafalaya, skirmish at the.
June 4—Lake Saint Joseph, affair at.
June 7—Battle of Milliken's Bend.
June 7—Young's Point, attack on.
June 9—Lake Providence, action near.
June 11—Port Hudson, capture of Confederate outposts.
June 14—Port Hudson, assault on.
June 15—Richmond, skirmish at.
June 16—Waterloo, demonstration on.
June 18—Plaquemine, skirmish at.

June 20—Thibodeaux, capture of.
June 20-21—Battle of La Fourche Crossing.
June 21—Brashear City, skirmish at.
June 23—Berwick Bay, action at.
June 23—Brashear City, capture of.
June 24—Bayou Boeuf Crossing, capture of Union forces at.
June 24—Chacahoula Station, skirmish at.
June 24—Mound Plantation, near Lake Providence, skirmish at.
June 25—Milliken's Bend, skirmish at.
June 28—Second Battle of Donaldsonville.
June 28—Lake Providence, skirmish at.
June 29—Mound Plantation, skirmish at.
June 29-30—Battle of Goodrich's Landing.
July 2—Springfield Landing, affair at.
July 8—*Saint Mary's Steamer*, attack on the.
July 12-13—Battle of Bayou La Fourche, also known as the Battle of La Fourche, the Battle of Kock's Plantation, and the Battle of Cox's Plantation; near Donaldsonville.
July 18—Des Allemands, skirmish at.
Aug. 3—Jackson, skirmish at.
Aug. 10—Bayou Tensas, skirmish at.
Aug. 24—Bayou Macon, skirmish at.
Aug. 24—Floyd, skirmish at.
Sept. 2—Trinity, skirmish at.
Sept. 4—Fort Beauregard, capture of.
Sept. 4—Harrisonburg, skirmish near.
Sept. 7, 20—Morgan's Ferry, on the Atchafalaya, skirmishes at.
Sept. 8-9—Atchaulaya, skirmishes on the.
Sept. 10—Battle of Little Rock, also known as the Battle of Bayou Fourche, and the Battle of Fourche Bayou.
Sept. 12—Stirling's Plantation, on the Fordoche, skirmish at, near Morganza.
Sept. 14—Vidalia, attack on.
Sept. 19—Baton Rouge, skirmish on the Greenwell Springs Road, near.
Sept. 20—Atchafalaya, skirmish at Morgan's Ferry, on the.
Sept. 23—Donaldsonville, affair opposite.
Sept. 29—Battle of Stirling's Plantation; on the Fordoche.
Oct. 3—Teche Bayou, skirmish on the.
Oct. 4—Nelson's Bridge, near New Iberia, affair at.
Oct. 5—Greenwell Springs Road, skirmish on the.
Oct. 9-10—Vermillion Bayou, skirmishes at.
Oct. 14—Red River, skirmish at.

Oct. 14, 15, 18—Carrion Crow Bayou, skirmishes at.
Oct. 16, 19—Grand Coteau, skirmishes at.
Oct. 21—Opelousas and Barre's Landing, skirmishes at.
Oct. 24, 31—Washington, skirmishes at.
Oct. 30—Opelousas, affair near.
Nov. 3—Bayou Bourbeau, engagement at.
Nov. 3, 18—Carrion Crow Bayou, skirmishes at.
Nov. 5, 8—Vermillionville, skirmishes at.
Nov. 8—Tunica Bend, or Bayou Tunica, skirmish at.
Nov. 9—Bayou Sara, skirmish near.
Nov. 9—Indian Bayou, skirmisli near.
Nov. 11—Carrion Crow and Vermillion Bayous, skirmishes at.
Nov. 11, 30—Vermillion Bayou, skirmishes at,
Nov. 20—Camp Pratt, skirmish at.
Nov. 22—Lake Borgne, affair on.
Nov. 23—Bayou Portage, Grand Lake, affair at.
Nov. 25—Camp Pratt, affair at.
Nov. 25—Vermillion Bayou, skirmish near.
Nov. 30—Port Hudson, skirmish near.
Dec. 3—Saint Martinsville, affair at.

1864

Feb. 4—Columbia, skirmish at.
Feb. 7—Vidalia, skirmish at.
Feb. 8—Donaldsonville, skirmish at.
Feb. 9—New River, skirmish at.
Feb. 11—Madisonville, skirmishes near.
Feb. 19—Grossetete, skirmish at.
March 1-4—Harrisonburg, action at.
March 1-4—Trinity, action at.
March 3—Jackson, skirmishes at, and near Baton Rouge.
March 3, 8—Baton Rouge, skirmishes near.
March 8—Cypress Creek, skirmish at.
March 12—Battle of Fort De Russy.
March 14—Fort de Russy, capture of.
March 15—Marksville Prairie, skirmish at.
March 19—Black Bayou, skirmish at.
March 20—Bayou Rapides, skirmish at.
March 21—Henderson's Hill, affair at.
March 24—Goodrich's Landing, skirmish near.

March 26—Campti, skirmish at.
March 29-30—Monett's Ferry and Cloutierville, skirmishes about.
March 31—Natchitoches, skirmish at.
April 2—Bayou Grossetete, skirmish at.
April 2—Crump's Hill, skirmish at.
April 3, 16, 29—Grand Ecore, skirmishes at.
April 4—Campti, skirmish at.
April 5—Natchitoches, skirmish at.
April 7—Port Hudson, skirmishes near.
April 7—Wilson's Plantation, near Pleasant Hill, skirmish at.
April 8—Bayou De Paul (Carroll's Mill), near Pleasant Hill, skirmish at.
April 8—Battle of Mansfield (Yankee name: Battle of Sabine Cross-Roads).
April 9—Battle of Pleasant Hill.
April 12-13—Battle of Fort Bisland.
April 12-13—Battle of Blair's Landing, also known as the Battle of Pleasant Hill Landing.
April 14—Bayou Saline, skirmish at.
April 14—Battle of Irish Bend.
April 15—Baton Rouge, skirmish near.
April 17—Battle of Vermillion Bayou.
April 20—Waterproof, skirmish at.
April 20-21—Natchitoches, skirmishes about.
April 21—Tunica Bend, affair at.
April 22-24—Cloutierville, skirmishes at and near.
April 23—Cane River Crossing, engagement at.
April 23—Battle of Monett's Ferry, also known as the Battle of Cane River Crossing.
April 24—Pineville, skirmish at.
April 25—Cotile Landing, skirmish at.
April 26—Bayou Rapides Bridge, near McNutt's Hill, skirmish at.
April 26—Berwick, skirmish at.
April 26—Deloach's Bluff, engagement at, and destruction of the U.S.S. *Eastport*.
April 26-27—Cane and Red Rivers, engagement at junction of the.
May 1—Ashton, skirmish at.
May 1—Berwick, affair at.
May 1—Clinton, skirmish at.
May 1, 4—Ashwood Landing, skirmishes at.
May 1-4—Governor Thomas Overton Moore's Plantation, skirmishes at.
May 2-3—Bayou Pierre, skirmishes at.

May 2, 6—Wells' Plantation, skirmishes at.
May 2, 14—Wilson's Landing, skirmishes at.
May 3—Baton Rouge, skirmish near.
May 4-5—David's Ferry, Red River, engagement at, destruction of U.S.S. *Covington*, and capture of the U.S.S. *Signal* and Steamer *Warner*.
May 5—Dunn's Bayou, engagement at.
May 5—Graham's Plantation, skirmish at.
May 5—Natchitoches, skirmish at.
May 6—Boyce's Plantation, skirmish at.
May 6-7, 12—Bayou Lamourie, skirmishes at.
May 7—Bayou Boeuf, skirmish at.
May 8—Bayou Robert, skirmish at.
May 15—Avoyelles, or Marksville, Prairie, skirmish at.
May 15—Mount Pleasant Landing, attack on.
May 16—Battle of Mansura, also known as the Battle of Belle Prairie, and the Battle of Smith's Plantation.
May 17—Moreauville, action near.
May 18—Battle of Yellow Bayou, also known as the Battle of Bayou De Glaize, and the Battle of Old Oaks.
May 24, 30—Morganza, skirmishes near.
May 28—Pest-house opposite Port Hudson, attack on.
May 29—Bayou Fordoche Road, skirmish on.
June 8—Simsport, engagement at.
June 15—Magnolia Landing, attack on Union gunboats at.
June 15—Ratliff's Landing, attack on Union gunboats at.
June 15-16—Como Landing, attacks on Union gunboats at.
June 17—Newport Cross-Roads, skirmish at.
June 19—Bayou Grossetete, affair at.
June 25—Point Pleasant, affair at.
June 29—Davis' Bend, skirmish at.
July 4—Cross Bayou, skirmish at.
July 21—Atchafalaya, skirmish at.
July 22—Concordia, skirmish at.
July 22—Vidalia, skirmish near.
July 25—Amite River, skirmish on, near Benton's Ferry.
July 28—Morgan's Ferry Road, skirmish on.
July 28—Morganza, skirmish near.
July 29—Baton Rouge, affair near, at Highland Stockade.
July 29—Napoleonville, skirmishes near.
July 30—Bayou Tensas, skirmish at.
July 31—Orange Grove, affair at.
Aug. 5—Concordia Bayou, skirmish at.

Aug. 5—Doyal's Plantation, affair at.
Aug. 5, 25—Olive Branch, skirmishes at.
Aug. 6—Indian Village, skirmish at.
Aug. 6—Plaquemine, skirmish at.
Aug. 15-21—Grand River, skirmish on.
Aug. 25—Atchafalaya River, skirmish on.
Aug. 25—Comite River, skirmish at.
Aug. 25—Morgan's Ferry, skirmish at.
Aug. 26—Bayou Tensas, skirmish near.
Aug. 29—Port Hudson, attack on steamer *White Cloud* near.
Sept. 1—Gentilly's Plantation, skirmish near.
Sept. 8—Labadieville, affair at.
Sept. 11—Hodge's Plantation, skirmish at.
Sept. 13, 16—Bayou Maringouin, skirmishes near.
Sept. 14—Bullitt's Bayou, skirmish at.
Sept. 15—Rosedale, skirmish near.
Sept. 16—Williamsport, skirmish at.
Sept. 17—Atchafalaya River, skirmish at.
Sept. 20—Bayou Alabama, skirmish at.
Oct. 3-6—Bayou Sara skirmishes.
Oct. 4—Bayou Sara, skirmish at and near.
Oct. 5—Alexander's Creek, near Saint Francisville, skirmish at.
Oct. 5—Atchafalaya, skirmish at.
Oct. 5—Jackson, skirmish near.
Oct. 5—Saint Charles, skirmish at.
Oct. 9-10—Bayou Sara, skirmishes near.
Oct. 15—Bayou Liddell, skirmish at.
Oct. 16—Morganza, skirmish near.
Oct. 20—Waterloo, skirmish near.
Nov. 15—Clinton, skirmish at.
Nov. 18—Lake Fausse Pointe, skirmish at.
Nov. 23—Bayou Grand Caillou, affair at.
Nov. 23—Morganza, skirmislies at.
Nov. 25—Raccourci, affair at.
Nov. 25—Williamsport, affair near.
Nov. 29—Doyal's Plantation, skirmish at.
Dec. 4—Morganza, skirmish near.
Dec. 4—New Texas Road, skirmish on.
Dec. 12—Amite River, skirmish on.

1865

Jan. 12-15—Morganza, expedition from, with skirmishes.
Jan. 23—Thompson's Plantation, skirmish at.
Jan. 24—Bayou Goula, skirmish near.
Jan. 30—Lake Verret, skirmish near.
Jan. 30—Richland Plantation, skirmish at.
Jan. 31—Bayou Bonfouca, skirmish at.
Feb. 4—The Park, skirmish at.
Feb. 10—Kittredge's Sugar House, skirmish at. (See Napoleonville La.)
Feb. 10—Napoleonville, skirmish near, at Kittredge's Sugar House.
Feb. 15—Martin's Lane, skirmish at.
March 12—Morganza Bend, skirmish at.
March 18—Amite River, skirmish at.
March 21—Bayou Teche, skirmish at.
April 4—Grand Bayou, skirmish at.
May 3—Chacahoula, skirmish at.
May 4—Bayou Black, skirmish at.
May 9—Bayou Goula, skirmish at.
May 11—Brown's Plantation, skirmish at.
May 27—Bayou De Large, affair at.

First Battle of Fort Sumter.

Confederate Commodore Franklin Buchanan, C.S. navy, circa 1862.

CHAPTER NINETEEN
MAINE

1863

July 27—Battle of Portland Harbor. (Note: This engagement was not recognized by 19th-Century Southern historians.)

Confederate ordnance officers examining damage to Fort Sumter after battle, 1861.

Confederate Chaplain Thomas Nelson Conrad, Third Virginia Cavalry Regiment, detailed to Confederate Secret Service and Army Intelligence Office, 1864.

CHAPTER TWENTY
MARYLAND

1861

June 14—Seneca Mills, skirmish at.
June 17—Conrad's Ferry, skirmish at.
June 18—Edward's Ferry, skirmish at.
July 7—Great Falls, skirmish at.
Aug. 5—Point of Rocks, skirmish at.
Aug. 18—Sandy Hook, skirmish at.
Aug. 27—Antietam Iron Works, skirmish at.
Sept. 4—Great Falls, skirmish at.
Sept. 16—Seneca Creek, skirmish opposite.
Sept. 18-29—Berlin, skirmishes at and near.
Sept. 20—Seneca Creek, skirmish opposite.
Sept. 24—Point of Rocks, skirmish at.
Oct. 28—Budd's Ferry, skirmish near.
Nov. 14—Mattawoman Creek, affair at mouth of.
Dec. 19—Point of Rocks, skirmish at.
Dec. 25—Fort Frederick, skirmish at.

1862

Jan. 5-6—Battle of Hancock; bombardment of.
Sept. 3-4—Edward's Ferry, skirmish at.
Sept. 4—Monocacy Aqueduct, skirmish at.
Sept. 4-5—Berlin, skirmishes at.
Sept. 4-5, 7—Point of Rocks, skirmishes at.
Sept. 4, 5, 8—Poolesville, skirmishes at.

Sept. 9—Barnesville, skirmish at.
Sept. 9—Monocacy Church, skirmish at.
Sept. 10-11—Sugar Loaf Mountain, skirmishes a
Sept. 11, 19, 20—Williamsport, skirmishes near.
Sept. 12—Frederick City, skirmishes at.
Sept. 12-13—Maryland Heights, action on.
Sept. 13—Catoctin Mountain, skirmish at.
Sept. 13—Jefferson, skirmish at.
Sept. 13—Middletown, skirmish at.
Sept. 13—South Mountain, skirmish at.
Sept. 14—Battle of Boonsboro Gap (Yankee name: Battle of South Mountain).
Sept. 14—Battle of Burkittsville (Yankee name: Battle of Crampton's Pass).
Sept. 14—Battle of Slaughter's Gap.
Sept. 14—Battle of Turner's Pass.
Sept. 15—Antietam Creek, skirmish on.
Sept. 16-17—Battle of Sharpsburg (Yankee name: Battle of Antietam).
Sept. 20—Hagerstown, skirmish near.
Oct. 9—Four Locks, skirmish at.
Oct. 10—Fairview Heights, capture of signal station on.
Oct. 10—Green Spring Furnace, skirmish at.
Oct. 10—McCoy's Ferry, skirmish at.
Oct. 12—White's Ford, skirmish at.

1863

April 26—Altamont, affair at.
April 26—Cranberry Summit, affair at.
April 26—Oakland, skirmish at.
June 10—Seneca Mills, skirmish at.
June 15—Williamsport, skirmish near.
June 17—Catoctin Creek and Point of Rocks, skirmishes at.
June 20—Middletown, skirmish at.
June 21—Frederick, skirmish at.
June 24—Sharpsburg, skirmish at.
June 28—Offutt's Cross-Roads and Seneca, skirmish between.
June 28—Rockville, skirmish near.
June 29—Lisbon and Poplar Springs, affairs at.
June 29—Muddy Branch, skirmish at.

June 29-30—Westminster, skirmishes at.
July 4—Emmitsburg, skirmish near.
July 5—Smithsburg, skirmish at.
July 6—Hagerstown, action at.
July 6-16—Battle of Williamsport.
July 7—Downsville, skirmish at.
July 7—Funkstown, skirmish at.
July 8—Battle of Boonsboro.
July 8, 14—Williamsport, skirmishes near.
July 9—Benevola (or Beaver Creek), skirmish at.
July 10—Clear Spring, skirmish near.
July 10—Old Antietam Forge, near Leitersburg, skirmish at.
July 10, 13—Funkstown, skirmishes at and near.
July 10-13—Hagerstown, skirmishes at and near.
July 10-13—Jones' Cross-Roads, near Williamsport, skirmishes at.
July 14—Falling Waters, action at.
Aug. 27—Edward's Ferry, skirmish at.
Sept. 22—Rockville, skirmish at.

1864

July 5—Keedysville, affair at.
July 5—Noland's Ferry, affair at.
July 5—Point of Rocks, skirmish at.
July 5, 7—Solomon's Gap, affairs at.
July 6—Antietam, affair at the.
July 6—Hagerstown, capture of.
July 7—Brownsville, affair at.
July 7—Hager's (or Catoctin) Mountain, affair at.
July 7—Middletown, skirmish at.
July 7, 8, 11—Frederick, skirmishes at.
July 8—Antietam Bridge, skirmish at.
July 8—Sandy Hook, skirmish at.
July 9—Battle of Monocacy.
July 9—Urbana, skirmish at.
July 10—Monocacy, skirmish near.
July 10—Rockville, skirmish at.
July 13—Rockville, affair at.
July 25—Williamsport, skirmish at.
July 29—Clear Spring, skirmish at.
July 29—Hagerstown, skirmish at.

July 30—Emmitsburg, affair at.
July 30—Monocacy Junction, skirmish at.
July 31—Hancock, skirmish at.
Aug. 1—Cumberland, attack on.
Aug. 1—Flintstone Creek, affair at.
Aug. 1—Battle of Folck's Mill, also known as the Battle of Cumberland.
Aug. 2—Hancock, skirmish at.
Aug. 2—Old Town, skirmish at.
Aug. 4—Antietam Ford, skirmish at.
Aug. 5, 15—Hagerstown, skirmishes at.
Aug. 5—Keedysville, skirmish at.
Aug. 5—Williamsport and Hagerstown, skirmishes at.
Aug. 22—Cove Point, affair at.
Aug. 26—Williamsport, affair at.
Oct. 14—Adamstown, skirmish at.

1865

Feb. 21—Cumberland, raid on.

Richmond, VA, in ruins, April 1865; from my book *The Unholy Crusade: Lincoln's Legacy of Destruction in the American South.*

CHAPTER TWENTY-ONE
MEXICO

1863

Sept. 2—Mier, affair with Zapata's banditti near.

1864

Jan. 12-13—Matamoras, affair at.

Battle of Fort Henry.

Confederate Colonel John S. Green, circa 1863.

CHAPTER TWENTY-TWO
MINNESOTA

1862

Aug. 20-22—Fort Ridgely, actions at.
Sept. 2—Birch Cooley, action at.
Sept. 4—Hutchinson, skirmish at.
Sept. 10—Sauk Centre, skirmish at.
Sept. 23—Wood Lake, near Yellow Medicine, skirmish at.

1864

May 16—Spirit Lake, affair at.

1865

May 2—Blue Earth River, affair on.
May 18—Couteau, Minn., skirmish with Indians on.

Camp Dennison, Cincinnati, OH.

Statue of U.S. Secretary of War and C.S. President Jefferson Davis in National Statuary Hall, U.S. Capitol, Washington, D.C., photo circa 1940. The two men saluting him are probably members of the Sons of Confederate Veterans, founded in 1896. Davis' statue was long ago removed from the main viewing chamber by enemies of the Truth.

CHAPTER TWENTY-THREE
MISSISSIPPI

1861

Sept. 17—Ship Island, affair at.

1862

April 3-4—Biloxi and Pass Christian, affairs at.
April 24-25—Corinth Road, skirmishes on the.
April 29-June 10—First Battle of Corinth, advance upon and siege of.
May 3-22—Farmington, skirmishes at and near.
May 4—Farmington Heights, skirmish at.
May 8—Glendale, skirmish at.
May 9—Corinth, skirmish near.
May 9—Farmington, engagement at.
May 17—Corinth, action at Russell's house, near.
May 21-29—Corinth, skirmishes near.
May 26—Grand Gulf, affair at.
May 29—Booneville, skirmish near.
May 30—Booneville, expedition to and capture of.
June 2—Rienzi, affair at.
June 3—Blackland, skirmish at.
June 4—Osborn's Creek, skirmish at.
June 4—Wolf's Creek, skirmish at.
June 9—Grand Gulf, engagement at.
June 11—Booneville, skirmish near.
June 14—Baldwyn, skirmish at.

June 14—Clear Creek, skirmish at.
June 21—Coldwater Station, skirmish at.
June 24—Grand Gulf, skirmish near.
June 24—Hamilton's Plantation, skirmish at.
June 28—Blackland, skirmishes at and near.
June 28—Vicksburg, bombardment of.
July 1—Battle of Booneville.
July 1—Holly Springs, skirmish at.
July 5—Hatchie River, skirmish on the.
July 15, 22—*Arkansas* C.S.S., engagements with.
July 20—Hatchie Bottom, affair at.
July 24—White Oak Bayou, skirmish at.
Aug. 2—Austin, Tunica County, skirmish at.
Aug. 2—Totten's Plantation, Coahoma County, skirmish near.
Aug 11—Brown's Plantation, skirmish at.
Aug. 16—Horn Lake Creek, skirmish at.
Aug. 23—Greenville, skirmish at.
Aug. 25—Bolivar, skirmish at.
Aug. 26—Rienzi, skirmish at.
Aug. 27—Kossuth, skirmish near.
Aug. 2S—Corinth, skirmish near.
Aug. 31—Marietta, skirmish near.
Sept. 6—Olive Branch, skirmish at.
Sept. 9—Cockrum's Cross-Roads, skirmish at.
Sept 9, 18—Rienzi, skirmish near.
Sept. 12—Coldwater Railroad Bridge, skirmish at.
Sept. 13, 20, 27—Iuka, skirmishes near.
Sept. 14—Burnsville, skirmish at.
Sept. 19—Barnett's Corners, skirmish at.
Sept. 19—Bolivar, attack on *Queen of the West*, near.
Sept. 19—Battle of Iuka.
Sept. 19—Peyton's Mill, skirmish at.
Sept. 19—Prentiss, skirmish at.
Sept. 20—Fulton Road, skirmish on the.
Sept. 28—Friar's Point, skirmish near.
Oct. 1, 7—Ruckersville, skirmishes at and near.
Oct. 2—Baldwyn, skirmish near.
Oct. 2—Ramer's Crossing, Mobile & Ohio Railroad, skirmish near.
Oct. 3-4—Second Battle of Corinth.
Oct. 5—Corinth, attack on the camp of the "Union brigade" at.
Oct. 7—Box Ford, Hatchie River, skirmish at.
Oct. 7—Ripley, skirmish at.

Nov. 5—Jumpertown, skirmish at.
Nov. 6—Worsham's Creek, skirmish at.
Nov. 6-8—Old Lamar, skirmishes at.
Nov. 8—Hudsonville, skirmish at.
Nov. 13—Holly Springs, skirmish near.
Nov. 28—Tallahatchie River, skirmish on the.
Nov. 29—Lumpkin's Mill, skirmish at.
Nov. 30—Chulahoma, skirmish at.
Dec. 1—Hudsonville, skirmish at.
Dec. 1—Mitchell's Cross-Roads, skirmish near.
Dec. 1—Yocknapatalfa River, skirmish on the.
Dec. 3—Free Bridge, skirmish at.
Dec. 3—Oakland, skirmish at.
Dec. 3—Prophet Bridge, skirmish at.
Dec. 3—Spring Dale Bridge, skirmish at.
Dec. 4, 18—Water Valley, skirmishes at and near.
Dec. 5—Coffeeville, engagement at.
Dec. 20—Coldwater, skirmish at.
Dec. 20—Holly Springs, capture of.
Dec. 21—Davis' Mill, skirmish at.
Dec. 23, 25—Ripley, skirmishes near.
Dec. 26-29—Battle of Chickasaw Bayou.
Dec. 27—Snyder's Mill, Yazoo River, affair at.
Dec. 27-28—Chickasaw Bayou, skirmishes at.
Dec. 29—Chickasaw Bluffs, assault on.

1863

Jan. 1—Bath Springs, skirmish at.
Jan. 3—Burnsville, skirmish at.
Feb. 3—*Berwick Bay*, (C.S.S.) steamer, capture of.
Feb. 16, 19—Yazoo Pass, skirmishes at and near.
Feb. 19—Coldwater River, skirmish near.
Feb. 23—Deer Creek, skirmish on.
Feb. 23—Fish Lake Bridge, skirmish at.
March 11, 13, 16—Fort Pemberton, engagements at.
March 15-16—Hernando, skirmishes near.
March 22—Deer Creek, skirmish on.
March 23—*Hartford*, U.S.S., attack on Warrenton batteries by.
March 23—*Monongahela*, U.S.S., attack on Warrenton batteries by.

March 31—Grand Gulf, engagement at.
April 2, 4—Fort Pemberton, engagements at.
April 7-10—Deer Creek, skirmishes on.
April 11—Courtney's Plantation, skirmish at.
April 18—Hernando, action at.
April 18-19—New Albany, skirmishes at.
April 19—Perry's Ferry, Coldwater River, skirmish at.
April 19—Pontotoc, skirmish at.
Ajiril 21—Palo Alto, skirmish at.
April 24—Birmingham, skirmish at.
April 28—Union Church, skirmish at.
April 29—Brookhaven, skirmish at.
April 29—Battle of Grand Gulf.
April 29—Haynes' Bluff, demonstration on.
April 29-May 1—Battle of Snyder's Bluff.
April 29-May 1—Drumgould's Bluff, demonstration on.
April 30-May 1—Snyder's Mill, engagement at.
May 1—Battle of Anderson's Hill.
May 1-14—Bayou Pierre, skirmishes on.
May 1—Haynes' Bluff, demonstration on.
May 1—Battle of Port Gibson.
May 3—Forty Hills, skirmish at.
May 3—Ingraham Heights, skirmish at.
May 3—Jones' Cross-Roads, skirmish at.
May 3—North Fork of Bayou Pierre, skirmish on the.
May 3—Willow Springs, skirmish at.
May 3, 4—Hankinson's Ferry, Big Black River, skirmishes at.
May 5—Big Sandy Creek, skirmish at.
May 5—Blackland, action near.
May 5—King's Creek, near Tupelo, action at.
May 8, 9—Big Sandy Creek, skirmishes at and near.
May 9-10—Utica, skirmishes at and near.
May 11—Coldwater River, skirmish at the.
May 12—Fourteen-Mile Creek, skirmish at.
May 12—Greenville, skirmish at.
May 12—Battle of Raymond.
May 13—Baldwin's Ferry, skirmish at.
May 13—Hall's Ferry, skirmish at.
May 13—Mississippi Springs, skirmish at.
May 13—Raymond, skirmish near.
May 14—Battle of Jackson.
May 14—Walnut Hill, skirmishes at and near.
May 15—Bolton Station, skirmish at and capture of.

May 15, 31—Edwards Station, skirmishes near.
May 16—Battle of Champion Hill, also known as the Battle of Champion's Hill, or the Battle of Baker's Creek.
May 17—Battle of Big Black River Bridge.
May 17—Bridgeport, skirmish near.
May 18—Greenville, skirmish near Island No. 82, above.
May 18—Haynes' Bluff, capture of.
May 18-July 4—Battle of Vicksburg.
May 23—Haynes' Bluff, skirmish at.
May 23—Liverpool Landing, skirmish at.
May 23—Senatobia, skirmish near.
May 24-28—Austin, skirmislics near.
May 24—Raymond, capture of.
May 24-29—Mechanicsburg, skirmishes at.
May 27—*Cincinnati*, U.S.S., engagement with Vicksburg batteries.
May 27—Greenwood, attack on Union gunboats, near.
June 4—Mechanicsburg, skirmish at.
June 6, 10—Edwards Station, skirmishes at.
June 9—Macon Ford, Big Black River, skirmish at.
June 11—Burnsville, skirmish at.
June 11—Corinth, skirmish at Smith's Bridge, near.
June 12—Birdsong Ferry, skirmish at.
June 16—Quinn's Mills, skirmish at.
June 16-17—Holly Springs, skirmishes near.
June 17—Commerce, attack on transports in Mississippi River, near.
June 17—Obion River, skirmish on the.
June 18—Belmont, skirmish at.
June 18—Birdsong Ferry, affair on Big Black River, at.
June 18—Coldwater Bridge, skirmish at.
June 19—Hernando, action on the Coldwater, near.
June 19—New Albany, skirmish at.
June 19, 20—Panola, skirmishes near.
June 20—Matthews' Ferry, skirmish on the Coldwater, at.
June 20—Mud Creek, skirmish at.
June 20—Rocky Ford, Tallahatchie River, skirmish near.
June 20—Senatobia, skirmish near.
June 21—Hudsonville, skirmish at.
June 22—Bear Creek, action near.
June 22—Big Black River, skirmish on.
June 22—Jones' Plantation, near Birdsong Ferry, skirmish at.
June 25—Ellisville, skirmish at Rocky Creek, near.
June 28—Jones' Ferry, Big Black River, skirmish at.

June 29-30—Big Black River, skirmishes at Messinger's Ferry, the.
July 1—Edwards Station, skirmish at.
July 1—Hankinson's Ferry, Big Black River, skirmish at.
July 3-4—Big Black River, skirmishes at Messinger's Ferry, the.
July 6—Jones' and Messinger's Ferry, skirmishes at.
July 7—Baker's Creek, skirmish near.
July 7—Iuka, action at.
July 7—Ripley, skirmish at.
July 7—Queen's Hill, skirmish at.
July 8—Bolton Station, skirmish near.
July 8-9—Clinton, skirmishes near.
July 9-22—Jackson, skirmishes near.
July 12—Canton, skirmish near.
July 12—Jackson, assault on.
July 14—Iuka, skirmish near.
July 16—Bolton Station, skirmish at.
July 16—Clinton, skirmish at.
July 16—Grant's Ferry, skirmish on Pearl River, at.
July 17—Bear Creek, skirmish near Canton, at.
July 18—Brookhaven, skirmish at.
July 19—Brandon, action at.
July 31—Natchez, skirmish near.
Aug. 3—Ripley, skirmish at.
Aug. 5—Mount Pleasant, skirmish at.
Aug. 8—Rienzi, skirmish at.
Aug. 12—Big Black River Bridge, skirmish at.
Aug. 13—Jacinto, skirmish at.
Aug. 14—Craven's Plantation, skirmish at.
Aug. 16—Corinth, skirmish near.
Aug. 17—Grenada, skirmish at.
Aug. 17—Panola, skirmish near.
Aug. 18—Payne's Plantation, near Grenada, skirmish at.
Aug. 20—Panola, skirmish at.
Aug. 21—Coldwater, skirmish at the.
Aug. 27—Mount Pleasant, skirmish at.
Sept. 7—Glendale, skirmish near.
Sept. 7—Holly Springs, skirmish at.
Sept. 7—Jacinto (or Glendale), skirmish near.
Sept. 11—Baldwin's Ferry, Big Black River, skirmish at.
Sept. 28—Brownsville, skirmish at.
Sept. 29—Benton, skirmish at Moore's Ford, near.
Oct. 3—Forked Deer Creek, skirmish at.
Oct. 5—New Albany, skirmish at.

Oct. 6—Lockhart's Mill, on Coldwater River, skirmish at.
Oct. 8—Salem, action at.
Oct. 10—Port Gibson, skirmish at Ingraham's Plantation, near.
Oct. 11—Hernando, skirmish near.
Oct. 12—Byhalia, skirmish at Ingram's Mill, near.
Oct. 12—Quinn and Jackson's Mill, skirmish at.
Oct. 13—Wyatt, action at.
Oct. 15—Brownsville, skirmish at.
Oct. 15-16—Canton Road, near Brownsville, skirmishes on the.
Oct. 16—Clinton and Vernon Cross-Roads, skirmish at Treadwell's, near.
Oct. 17—Bogue Chitto Creek, action at.
Oct. 17—Livingston, skirmish at Robinson's Mills, near.
Oct. 17—Satartia, skirmish near.
Oct. 18—Clinton, skirmish on the Livingston road, near.
Oct. 19—Smith's Bridge, skirmish at.
Oct. 20—Treadwell's Plantation, skirmish at.
Oct. 22—Brownsville, skirmish at.
Oct. 26—Vincent's Cross-Roads, near Bay Springs, skirmish at.
Oct. 31—Yazoo City, skirmish at.
Nov. 1, 3—Quinn and Jackson's Mill, Coldwater River, skirmishes at.
Nov. 2, 12—Corinth, skirmishes at.
Nov. 5—Holly Springs, skirmish at.
Nov. 11—Natchez, skirmish near.
Nov. 14, 15—Danville, skirmishes at.
Nov. 17—Bay Saint Louis, skirmish at.
Nov. 22—Camp Davies, skirmish at.
Nov. 22—Fayette, skirmish at.
Nov. 28—Molino, skirmish near.
Dec. 1—Ripley, skirmish at.
Dec. 4—Ripley, affair at.
Dec. 7—Independence, skirmish at.
Dec. 9—Okolona, skirmish at.
Dec. 17, 24—Rodney, skirmishes at.
Dec. 22—Fayette, skirmish at.
Dec. 23—Corinth, skirmish near.
Dec. 26—Port Gibson, skirmish at.
Dec. 28—Mount Pleasant, skirmish at.
Dec. 29—Coldwater, skirmish at.

1864

Jan. 6—*Delta*, steamer, attack on, on the Mississippi River.
Jan. 16—Oak Ridge, skirmish at.
Jan. 18—Grand Gulf, skirmish at.
Jan. 25—Mount Pleasant, skirmish at.
Feb. 3—Liverpool Heights, Yazoo River, action at.
Feb. 4—Bolton Depot, skirmish near.
Feb. 4—Champion's Hill, skirmish at.
Feb. 4—Edwards' Ferry, skirmish at.
Feb. 4—Liverpool Heights, Yazoo River, skirmish opposite.
Feb. 4—Queen's Hill, skirmish at.
Feb. 5—Baker's Creek, skirmish, on.
Feb. 5—Clinton, skirmish at.
Feb. 6, 10—Hillsboro, skirmishes at.
Feb. 7—Brandon, skirmish at.
Feb. 7—Satartia, skirmish at
Feb. 7, 8, 10—Morton, skirmishes at and near.
Feb. 8—Coldwater Ferry, affair at.
Feb. 8-9—Senatobia, skirmishes at and near.
Feb. 11—Raiford's Plantation, near Byhalia, affair at.
Feb. 12—Holly Springs, skirmish at.
Feb. 12—Wall Hill, affair at.
Feb. 13—Wyatt, skirmish at.
Feb. 13-14—Chunky Creek and Meridian, skirmishes between.
Feb. 13-14, 19—Meridian, skirmishes near.
Feb. 14-20—Battle of Meridian.
Feb. 15-17—Marion Station, skirmishes at.
Feb. 16—Lauderdale Springs, skirmish at.
Feb. 17—Houlka Swamp, near Houston, skirmish in the.
Feb. 17—Pontotoc, skirmish near.
Feb. 18—Aberdeen, skirmish at.
Feb. 19—Egypt Station, skirmish at.
Feb. 21—Ellis' Bridge, skirmish at.
Feb. 21—Prairie Station, skirmish at.
Feb. 21—Battle of West Point.
Feb. 21-22—Union, skirmishes at.
Feb. 22—Ivey's Hill, or Farm, skirmish at.
Feb. 22—Battle of Okolona.
Feb. 22—Tallahatchie River, skirmish on the.
Feb. 23—New Albany, skirmish near.
Feb. 24, 26, 29—Canton, skirmishes at and near.

Feb. 24—Tippah River, skirmish at.
Feb. 24—Madisonville, affair at.
Feb. 27—Sharon, skirmish at.
Feb. 28—Pearl River, skirmishes on.
Feb. 28—Yazoo City, skirmish near.
March 2—Canton, skirmish at.
March 3, 7-8—Brownsville, skirmishes at.
March 3—Liverpool, skirmish at.
March 4—Rodney, skirmish at.
March 5—Yazoo City, attack on.
March 22—Langley's Plantation, Issaquena County, skirmish at.
March 26—Clinton, skirmish at.
March 27—Livingston, skirmish at.
March 30—Snyder's Bluff, attack on outpost at.
April 3—Clinton, skirmish at.
April 17—Holly Springs, skirmish at.
April 19-23—Mechanicsburg, skirmishes at and near.
April 21—Red Bone, skirmish at.
April 25—Natchez, skirmish near.
May 7-9—Benton, skirmishes at.
May 15—Luce's Plantation, skirmish at.
May 20, 27—Greenville, skirmishes at.
May 22—Mount Pleasant, skirmish near.
May 29—Yazoo River, skirmish at.
June 4—Vicksburg, skirmish near.
June 7—Ripley, skirmish at.
June 8—Indian Bayou, affair at.
June 10—Battle of Brice's Cross-Roads.
June 10—Guntown, engagement near.
June 11—Battle of Ripley.
June 11—Salem, skirmish at.
June 11—Battle of Tallahatchie.
June 12—Davis' Mills, skirmish at.
June 23—Okolona, skirmish at.
June 25—Ashwood, skirmish at.
July 6—Bolivar, skirmish near.
July 7—Jackson, engagement near.
July 7—Ripley, skirmish near.
July 8—Kelly's Mill, skirmish near.
July 10—Cherry Creek and Plentytude, skirmishes at.
July 11-12—Pontotoc, skirmishes at and near.
July 13—Camargo Cross-Roads, action near.
July 13—Utica, skirmish at.

July 14—Port Gibson, skirmish at.
July 14-15—Battle of Tupelo.
July 15—Battle of Old Town Creek.
July 16—Ellistown, skirmish at.
July 16—Grand Gulf, skirmish at.
July 22—Coldwater River, skirmish at.
Aug. 7-9, 10—Tallahatchie River, skirmishes at the.
Aug. 9, 13-14, 19—Hurricane Creek, skirmishes at.
Aug. 9—Oxford, skirmish at.
Aug. 14—Lamar, skirmish at.
Aug. 16—Battle of Hurricane Creek.
Aug. 23—Abbeville, skirmish at.
Aug. 29—Mississippi River, attack on steamer *White Cloud* on.
Sept. 6—Natchez and Liberty Road, skirmish on, near the Eight-Mile Post.
Sept. 22-23—Rolling Fork, skirmishes near.
Sept. 28—Brownsville, skirmish at.
Sept. 29—Moore's Bluff, skirmish at.
Sept. 30—Port Gibson, skirmish at.
Oct. 2—Fayette, descent on.
Oct. 4-12—Woodville, expedition from Natchez to, and skirmishes, etc.
Oct. 10—Eastport, action at.
Oct. 15—Hernando, skirmish at.
Oct. 25—Steele's Bayou, skirmish at.
Nov. 14-21—Brookhaven, expedition to, from Baton Rouge, La., and skirmishes.
Nov. 27—Big Black Bridge, skirmish at.
Dec. 1—Concord Church, action at.
Dec. 10—Chickasaw Bridge, skirmish at.
Dec. 21-22—Franklin Creek, skirmish at.
Dec. 25—Verona, engagement at.
Dec. 27—Okolona, skirmish at.
Dec. 28—Egypt, engagement at.

1865

Jan. 2—Franklin, engagement at.
Jan. 2—Lexington, skirmish at.
Jan. 3—Mechanicsburg, skirmish near.
Jan. 4—The Ponds, skirmish at.

Jan. 19—Corinth, skirmish at.
May 3-6—Fort Adams, operations about.
May 3-6—Port Gibson, expedition from Rodney to, with skirmishes.

Confederate officer, name unknown, New Orleans, LA, circa 1861.

Confederate Secretary of the Navy Stephen Russell Mallory, circa 1862.

CHAPTER TWENTY-FOUR
MISSOURI

1861

June 17—First Battle of Boonville.
June 19—Battle of Cole Camp.
June 24—Jackson, skirmish at.
July 4—Farmington, skirmish at.
July 5—Brier Fork, action at.
July 5—Battle of Carthage.
July 5—Dry Fork, action at.
July 9-11—Monroe Station, skirmishes near and at.
July 15—Mexico, skirmish at.
July 15-17—Wentzville, skirmish at.
July 17—Fulton, skirmish at.
July 17-19—Parkersville, skirmish at.
July 18—Harrisonville, action near.
July 18—Martinsburg, skirmish at.
July 22—Etna, skirmish at.
July 22—Forsyth, skirmish at.
July 24—Blue Hills, action at.
July 25—Dug Springs, skirmish at.
July 25-27—Harrisonville, skirmishes at.
July 26—McCulla's Store, skirmish at.
Aug. 1—Edina, skirmish at.
Aug. 2—Dug Springs, skirmish at.
Aug. 3—McCulla's Store, skirmish at.
Aug. 5—Athens, skirmish at.
Aug. 6-9—Battle of Kirksville.
Aug. 10—Battle of Oak Hills (Yankee name: Battle of Wilson's Creek).

Aug. 11 or 12—Hamburg, affair at.
Aug. 16-21—Kirksville, operations around.
Aug. 17—Brunswick, skirmish at.
Aug. 17—Hunnewell, affair at.
Aug. 17—Palmyra, affair at.
Aug. 19—Klapsford, skirmish at.
Aug. 19-20—Fish Lake, skirmish at.
Aug. 19-20—Charleston, skirmishes at.
Aug. 21-22—Jonesboro, skirmishes at.
Aug. 23—Medoc, skirmish at.
Aug. 28—Ball's Mill, skirmish at.
Aug. 29—Morse's Mills, skirmish at.
Sept. 1—Rennight's Mills, skirmish at.
Sept. 2—Dallas, skirmish at.
Sept. 2—Battle of Dry Wood Creek.
Sept. 5—Papinsville, skirmish at.
Sept. 6—Monticello Bridge, skirmish at.
Sept. 8-10—Lucas Bend, engagements at.
Sept. 13—Second Battle of Boonville.
Sept. 13-20—First Battle of Lexington, also known as the Battle of the Hemp Bales.
Sept. 14—Old Randolph, skirmish at.
Sept. 17—Blue Mills Landing, action at.
Sept. 17—Battle of Liberty.
Sept. 17—Morristown, skirmish at.
Sept. 22—Osceola, skirmish at and destruction of.
Sept. 27—Norfolk, skirmish near.
Oct. 13—Pomme de Terre, skirmish on the.
Oct. 13—Wet Glaze, action at.
Oct. 14—Bird's Point, skirmish at Underwood's Farm near.
Oct. 14—Linn Creek, affair at.
Oct. 15—Blackwell's Station, skirmishes near and at.
Oct. 16—Linn Creek, skirmish near.
Oct. 17-18—Fredericktown, skirmishes at.
Oct. 18—Warrensburg, skirmish at.
Oct. 19—Second Battle of Lexington.
Oct. 19—Big Hurricane Creek, action at.
Oct. 21—Battle of Fredericktown.
Oct. 25—First Battle of Springfield.
Oct. 27—Spring Hill, skirmish near.
Nov. 6—Little Santa Fe, action at.
Nov. 7—Battle of Belmont.
Nov. 11—Little Blue River, action at.

Nov. 18—Price's Landing, attack on steamboat *Platte Valley* at.
Nov. 20—Butler, skirmish at.
Nov. 20—Little Santa Fe, skirmish at.
Nov. 24—Johnstown, skirmish at.
Nov. 24—Lancaster, skirmish at.
Nov. 26—Independence, skirmish at.
Nov. 30—Grand River, skirmish at.
Dec. 1—Shanghai, skirmish at.
Dec. 3—Salem, action at.
Dec. 9—Union Mills, skirmish at.
Dec. 11—Bertrand, skirmish near.
Dec. 13—Charleston, skirmish at.
Dec. 18—Blackwater Creek, skirmish on the.
Dec. 18—Milford, skirmish at.
Dec. 23—Dayton, skirmish at.
Dec. 24—Wadesburg, skirmish at.
Dec. 27—Hallsville, skirmish near.
Dec. 28—Battle of Mount Zion Church.
Dec. 29—*City of Alton*, steamboat, attack on.
Dec. 29—Commerce, descent on.

1862

Jan. 1-3—Dayton, expedition to, skirmish near, and destruction of.
Jan. 3—Hunnewell, skirmish at.
Jan. 8—Charleston, skirmish at.
Jan. 8—Battle of Roan's Tan-Yard; Silver Creek, action at.
Jan. 9—Columbus, skirmish at.
Jan. 22—Knobnoster, skirmish at.
Feb. 8—Bolivar, affair at.
Feb. 9—Marshfield, skirmish at.
Feb. 12—Springfield, skirmish at.
Feb. 14—Crane Creek, skirmish at.
Feb. 15—Flat Creek, skirmish near.
Feb. 19—West Plains, skirmish at.
Feb. 22—Independence, skirmish at.
Feb. 23-24—Pea Ridge Prairie, reconnoissance to and skirmish on.
Feb. 23-25—Saint Francisville, reconnoissance to and skirmish near.
Feb. 25—Keytesville, skirmish at.

Feb. 28-April 8—Battle of New Madrid, also known as the Battle of Island No. 10; advance upon and siege of.
March 1—Sikeston, skirmish near.
March 7—Bob's Creek, skirmish at.
March 7—Fox Creek, skirmish at.
March 7 and 18—Point Pleasant, engagements at.
March 9—Big Creek, skirmish on.
March 9—Mountain Grove, skirmish at.
March 10—La Fayette County, skirmish in.
March 15-16—Marshall, skirmish near.
March 17—Riddle's Point, action at.
March 19—Leesville, skirmish near.
March 21—McKay's Farm, affair at.
March 22—Little Santa Fe, skirmish at.
March 22—Post Oak Creek, skirmish on.
March 25—Monagan Springs, skirmish at.
March 25-28—Moniteau County, expedition in, and skirmish en route.
March 26—Gouge's Mill, skirmish near.
March 26—Humansville, action at.
March 26—Post Oak Creek, action on.
March 20—Blackwater Creek, skirmish on the.
March 30—Clinton, skirmish near.
March 31—Pink Hill, skirmish at.
April 1—Doniphan, skirmish at.
April 1—Little Sni, skirmish on the.
April 2—Walkersville, skirmish near.
April 8—Medicine Creek, skirmish at.
April 8—Warrensburg, skirmish near
April 9—Jackson, skirmish at.
April 11—Shiloh, skirmish near.
April 14—Diamond Grove, skirmish at.
April 14—Montevallo, skirmish at.
April 14—Santa Fe Road, skirmish near the.
April 15—Lost Creek, skirmish at.
April 16—Blackwater, skirmish on.
April 17-28—Warsaw, skirmishes at.
April 25—Monagan Springs, skirmish at.
April 25—Osage River, skirmish on, near Monagan Springs.
April 26—Neosho, skirmish at.
April 26—Turnback Creek, skirmish at.
May 7—Horse Creek, skirmish at.
May 10—Bloomfield, skirmish at.

May 15—Butler, skirmish near.
May 17—Independence, skirmish near.
May 26—Crow's Station, near Licking, skirmish at.
May 26—Miami, skirmish at.
May 26—Waverly, skirmish at.
May 27—Monagan Springs, skirmish near.
May 27—Osceola, skirmish near.
May 31—Florida, skirmish at.
May 31—Neosho, skirmish near.
May 31—Salt River, skirmish on.
May 31—Waynesville, skirmish near.
June 1—Eleven Points, skirmish at.
June 2—Little Blue River, skirmish on the.
June 5—Sedalia, skirmish near.
June 11—Deep Water, skirmish at.
June 11—Pink Hill, skirmish at.
June 17—Eminence, skirmish at.
June 17—Warrensburg, skirmish near.
June 18—Hambright's Station, skirmish at.
June 23—Pineville, skirmish at.
June 23—Raytown, skirmish near.
June 26—Cherry Grove, Schuyler County, skirmish at.
July 1—Cherry Grove, Schuyler County, skirmish near.
July 6—Salem, skirmish at.
July 7—Inman Hollow, skirmish at.
July 7—Newark, skirmish near.
July 8—Black Run, skirmish at.
July 8-11—Pleasant Hill, skirmishes at and near.
July 9—Lotspeich Farm, on Sugar Creek, skirmish at.
July 9—Wadesburg, skirmish near.
July 11—Big Creek Bluffs, near Pleasant Hill, skirmish at.
July 11—Cassville, skirmish at.
July 11—Sears' House, near Pleasant Hill, skirmish at.
July 18—Memphis, skirmish near.
July 20—Greenville, skirmish at.
July 20—Taberville, skirmish at.
July 22—Florida, skirmish near.
July 23—Blackwater, skirmish near the.
July 23—Boles' Farm, skirmish at.
July 24—Fulton, skirmish near.
July 24—Moore's Mill, skirmish at.
July 24, 25—Santa Fe, skirmishes near.
July 25-26—Mountain Store, skirmishes near.

July 27—Brown's Spring, skirmish at.
July 28—Bollinger's Mill, skirmishes at and near.
July 28—Cross Timbers, skirmish at.
July 28—Fulton, action near.
July 28—Moore's Mill, action at.
July 29—Arrow Rock, skirmish at.
July 29—Bloomfield, skirmish near.
July 30—Clark's Mill, Chariton County, skirmish at.
Aug. 1—Carrollton, skirmish near.
Aug. 1—Grand River, skirmish at.
Aug. 1—Ozark, skirmish at.
Aug. 2, 19—Clear Creek, skirmishes on.
Aug. 2-11—Taberville, skirmishes near.
Aug. 3—Chariton Bridge, skirmish at.
Aug. 4—Forsyth, skirmish near.
Aug. 4—Gayoso, skirmish at.
Aug. 4—White River, skirmish on.
Aug. 5—Cravensville, skirmish near.
Aug. 5-7—Montevallo, skirmishes near.
Aug. 6—Kirksville, action at.
Aug. 6—Salem, skirmish at.
Aug. 7—Rocky Bluff, Platte County, skirmish at.
Aug. 8—Newtonia, skirmish at.
Aug. 8—Panther Creek, skirmish at.
Aug. 8—Stockton, Macon County, skirmish near.
Aug. 9—Sears' Ford, skirmish at.
Aug. 9—Walnut Creek, skirmish at.
Aug. 10—Linn Creek, skirmish at.
Aug. 10—Switzler's Mill, skirmish at.
Aug. 11—Compton's Ferry, Grand River, skirmish at.
Aug. 11—First Battle of Independence; surrender of.
Aug. 11—Little Compton, Grand River, skirmish at.
Aug. 11—Sinking Creek, skirmish on.
Aug. 12—Humansville and Stockton, skirmish between.
Aug. 12—Van Buren, skirmish at.
Aug. 13—Muscle Fork, Chariton River, skirmish at.
Aug. 13—Yellow Creek, skirmish at.
Aug. 14—Barry, skirmish near.
Aug. 15-16—Battle of Lone Jack.
Aug. 18—White Oak Ridge, skirmish at.
Aug. 20—Pilot Knob, skirmish at.
Aug. 21—Neosho, skirmish near.
Aug. 23—Columbus, skirmish near.

Aug. 23—Four Mile, skirmish at.
Aug. 23—Hickory Grove, skirmish at.
Aug. 23—Wayman's Mill, on Spring Creek, skirmish near.
Aug. 24—Bloomfield, affair near.
Aug. 24—Coon Creek, near Lamar, skirmish on.
Aug. 24—Crooked Creek, near Dallas, skirmish on.
Aug. 24—Dallas, skirmish near.
Aug. 24—Lamar, skirmish near.
Aug. 28—Ashley, skirmish at.
Aug. 28—Howard County, skirmish in.
Aug. 29—Bloomfield, skirmish near.
Aug. 29—California House, skirmish at.
Aug. 29—Iberia, skirmish near.
Aug. 31—Little River Bridge, skirmish at.
Sept. 1, 3, 5—Neosho, skirmishes near.
Sept. 1—Putnam, skirmish at.
Sept. 1—Spring River, skirmish at.
Sept. 4—Prairie Chapel, skirmish at.
Sept. 6—Roanoke, skirmish near.
Sept. 7—Lancaster, skirmish at.
Sept. 9—Big Creek, skirmish at.
Sept. 11—Bloomfield, action at.
Sept. 13—Bragg's Farm, near Whaley's Mill, skirmish near.
Sept. 13—Newtonia, skirmish near.
Sept. 13—Strother Fork of Black River, Iron County, skirmish on.
Sept. 19—Hickory Grove, skirmish at.
Sept. 19—Mount Vernon, affair at.
Sept. 20—Shirley's Ford, Spring River, action at.
Sept. 21—Cassville, skirmish near.
Sept. 24—Granby, skirmish at.
Sept. 30—First Battle of Newtonia.
Oct. 2—Columbia, skirmish near.
Oct. 3—Jollification, skirmish at.
Oct. 4—Granby, affair at.
Oct. 4, 7—Newtonia, skirmishes near.
Oct. 5—Cole Camp, skirmish at.
Oct. 5—Sims' Cove, skirmish near.
Oct. 6—Liberty, skirmish at.
Oct. 6—Sibley, skirmish at.
Oct. 7, 13—New Franklin, skirmishes at and near.
Oct. 12—Arrow Rock, skirmish near.
Oct. 14—Hazel Bottom, skirmish at.
Oct. 16—Auxvasse Creek, Callaway County, skirmish at.

Oct. 16—Portland, affair at.
Oct. 16—Shell's Mill, skirmish at.
Oct. 17—Lexington, skirmish at.
Oct. 18—California House, skirmish at.
Oct. 18—Uniontown, Scotland County, skirmish near.
Oct. 20—Marshfield, skirmish near.
Oct. 22—Van Buren, skirmish near.
Oct. 21—Clarkston, skirmish at.
Oct. 25—Eleven Points River, skirmish near.
Oct. 25—Pike Creek, skirmish near.
Oct. 29—Island Mound, skirmish at.
Nov. 3—Harrisonville, Cass County, skirmish near.
Nov. 5—Lamar, action at.
Nov. 7—Battle of Clark's Mill, Douglas County.
Nov. 9—Drywood, skirmish at.
Nov. 9—Huntsville, skirmish at.
Nov. 15—Yocum Creek, skirmish at.
Nov. 17-18—Keytesville, operations about.
Nov. 19—Pineville, skirmish at.
Nov. 26-29—La Fayette County, affairs in.
Nov. 30-Dec. 6—Ozark Mountains, expedition to the, and skirmishes.

1863

Jan. 6—Fort Lawrence, skirmish at.
Jan. 8—Second Battle of Springfield.
Jan. 9-11—Battle of Hartville.
Jan. 21—Columbia, skirmish near.
Jan. 27—Bloomfield, affair at.
Feb. 2-13—Mingo Swamp, scouts and skirmishes, etc.
Feb. 8—Independence, skirmish near.
March 1-2—Bloomfield, capture of, and skirmish near.
March 9—Sherwood, skirmish near.
March 22—Blue Springs, near Independence, skirmish at.
April 17—White River, skirmish at.
April 20—Patterson, skirmish at.
April 22—Fredericktown, skirmish at.
April 24—Mill Creek Bridge, skirmish at.
April 26—Battle of Cape Girardeau.
April 26, 27—Jackson, skirmishes.

April 27—White Water Bridge, skirmish near.
April 29—Castor River, skirmish at.
April 30—Bloomfield, skirmish at.
May 9—Stone County, skirmish in.
May 15—Big Creek, skirmish at.
May 15—Centre Creek, skirmish at.
May 15—Pleasant Hill, skirmish near.
May 18—Hog Island, Bates County, affair at.
May 18—Sherwood, skirmish near.
May 19—Richfield, Clay County, skirmish near.
May 26—Carthage, skirmish near.
June 1—Doniphan, skirmish near.
June 1—Rocheport, skirmishes near.
June 1—Waverly, affair at.
June 17—Wellington, affair near.
June 17—Westport, skirmish near.
June 23—Papinsville, skirmish near.
June 23—Sibley, skirmish at and destruction of.
July 4—Black Fork Hills, affair in the.
July 7—Drywood, skirmish near.
July 11—Stockton, skirmish at.
July 12—Switzler's Mill, Chariton County, skirmish near.
July 24—Dade County, skirmish in.
July 27—Cassville, affair near.
July 30—Lexington, skirmish near.
Aug. 1—Little Blue River, skirmish at Taylor's Farm, on the.
Aug. 1—Round Ponds, near Castor River, affair at.
Aug. 2—Stumptown, skirmish at.
Aug. 6-11—Spring River Mills, scout to, and skirmishes.
Aug. 8—Ball Town, affair on Clear Creek, near.
Aug. 9—Garden Hollow, near Pineville, skirmish at.
Aug. 9, 13—Pineville, skirmishes.
Aug. 10—Dayton, skirmish at.
Aug. 13—Ash Hills, skirmish at the.
Aug. 14—Jack's Ford, skirmish near.
Aug. 14—Wellington, skirmish near.
Aug. 22—Big Creek, skirmish at.
Aug. 23—Bennett's Bayou, skirmishes on.
Aug. 25—Independence, skirmish near.
Aug. 25—Waynesville, skirmish near.
Aug. 25-26—Hopewell, skirmishes near.
Aug. 26—Clear Fork, skirmish at.
Aug. 29—Texas Prairie, skirmish at.

Sept. 4—Quincy, affair at.
Sept. 13—Salem, attack on and skirmish near.
Sept. 15—Enterprise, skirmish near.
Sept. 15—Jackson County, skirmish in.
Sept. 22-25—La Fayette County, skirmishes.
Oct. 4—Bowers' Mill, skirmish at.
Oct. 4—Neosho, action at.
Oct. 4—Neosho, skirmish at Widow Wheeler's, near.
Oct. 4—Oregon, skirmish at.
Oct. 5—Greenfield, skirmish at.
Oct. 5—Stockton, skirmish at.
Oct. 5, 10—Syracuse, skirmishes.
Oct. 6—Humansville, affair near.
Oct. 7—Warsaw, skirmish near.
Oct. 9—Cole Camp, skirmish near.
Oct. 10—La Mine Bridge, affair at.
Oct. 10—Tipton, affair at.
Oct. 11-12—Third Battle of Boonville.
Oct. 12—Dug Ford, near Jonesboro, skirmish at.
Oct. 12—Merrill's Crossing, skirmish at.
Oct. 13—Marshall, action at.
Oct. 14—Man's Creek, Shannon County, skirmish near.
Oct. 14—Scott's Ford, skirmish at.
Oct. 15—Cross Timbers, skirmish at.
Oct. 16—Deer Creek, skirmish on.
Oct. 16—Humansville, skirmishes at and near.
Oct. 16—Johnstown, skirmish at.
Oct. 17—Cedar County, skirmish in.
Oct. 18—Carthage, skirmish at.
Oct. 19—Honey Creek, affair on.
Oct. 21—Greenton Valley, near Hopewell, affair in.
Oct. 24—Harrisonville, skirmish near.
Oct. 26—King's House, near Waynesville, skirmish at.
Oct. 29—Warsaw, affair near.
Nov. 4—Lexington, skirmish near.
Nov. 4-6—Neosho, skirmishes at and near.
Nov. 29-30—Bloomfield, attack on.
Dec. 23-25—Centreville, attack on, etc.
Dec. 25—Pulliam's, skirmish at.

1864

Jan. 14—Bollinger County, skirmish in.
Jan. 23—Cowskin Bottom, Newton County, affair at.
Feb. 2—Halcolm Island, skirmish on.
Feb. 5—Cape Girardeau, skirmish near.
Feb. 10—Pocahontas, skirmish at.
Feb. 12—California House, affair near the.
Feb. 12—Macon, skirmish at.
Feb. 15—Charleston, affair near.
Feb. 18—Piney River, affair near headwaters of the.
Feb. 19—Independence, skirmish near.
Feb. 22—Lexington, skirmish at.
Feb. 27—Poplar Bluff, affair near.
March 27—Deepwater Township, affair in.
March 30—Greenton, affair near.
April 1—Bloomfield, affair near.
April 11—Chariton County, affair in.
April 18—Hunnewell, affair at.
April 19-20—Charleston, skirmishes near.
April 23—Independence, skirmish at.
April 26—Wayne County, skirmish in.
April 27—Dayton, skirmish at.
April 28-30—Johnson County, skirmishes in.
May 2—Bee Creek, affair on.
May 13—Cuba, skirmish near.
May 16—Drywood Creek, skirmish near.
May 20—Lamar, skirmish at.
May 21—Blue River, affair on the.
May 26—Lane's Prairie, Maries County, affair on.
May 27—Shanghai, skirmish near.
May 28—Pleasant Hill, skirmish at.
May 28—Warrensburg, skirmish at.
May 30-31—Mill and Honey Creeks, skirmishes on.
June 3—Neosho, skirmish near.
June 7—Sikeston, affair at.
June 9—Breckinridge, affair near.
June 10—Saint James, affair near.
June 11—Ridgely, skirmish at.
June 12—Kingsville, skirmish near.
June 12—Montevallo, affair at.
June 14—Lexington, skirmish near.

June 15—White Hare, skirmish near.
June 16—Big North Fork, near Preston, affair on.
June 16—Preston, affair near.
June 17—Columbia, skirmish near.
June 26—Sedalia and Marshall Road, affair near the.
June 27-28—Dunksburg, affairs near.
July 1—Fayette, skirmish near.
July 3—Platte County, skirmish in.
July 4—Clay County, skirmish in.
July 6—Little Blue River, Jackson County, western Missouri, skirmish near the.
July 7—Parkville, attack on.
July 8—Richmond, skirmish near.
July 10—Platte City, affair at.
July 10—Warder's Church, skirmish at.
July 12—Columbus, skirmish at.
July 13—Camden Point, action at.
July 13—Versailles, affair at.
July 14—Bloomfield, skirmish near.
July 14—Fredericksburg, skirmish near.
July 15—Huntsville, attack on.
July 15—Lindley, affair at, in Grundy County.
July 16—Clear Fork, near Warrensburg, skirmish on the.
July 16—Fayette Road, near Huntsville, skirmish on the.
July 16, 24—Huntsville, skirmishes.
July 16—Warrensburg, skirmish near.
July 17—Fredericksburg, Ray County, action near.
July 19—Webster, Washington County, attack on.
July 20—Arrow Rock, attack on.
July 21—Carthage, skirmish near.
July 21—Plattsburg, attack on.
July 22—Camden Point and Union Mills, skirmishes near.
July 22—Wright County, skirmish in.
July 23—Allen, skirmish at.
July 23—Liberty, skirmish near.
July 26—Shelbina, attack on.
July 27—Blackwater River, skirmish on.
July 28—Big Creek, skirmish on.
July 30—Chapel Hill, skirmish near.
July 30—Chariton Road, skirmish on.
July 30—Keytesville, skirmish near.
July 30—Union Church, skirmish at.
Aug. 1—Diamond Grove Prairie, skirmish at.

Aug. 1—Independence, skirmish near.
Aug. 1—Rolla, skirmish at.
Aug. 3—Fayette, skirmish near.
Aug. 4—Elk Chute, skirmish at.
Aug. 4—Rutledge, skirmish at.
Aug. 7—Arrow Rock, skirmishes at.
Aug. 7—Buffalo Creek, skirmish on.
Aug. 7—Enterprise, skirmishes at and near.
Aug. 7—Huntsville, skirmish near.
Aug. 8—Norris Creek, skirmish on.
Aug. 8-9—Little Missouri River, action on the.
Aug. 11—Hartville, skirmish at.
Aug. 12—Fredericksburg, skirmish at.
Aug. 12—Holden, skirmish near.
Aug. 15—Dripping Spring, skirmish at.
Aug. 16, Sept. 16—Columbia, skirmishes at.
Aug. 20, 28—Rocheport, skirmishes near.
Aug. 21—Diamond Grove, skirmish at.
Aug. 23—Webster, affair at.
Aug. 26—Pleasant Hill, skirmish near.
Aug. 31—Steelville, affair at.
Sept. 1—Lone Jack, skirmish near.
Sept. 1—Tipton, attack on.
Sept. 2—Mount Vernon, skirmish near.
Sept. 3, 23—Rocheport, skirmishes near.
Sept. 6—Brunswick, affair near.
Sept. 7-8—Boone County, skirmishes in.
Sept. 7, 27—Centralia, affairs at.
Sept. 8—Gayoso, skirmish near.
Sept. 8—Hornersville and Gayoso, skirmishes near.
Sept. 9—Warrensburg, affair near, on the Warrensburg Road.
Sept. 10—Dover, skirmish near.
Sept. 10—Pisgah, skirmish near.
Sept. 10—Roanoke, skirmish near.
Sept. 12, 28—Caledonia, skirmishes at.
Sept. 13, 22—Longwood, skirmishes at and near.
Sept. 18—Lexington, skirmish near.
Sept. 18—Thomasville, skirmish at.
Sept. 19—Doniphan, affair at.
Sept. 20—Keytesville, surrender of.
Sept. 20—Fender's Mill, Little Black River, skirmish at.
Sept. 22—Carthage, skirmish at.
Sept. 22—Patterson, affair at.

Sept. 22—Sikeston, skirmish near.
Sept. 24—Fayette, attack on.
Sept 24, 25—Farmington, skirmishes at.
Sept. 24—Jackson, skirmish at.
Sept. 25—Huntsville, affair at.
Sept. 26—Arcadia Valley, Shut-in Gap, and Ironton, skirmishes at.
Sept. 26, 27—Ironton, skirmishes at.
Sept. 27—Arcadia and Ironton, skirmishes at.
Sept. 27—Battle of Fort Davidson; Pilot Knob, attack on.
Sept. 27—Mineral Point, skirmish at.
Sept. 28—Centralia, skirmish near.
Sept. 29—Cuba, affair at.
Sept. 29-Oct. 1—Leasburg, or Harrison, skirmishes at.
Sept. 30—Waynesville, skirmish at.
Oct. 1—Franklin, skirmish at.
Oct. 1—Lake Springs, skirmish near.
Oct. 1—Union, skirmish at.
Oct. 3—Hermann, skirmish at.
Oct. 4—Richwoods, skirmish at.
Oct. 5-6—Osage River, skirmishes on the.
Oct. 6—Cole County, skirmish in.
Oct. 7—Moreau Creek, skirmish at.
Oct. 7—Tyler's Mills, Big River, skirmish at.
Oct. 7, 8—Jefferson City, skirmishes at and near.
Oct. 8, 18, 29—Barry County, skirmishes in.
Oct. 9, 11-12—Boonville, skirmishes.
Oct. 9—California, skirmish at.
Oct. 9—Russellville, skirmish at.
Oct. 11—Fourth Battle of Boonville.
Oct. 11—Brunswick, skirmish at.
Oct. 14—Danville, attack on.
Oct. 14, 26—Glasgow, skirmishes near.
Oct. 15—Battle of Glasgow.
Oct. 15—Paris, surrender of.
Oct. 15—Sedalia, affair at.
Oct. 16—Ridgely, capture of.
Oct. 17—Carrollton, surrender of.
Oct. 17—Lexington, skirmish near.
Oct. 19—Lexington, action at.
Oct. 19—Montevallo, skirmish near.
Oct. 20—Dover, skirmish at.
Oct. 21—Battle of Little Blue River.
Oct. 22-23—Battle of Big Blue River, also known as the Battle of

Byram's Ford.
Oct. 22—Second Battle of Independence.
Oct. 22—State Line, action at.
Oct. 23—Battle of Westport.
Oct. 25—Battle of Charlotte.
Oct. 25—Clinton, attack on.
Oct. 25—Battle of Marmiton River.
Oct. 26—Albany, skirmish at.
Oct. 28—Second Battle of Newtonia.
Oct. 29—Upshaw's Farm, Barry County, skirmish at.
Oct. 29—Warrenton, skirmish near.
Nov. 1—Big Piney, skirmish on.
Nov. 1—Greenton, affair at.
Nov. 1—Lebanon, skirmish near.
Nov. 1—Rolla, skirmish at.
Nov. 1—Waynesville, skirmish near.
Nov. 1-2—Quincy, skirmishes at.
Nov. 3—Vera Cruz, skirmish at.
Nov. 5—Charleston, skirmish at.
Nov. 6—Sikeston, skirmish near.
Nov. 9—Licking, Texas County, skirmish near.
Nov. 10—Neosho, skirmish at.
Nov. 12—Centreville, skirmish near.
Nov. 18—Fayette, skirmish at.
Nov. 19—Reeves' Mill, skirmish at.
Nov. 26—Osage, skirmish at.
Nov. 28—Fulton, skirmish near.
Dec. 2—Big Piney, skirmish on.
Dec. 3—New Madrid, skirmish near.
Dec. 7—Franklin, affair near, at the Moselle Bridge.
Dec. 7—Moselle Bridge, affair at.
Dec. 8—Tuscumbia, affair at.
Dec. 14—Cape Girardeau, skirmish near.
Dec. 18—Little River, New Madrid County, skirmish on.
Dec 30—Caruthersville, skirmish near.

1865

Jan. 9-11—Texas County, skirmishes in.
Jan. 10—Glasgow, skirmish near.
Jan. 11—Lexington, skirmish near.

Jan. 30—La Fayette County, skirmish in.
Feb. 12—Columbia, skirmish near.
Feb. 12—Macon, skirmish at.
Feb. 13—Mississippi County, skirmish in.
Feb. 20—Center Creek, skirmish at.
Feb. 24—Switzler's Mill, affair at.
Feb. 27—Sturgeon, skirmish near.
March 3, 7—Bloomfield, skirmishes near.
March 4—Dunklin County, skirmish in.
March 11—Little Blue River, affair near.
March 12—Lone Jack, affair near.
March 19-23—Columbus, scout from Warrensburg to, with skirmish near Greenton.
March 24—Rolla, affair near.
March 28—Bull Creek, Christian County, skirmish at.
March 29—Southwest Missouri, skirmish in.
April 15—Patterson, skirmish at McKenzie's Creek near.
April 22—Big Gravois, skirmish near mouth of.
April 22, 25—Linn Creek, skirmishes.
April 23—Spring Valley, skirmish at.
April 24—Miami, skirmish near.
April 27—James Creek, affair near.
May 3—Boonville, skirmishes on Missouri River, near.
May 4—Star House, near Lexington, skirmish at.
May 5—Perche Hills, skirmish in.
May 8—Readsville, skirmish near.
May 14—Little Piney, skirmish on.
May 20—Longwood, skirmish on the Blackwater near.
May 22—Valley Mines, skirmish at.
May 23—Waynesville, skirmish near.
May 24—Rocheport, skirmish near.
May 26-27—Carroll and Ray Counties, scout and skirmish.
May 27—Chariton County, skirmish in.
May 27—Switzler's Mill, Chariton County, skirmish at.

Remains of the redoubt at Hampton Bridge, VA.

CHAPTER TWENTY-FIVE
MONTANA TERRITORY

1865

Sept. 1, 2, 4, 7—Powder River, skirmishes at.
Sept. 5, 8—Powder River, engagements at.

Battle of Gaines' Mill.

Confederate woman, name unknown, circa 1860s; probably the wife, sister, or sweetheart of a Confederate soldier. From my book *I, Confederate: Why Dixie Seceded and Fought in the Words of Southern Soldiers*.

CHAPTER TWENTY-SIX
NEBRASKA

1863

June 23—Pawnee Agency, Neb., attack on.

1864

May 12—Smith's Station, skirmish at.
Dec. 8—Plum Creek, skirmish near.

Second Battle of Murfreesboro.

This photograph from the Spanish-American War period shows a Confederate veteran (left) shaking hands with a Union veteran (right), circa 1898. (The young girl, with broken shackles, represents an independent Cuba.) The portrayal symbolizes the postwar unification of the South and the North in the fight against Spanish dominance in the Americas.

CHAPTER TWENTY-SEVEN
NEBRASKA TERRITORY

1864

Sept. 20—Fort Cottonwood (NE), skirmish near.

1865

Feb. 4-6—Mud Springs (NE), action at.
Feb. 8-9—Rush Creek (NE), action on the North Platte River near.
May 5—Mullahla's Station (NE), attack on wagon train near.
May 18—Fort Kearny, Neb. Ter., skirmish with Indians near.

South view of Fort Moultrie, SC.

Confederate Private James Clarke, Co. 5, Washington Louisiana Light Artillery Battery, New Orleans, LA, circa 1863.

CHAPTER TWENTY-EIGHT
NEW MEXICO

1861

July 25—Mesilla, skirmish at.
Aug. 23—Fort Craig, skirmish near.
Sept. 25—Canada Alamosa, skirmish at.
Sept. 26—Fort Thorn, skirmish near.

1862

Feb. 20-21—Battle of Valverde.
March 3—Cubero, capture of.
March 26—Apache Canyon, skirmish at.
March 26-28—Battle of Glorieta Pass.
March 28—Pigeon's Ranch, engagement at.
April 15—Peralta, skirmish at.
April 25—Socorro, affair at.
May 21—Paraje, affair at.

May 23—Fort Craig, affair near.
July 15—Apache Canyon, skirmish at.

1863

Jan. 29—Pinos Altos Mines, skirmish at.
March 27—Bonito Rio, skirmish on the.
April 25—Apache Pass, skirmish at.
May 7—Cajoude Arivaypo, skirmish at.
June 16—Jornada del Muerto, skirmish on the.
July 4—Fort Craig, N. Mex., skirmish with Indians near.
July 10, 24—Cook's Canyon, N. Mex., skirmishes with at.
July 18—Rio Hondo, N. Mex., skirmish with Indians on the.
July 19—Rio de las Animas, N. Mex., skirmish with Indians on the.
July 29—Conchas Springs, N. Mex., skirmish with Indians at.
Aug. 18—Pueblo Colorado, N. Mex., skirmish with Indians at.

1864

Jan. 26—San Andres Mountains, affair in the.
April 7, 15—Spencer's Ranch, near Presidio del Norte, skirmish at.
May 4—Doubtful Canyon, skirmish in.
Aug. 12—San Andres Mountains, affair in the.
Aug. 26—Sacramento Mountains, skirmish at.
Nov. 25—Adobe Fort, N. Mex., engagement with Indians at.
Dec. 1—Red River, skirmish on.

1865

June 14—Santa Fe Road, action on.

CHAPTER TWENTY-NINE
NORTH CAROLINA

1861

Aug. 28-29—Battle of Hatteras Inlet Batteries; capture of Confederate batteries at.
Oct. 4—Chicamacomico, affair at.

1862

Feb. 7-8—Battle of Roanoke Island.
Feb. 18-21—Winton, expedition to and skirmish.
March 14—Battle of New Bern.
March 23-April 26—Battle of Fort Macon.
March 31—Deep Gully, Trenton Road, skirmish near.
April 7—Foy's Plantation, skirmish at.
April 7—Newport, skirmish near.
April 13—Gillett's Farm, Pebbly Run, skirmish at.
April 19—Battle of South Mills, Camden County, engagement at.

April 19—Trent Road, skirmish on the.
April 27—Haughton's Mill, Pollocksville Road, skirmish near.
April 29—Batchelder's Creek, skirmish near.
May 2—Deep Gully, Trenton Road, skirmish at.
May 15-16—Trenton Bridge, Young's Cross-Roads, and Pollocksville, skirmishes near.
May 22—Trenton and Pollocksville Cross-Roads, skirmish at the.
June 5—Battle of Tranter's Creek.
June 9—Hamilton, capture of.
June 26—Mill Creek, skirmish at.
June 26-29—Young's Cross-Roads, reconnoissance and skirmish.
Aug. 30—Plymouth, skirmish near.
Sept. 6—Washington, attack on.
Nov. 2—Little Creek, skirmish at.
Nov. 2—Rawle's Mill, skirmish at.
Nov. 11—New Bern, demonstration on.
Nov. 18—Core Creek, skirmish at.
Dec. 10—Plymouth, attack on.
Dec. 11-12—Kinston Road, skirmishes on the.
Dec. 13-14—Southwest Creek, skirmishes at.
Dec. 14—Battle of Kinston.
Dec. 15—White Hall Bridge, affair at.
Dec. 16—Goshen Swamp, affair at.
Dec. 16—Mount Olive Station, affair at.
Dec. 16—Battle of White Hall.
Dec. 17—Battle of Goldsboro Bridge.
Dec. 17—Thompson's Bridge, skirmish at.
Dec. 27—Elizabeth City, skirmish at.

1863

Jan. 19—White Oak Creek, skirmish at.
Jan. 20—Jacksonville, skirmish near.
Feb. 7—Edenton, skirmish near.
Feb. 10—Batchelder's Creek, skirmish at.
Feb. 13—Sandy Ridge, skirmish at.
Feb. 13—Washington, skirmish near.
Feb. 23—Fort Caswell, engagement at.
March 3—Fairfield, skirmish near.
March 4—Swan Quarter, skirmish near.

March 6-8—Kinston, demonstration on.
March 7—Core Creek, skirmish near.
March 7—Dover, skirmish near.
March 13-14—Deep Gully, skirmishes at and near.
March 13-15—Battle of Fort Anderson.
March 23—Winfield, skirmish at.
March 24—Rocky Hock Creek, skirmish at.
March 30—Rodman's Point, skirmish at.
March 30-April 20—Battle of Washington; siege of, and pursuit of Confederate forces.
April 1, 4, 5—Rodman's Point, engagements at.
April 2—Hill's Point, engagement at.
April 6—Nixonton, skirmish at.
April 9—Blount's Creek, action at.
April 16—Hill's Point, affair at.
April 16—Rodman's Point, affair at.
April 17-18—Core Creek, skirmish near.
April 19—Big Swift Creek, skirmish at.
April 20—Sandy Ridge, skirmish at.
April 28—Wise's Cross-Roads, skirmish at.
May 5—Peletier's Mill, skirmish at.
May 20-23—Kinston, demonstration on.
May 22—Gum Swamp, skirmish at.
May 23—Batchelder's Creek, skirmish at.
July 5—Kenansville, skirmish at.
July 5—Warsaw, skirmish at.
July 6—Free Bridge, near Trenton, skirmish at.
July 6—Trenton, skirmish near.
July 17-20—Swift Creek Village, skirmish at.
July 20—Sparta, skirmish at.
July 20—Tarboro and Sparta, skirmishes at.
July 21—Street's Ferry, skirmish at.
July 22—Scupperton, skirmish at.
July 26—Potecasi Creek, skirmish at.
Aug. 14—Washington, skirmish at.
Aug. 18—Pasquotank, skirmish near.
Sept. 12—South Mills, skirmish at.
Oct. 16-17—Pungo Landing, affairs at.
Oct. 17—Camden Court House, skirmish near.
Oct. 23, 26—Warm Springs, skirmishes at.
Oct. 27—Cherokee County, skirmish in.
Oct. 30—Ford's Mill, near New Bern, affair at.
Oct. 30—New Bern, affair at.

Nov. 4—Rocky Run, skirmish near.
Nov. 25—Greenville, skirmish near.
Nov. 26—Warm Springs, skirmish at.
Nov. 26—Plymouth, skirmish at.
Dec. 1—Cedar Point, skirmish at.
Dec. 10—Hertford, skirmish at.
Dec. 16—Free Bridge, skirmish near.
Dec. 18—Indiantown, or Sandy Swamp, skirmish at.
Dec. 30—Greenville, skirmish near.

1864

Jan. 4, 11—Lockwood's Folly Inlet, affairs at.
Jan. 30—Windsor, skirmish at.
Feb. 1—Batchelder's Creek, skirmish at.
Feb. 2—Bogue Sound Blockhouse, skirmish at.
Feb. 2—Gales' Creek, skirmish at.
Feb. 2, 6—Newport Barracks, skirmishes at and near.
Feb. 7—Waccomo Neck, affair at.
Feb. 16—Fairfield, affair at.
March 26—Black Jack Church, skirmish near.
April 1—Plymouth, skirmish near.
April 5—Blount's Creek, affair near.
April 17—Beaver Creek, skirmish at.
April 17-20—Battle of Plymouth; capture of.
April 27-29—Masonboro Inlet, affairs at.
May 4—Trent Road, skirmish on.
May 5—*Albemarle*, C.S.S., engagement with.
May 5—Battle of Albemarle Sound.
May 5—Trent River, skirmish on the south side of.
June 22—Southwest Creek, skirmish at.
June 28—Camp Vance, capture of.
Aug. 2—Murphy, skirmish near.
Dec. 7-27—First Battle of Fort Fisher; operations against.

1865

Jan. 13—Fort Fisher, bombardment of, by naval flee .
Jan. 13-15—Second Battle of Fort Fisher; combined military and

naval operations against.
Jan. 15—Fort Fisher, assault and capture of.
Jan. 16-17—Fort Caswell blown up, and works at Smithville and Reeves' Point abandoned by Confederates.
Jan. 19—Half-Moon Battery, skirmish at.
Feb. 11—Sugar Loaf, action near.
Feb. 11-22—Battle of Wilmington, also known as the Battle of Fort Anderson, the Battle of Town Creek, the Battle of Forks Road, and the Battle of Sugar Loaf Hill.
Feb. 17—Smithville, skirmish near.
Feb. 18—Fort Anderson, action at.
Feb. 18—Orton Pond, skirmish at.
Feb. 19—Fort Anderson, capture of.
Feb. 19-20—Town Creek, skirmish at.
Feb. 21—Eagle Island, skirmish at.
Feb. 21—Fort Strong, skirmish at.
Feb. 22—Northeast Ferry, skirmish at.
Feb. 22—Smith's Creek, skirmish at.
March 4—Phillips' Cross-Roads, skirmish at.
March 7—Rockingham, skirmish at.
March 7-10—Battle of Wyse Fork, also known as the Battle of Southwest Creek.
March 10—Battle of Monroe's Cross-Roads (at what is now Fort Bragg).
March 11, 13—Fayetteville, skirmishes at and near.
March 15—Smith's Mills, Black River, skirmish near.
March 15—South River, skirmish at.
March 16—Battle of Averasboro, also known as the Battle of Taylor's Hole Creek.
March 16—Little Cohera Creek, skirmish at.
March 17—Averasboro, skirmish at.
March 17, 20—Falling Creek, skirmishes at and near.
March 18—Benton's Cross-Roads, skirmish near.
March 18—Bushy Swamp, skirmish at.
March 18—Mingo Creek, skirmish at.
March 19—Goldsboro, skirmish at Neuse River Bridge, near.
March 19-20, 23—Cox's Bridge, Neuse River, skirmishes at and near.
March 19-21—Battle of Bentonville.
March 22—Black Creek, skirmish at.
March 22—Hannah's Creek, skirmish at.
March 22—Mill Creek, skirmish at.
March 24—Moccasin Creek, skirmish near.

March 28—Boone, skirmish at.
March 28—Snow Hill, skirmish near.
March 29—Moseley Hall, skirmish near.
March 29—Wilkesboro, skirmish at.
March 31—Gulley's, skirmish at.
March 31—Hookerton, skirmish at.
April 1—Snow Hill, skirmish near.
April 2—Goldsboro, skirmish near.
April 5-7—Neuse River, destruction of U.S. transports on.
April 8—Martinsville, action at.
April 10—Boonville, skirmish at.
April 10—Moccasin Swamp, skirmish at.
April 10—Nahunta Station, skirmish near.
April 11—Beulah, skirmish near.
April 11—Mocksville, skirmish near.
April 11—Pikeville, affair near.
April 11—Shallow Ford, skirmish at.
April 11—Smithfield, skirmish near.
April 12—Grant's Creek, near Salisbury, skirmish at.
April 12—Raleigh, action near.
April 12—Salisbury, engagement at.
April 12—Salisbury, skirmish at Grant's Creek, near.
April 12—Swift Creek, action at.
April 13—Raleigh, skirmish near.
April 13-15—Battle of Morrisville; skirmishes at and near.
April 14—Saunders' Farm, affair near.
April 15—Chapel Hill, skirmish near.
April 17—Catawba River, near Morganton, action at.
April 22—Howard's Gap, Blue Ridge Mountains, skirmish at.
April 23—Hendersonville, action near.
April 26—Bennett's House, near Durham Station, surrender of the Confederate army in North Carolina at.

Confederate Ironclad C.S.S. *Louisiana*.

CHAPTER THIRTY
OHIO

1863

June 16-20—Holmes County, affairs in.
July 14—Camp Dennison, skirmish at.
July 17—Berlin, skirmish at.
July 17—Hamden, skirmish near.
July 18—Pomeroy, skirmish at.
July 19—Battle of Buffington Island.
July 20—Cheshire, skirmish near.
July 20—Coal Hill, skirmish at.
July 20—Hockingport, skirmish near.
July 22—Eagleport, skirmish at.
July 23—Rockville, skirmish at.
July 24—Athens, skirmish at.
July 24—Washington, skirmish at.
July 25—Springfield, skirmish near.
July 25—Steubenville, skirmish near.
July 26—Salineville, skirmish at.

Battle of Elkhorn Tavern.

Confederate Captain Black Dog (also known as Young Black Dog), Co. B, First Osage Battalion, C.S.A., 1876, one of the 70,000 Native-Americans who served in the C.S. military. (Note bear claw necklace.) From my book *I, Confederate: Why Dixie Seceded and Fought in the Words of Southern Soldiers*.

CHAPTER THIRTY-ONE
PENNSYLVANIA

1862

Oct. 10—Chambersburg, capture of.
Oct. 11—Gettysburg, skirmish near.

1863

June 22—Greencastle, skirmish at.
June 25—McConnellsburg, skirmish near.
June 26—Gettysburg, skirmish near.
June 28—Fountain Dale, skirmish at.
June 28—Wrightsville, skirmish at.
June 28-29—Oyster Point, skirmish near.
June 29—McConnellsburg, skirmish at.
June 30—Fairfield, skirmish at.
June 30—Battle of Hanover.
June 30—Sporting Hill, near Harrisburg, skirmish at.
July 1—Carlisle, skirmish at.
July 1-3—Battle of Gettysburg.
July 2—Chambersburg, skirmish near.
July 2—Hunterstown, skirmish at.
July 3—Fairfield, action at.
July 4—Fairfield Gap, skirmish at.
July 4—Monterey Gap, action at.
July 5—Cunningham's Cross-Roads, skirmish at.
July 5—Fairfield, skirmish near.
July 5—Greencastle, skirmish near.
July 5—Green Oak, skirmish near.

July 5—Mercersburg, skirmish near.
July 5—Stevens' Furnace (or Caledonia Iron Works), skirmish at.

1864

July 29—Mercersburg, skirmish at.
July 30—McConnellsburg, skirmish at.
July 30—Chambersburg, burning of.

Jefferson Davis: The most conservative, intelligent, honest, righteous, hard-working, educated, Christian chief executive in American history.

CHAPTER THIRTY-TWO
SOUTH CAROLINA

1861

April 12-14—First Battle of Fort Sumter.
Nov. 3-7—Battle of Port Royal.
Nov. 7—Fort Beauregard, bombardment and capture of (part of the Battle of Port Royal).
Nov. 7—Fort Walker, bombardment and capture of (part of the Battle of Port Royal).
Dec. 17—Chisolm's Island, skirmish on.

1862

Jan. 1—Port Royal Ferry, Coosaw River, engagement at.
Feb. 10—Barnwell Island, skirmish on.
March 20—Buckingham, affair at.
March 20—Hunting Island, affair at.
March 29—Edisto Island, affair on.

April 19—Edisto Island, skirmish on.
April 29—Pineberry Battery, engagement at.
April 29—Willstown, engagement at.
April 29—White Point, engagement at.
May 20—Cole's Island, bombardment of.
May 21—Battery Island, affair near.
May 25—James and Dixon's Islands, affair between.
May 29—Pocotaligo, skirmish at.
June 3, 8, 10—James Island, skirmishes on.
June 6—Port Royal Ferry, affair at.
June 13—White House, near Hilton Head, affair at.
June 16—Battle of James Island, also known as the Battle of Secessionville.
June 21—Battle of Simmon's Bluff.
July 4—Port Royal Ferry, affair at.
July 9-10—Pocotaligo, demonstration against.
Aug. 13—Black River, engagement on.
Aug. 21—Pinckney Island, affair on.
Sept. 10—Kilkenny River, skirmish on the.
Oct. 18—Kirk's Bluff, affair at.
Oct. 22—Caston's Plantation, engagement at.
Oct. 22—Frampton's Plantation, engagement at.
Oct. 24—Saint Helena Island, affair on.

1863

Jan. 31—Bull Island, affair on.
Jan. 31—Charleston, attack on blockading squadron off.
April 7—First Battle of Charleston Harbor.
April 7—Fort Sumter, attack on.
April 10—Folly Island, skirmish on.
April 27—Murray's Inlet, affair at.
May 4—Murray's Inlet, affair at.
May 19—Pope's Island, skirmish at.
May 31—James Island, affair on.
June 18—Edisto Island, skirmish on.
June 21—Dixon's Island, affair on.
July 10—Willstown Bluff, Pon Pon River, engagement at.
July 11, 18—First Battle of Fort Wagner; Battery Wagner, Morris Island, assaults on.
July 16—Battle of Grimball's Landing; James Island, engagement

near.
July 18-Sept. 7—Second Battle of Charleston Harbor, also known as the Second Battle of Fort Wagner; Battery Wagner, Morris Island, assaults on.
July 20—Legare's Point, bombardment of.
Aug. 2—*Chesterfield*, steamer, attack on, at Cummings Point.
Aug. 4—Vincent's Creek, affair at the mouth of.
Aug. 17-Sept. 9—Second Battle of Fort Sumter; bombardment of.
Aug. 21-Dec. 31—Charleston, bombardment of.
Aug. 25-26—Morris Island, assault on, and capture of Confederate rifle-pits.
Sept. 7—Battery Island, affair on.
Sept. 7-8—Charleston Harbor, engagement in.
Sept. 8-9—Fort Sumter, boat attack on.
Oct. 19—Murrell's Inlet, affair at.
Nov. 16—Sullivan's Island Batteries, engagement between U.S. *Monitor* and.
Nov. 19-20—Fort Sumter, boat demonstration upon.
Nov. 24—Cunningham's Bluff, skirmish near.
Dec. 5—Murrell's Inlet, affair at.
Dec. 25—*Marblehead*, U.S.S., attack on, in Stono River.
Dec. 25—Stono River, attack on U.S.S. *Marblehead* in.

1864

Jan. 7—Waccamaw Neck, affair on.
Feb. 9, 11—Bugbee Bridge, skirmish near.
March 25—McClellarsville, affair at.
March 31—Spring Island, affair at.
April 8—James Island, demonstration on.
April 15—Battery Island, demonstration on.
May 10—Pine Island, skirmish on.
May 13—James Island, affair on.
May 16—Ashepoo River, skirmish, on the.
May 21-23—James Island, demonstration on.
July 2, 16—James Island, skirmishes on.
July 2—Secessionville, skirmish near.
July 3—Fort Johnson and Battery Simkins, assault on.
July 3, 7—John's Island, skirmishes on.
July 3—King's Creek, skirmish at.
July 3—White Point, skirmish near.

July 4-9—Battery Pringle, attack on.
July 9—Burden's Causeway, John's Island, action at.
July 10—Fort Johnson and Battery Simkins, attack on.
Nov. 29—Boyd's Landing, skirmish near.
Nov. 30—Battle of Honey Hill, near Grahamville.
Dec. 6-9—Charleston & Savannah Railroad, demonstration against.
Dec. 20—Pocotaligo Road, skirmish near.

1865

Jan. 3—Hardeeville, skirmish near.
Jan. 20—Salkehatchie River, reconnoissance from Pocotah, and skirmish.
Jan. 26—Pocotaligo, skirmish near.
Jan. 27—Ennis Cross-Roads, skirmish at.
Jan. 28—Combahee River, skirmish at.
Jan. 29—Robertsville, skirmish at.
Jan. 30—Lawtonville, skirmish near.
Feb. 1—Hickory Hill, skirmish at.
Feb. 1—Whippy Swamp Creek, skirmish at.
Feb. 2—Barker's Mill, Whippy Swamp, skirmish at.
Feb. 2—Duck Branch, near Loper's Cross-Roads, skirmish at.
Feb. 2—Lawtonville, skirmish at.
Feb. 2—Rivers' and Broxton's Bridges, Salkehatchie River, skirmishes at.
Feb. 3—Dillingham's Cross-Roads, or Duck Branch, skirmish at.
Feb. 3—Duck Branch, skirmish at.
Feb. 3—Battle of Rivers' Bridge; Salkehatchie River, action at.
Feb. 4—Angley's Post-Office, skirmish at.
Feb. 4—Buford's Bridge, skirmish at.
Feb. 5—Combahee Ferry, skirmish at.
Feb. 5—Duncanville, skirmish at.
Feb. 6—Barnwell, skirmish near,
Feb. 6—Cowpen Ford, Little Salkehatchie River, skirmish at.
Feb. 6—Lane's Bridge, action at Fishburn's Plantation, near.
Feb. 6—Little Salkehatchie River, skirmish at Cowpen Ford.
Feb. 7—Blackville, skirmish at.
Feb. 7—Edisto Railroad Bridge, skirmish at.
Feb. 8—Cannon's Bridge, South Edisto River, skirmish at.
Feb. 8—Walker's or Valley Bridge, Edisto River, skirmish at.
Feb. 8—White Pond, skirmish near.

Feb. 8—Williston, skirmish at.
Feb. 9—Binnaker's Bridge, South Edisto River, skirmish at.
Feb. 9—Holman's Bridge, South Edisto River, skirmish at.
Feb. 10—James Island, skirmish at.
Feb. 10—Johnson's Station, skirmish at.
Feb. 11—Aiken, action at.
Feb. 11—Battery Simkins, attack on.
Feb. 11—Johnson's Station, action at.
Feb. 11-12—Orangeburg, skirmishes about.
Feb. 14—Gunter's Bridge, North Edisto River, skirmish at.
Feb. 14—Wolf's Plantation, skirmish at.
Feb. 15—Bates' Ferry, Congaree River, skirmish at.
Feb. 15—Congaree Creek, skirmish at.
Feb. 15—Savannah Creek, skirmish at.
Feb. 15—Two League Cross-Roads, near Lexington, skirmish near.
Feb. 16-17—Columbia, skirmishes about.
Feb. 22—Wateree River, skirmish near.
Feb. 22, 23, 24—Camden, skirmishes.
Feb. 25—West's Cross-Roads, skirmish at.
Feb. 26—Lynch's Creek, skirmish at.
Feb. 26—Stroud's Mill, skirmish near.
Feb. 27—Cloud's House, skirmish at.
Feb. 27—Mount Elon, skirmish near.
Feb. 28—Cheraw, skirmish near.
Feb. 28—Rocky Mount, skirmish near.
March 1—Wilson's Store, skirmish at.
March 2—Chesterfield, skirmish at.
March 2—Thompson's Creek, near Chesterfield, skirmish at.
March 3—Big Black Creek, affair near.
March 3—Blakeny's, skirmish near.
March 3—Hornsboro, skirmish near.
March 3—Juniper Creek, near Cheraw, skirmish at.
March 3—Thompson's Creek, near Cheraw, skirmish at.
March 4-6—Florence, expedition from near Cheraw to, and skirmishes.
March 5—Cheraw, skirmish near.
March 8—Love's or Blue's Bridge, skirmish at.
April 9—Dingle's Mill, skirmish near Sumterville at.
April 15—Statesburg, skirmish near.
April 18—Boykins' Mill, skirmish at.
April 19—Denkins' Mill, skirmish at.
April 19—Statesburg, skirmish at Beech Creek near.

Confederate officer, name unknown, circa 1863. From my book *The Bittersweet Bond: Race Relations in the Old South as Described by White and Black Southerners*.

CHAPTER THIRTY-THREE
TENNESSEE

1861

Sept. 29—Travisville, affair at.

1862

Jan. 17-22—Fort Henry, demonstration on.
Feb. 2—Morgan County, skirmish in.
Feb. 6—Battle of Fort Henry.
Feb. 11-15—Fort Henry, action at.
Feb. 11-16—First Battle of Fort Donelson; siege and capture of.
Feb. 14—Cumberland Gap, skirmish near.
Feb. 18-22—Nashville, action at.
March 1—Pittsburg, engagement at.
March 9—Granny White's Pike, skirmish on.
March 11—Paris, skirmish near.
March 14—Jacksboro, skirmish at.
March 16—Pittsburg Landing, skirmishes near.
March 21-23—Cumberland Gap, reconnoissance to and skirmish.
March 24—Camp Jackson, skirmish at.
March 31—Adamsville, skirmish near.
March 31—Purdy Road, skirmish on, near Adamsville.
April 3, 17, 28, 20—Monterey, skirmishes near and at.
April 4—Lawrenceburg, skirmish at.
April 4—Pittsburg Landing, skirmishes near.
April 6-7—Battle of Shiloh (Yankee name: Battle of Pittsburg Landing).

April 8—Battle of Fallen Timbers.
April 10-11—Battle of Fort Pulaski.
April 11—Wartrace, skirmish at.
April 15-27—Pea Ridge, skirmishes at.
April 24—Lick Creek, skirmish at.
April 24—Shelbyville Road, skirmish on.
April 26—Atkins' Mill, skirmish at.
April 29—Cumberland Gap, skirmish near.
May 1,4, 11—Pulaski, skirmishes near and at.
May 5—Battle of Lebanon.
May 5—Lockridge's Mill, skirmish at.
May 9—Elk River, skirmish on, near Bethel.
May 10—Plum Point, naval engagement at.
May 20—Elk River, skirmishes at.
May 24—Winchester, skirmishes at.
June 1—Jasper, skirmish near.
June 4—Sweeden's Cove, near Jasper, skirmish at.
June 4, 10—Winchester, skirmishes at.
June 6—First Battle of Memphis; naval engagement off, and capture of.
June 7—Jackson, capture of.
June 7—Readyville, skirmish at.
June 7-8—First Battle of Chattanooga.
June 10, 16—Wilson's Gap, skirmishes at.
June 10, 16—Winchester, skirmishes at.
June 10—Rogers' Gap, skirmish at.
June 11-13—Big Creek Gap, skirmishes at.
June 21—Battle Creek, skirmishes at.
June 21—Rankin's Ferry, skirmish at.
June 25—La Fayette Station, affair near.
June 30—Powell River, affair at.
June 30—Rising Sun, skirmish at.
July 5—Walden's Ridge, affair at.
July 13-August 30—Middle Tennessee, action in.
July 13—First Battle of Murfreesboro.
July 13—Wolf River, skirmish near.
July 15—Wallace's Cross-Roads, skirmish at.
July 17—Mount Pleasant, skirmish near.
July 17—Columbia, skirmish at.
July 21—Nashville, skirmish around.
July 25—Clinton's Ferry, skirmish at.
July 26—Tazewell, skirmish at.
July 27—Lower Post Ferry, affair near.

July 27—Toone's Station, affair near.
July 28—Humboldt, skirmish at.
July 29—Denmark, affair near.
July 29—Hatchie Bottom, affair at.
Aug. 3—Nonconnah Creek, skirmish on.
Aug. 5—Sparta, skirmish at.
Aug. 6—Tazewell, skirmish near.
Aug. 7, 18—Dyersburg, skirmishes near.
Aug. 7—Wood Springs, skirmish at.
Aug. 11—Kinderhook, affair near.
Aug. 11—Saulsbury, skirmish at.
Aug. 11—Williamsport, skirmish near.
Aug. 13—Gallatin, skirmish, near.
Aug. 13—Huntsville, skirmish at.
Aug. 13, 31—Medon, skirmishes at and near.
Aug. 14—Mount Pleasant, skirmish near.
Aug. 16—Meriwether's Ferry, Obion River, skirmish at.
Aug. 17—Pine Mountain, skirmish at.
Aug. 20—Drake's Creek, skirmish near.
Aug. 20—Edgefield Junction, skirmishes near.
Aug. 20—Manscoe Creek, skirmish at.
Aug. 21—Gallatin, action near.
Aug. 21—Hartsville Road, action on the.
Aug. 23-25—Fort Donelson, skirmishes at and near.
Aug. 26—Cumberland Iron Works, skirmish at.
Aug. 26-27—Cumberland Gap, skirmishes near.
Aug. 27—Battle Creek, attack on Fort McCook.
Aug. 27—Pulaski, skirmish near.
Aug. 27—Reynolds' Station, skirmish near.
Aug. 27—Richland Creek, skirmish on and near.
Aug. 27—Murfreesboro, skirmish near.
Aug. 27—Round Mountain, skirmish at.
Aug. 27—Woodbury, skirmish near.
Aug. 29—Short Mountain Cross-Roads, skirmish at.
Aug. 30—Altamont, skirmish at.
Aug. 30—Bolivar, skirmishes at and near.
Aug. 30—Little Pond, skirmish at.
Aug. 30—Medon Station, skirmishes at and near.
Aug. 31—Rogers' Gap, skirmish at.
Aug. 31—Toone's Station, skirmish near.
Sept. 1—Britton's Lane, skirmish, at.
Sept. 1—Denmark, affair near.
Sept. 2—Memphis, skirmish near.

Sept. 2—Nashville, skirmish around.
Sept. 5—Burnt Bridge, skirmish at.
Sept. 5—Humboldt, skirmish near.
Sept. 6—New Providence, skirmish at.
Sept. 7—Murfreesboro, skirmish near.
Sept. 7—Pine Mountain, skirmish at.
Sept. 7—Riggin's Hill, skirmish at.
Sept. 9-10—Columbia, skirmishes near.
Sept. 18, 23—Fort Donelson, operations about and skirmishes.
Sept. 19-20—Brentwood, skirmishes at.
Sept. 20-22—Grand Junction, expedition to and skirmish.
Sept. 21—Van Buren, skirmish near.
Sept. 23—Wolf Creek Bridge, skirmish at.
Sept. 26—Pocahontas, skirmish at.
Sept. 30—Goodlettsville, skirmish at.
Oct. 1—Davis' Bridge, skirmish at.
Oct. 1, 5, 13, 20—Nashville, skirmishes around.
Oct. 3—La Fayette Landing, affair near.
Oct. 4—Middleton, skirmish near.
Oct. 5—Big Hatchie, engagement at.
Oct. 5—Big Hill, skirmish near.
Oct. 5—Chewalla, skirmish near.
Oct. 5—Davis' Bridge, Hatchie River, engagement at.
Oct. 5—Battle of Hatchie's Bridge, also known as the Battle of Davis Bridge, and the Battle of Metamora (also sometimes referred to in 19th-Century histories as the Battle of Hatchie Bridge).
Oct. 5-15—Neely's Bend, Cumberland River, skirmishes at.
Oct. 5—Fort Riley, skirmish at.
Oct. 7—La Vergne, skirmish near.
Oct. 9—Humboldt, affair near.
Oct. 10—Medon Station, skirmishes at and near.
Oct. 13—Lebanon Road, skirmish on the.
Oct. 17—Island No. 10, skirmish at.
Oct. 20—Gallatin Pike, skirmish on the.
Oct. 20—Hermitage Ford, skirmish at.
Oct. 21—Woodville, skirmish at.
Oct. 22-25—Waverly, expeditions to, with skirmishes.
Oct. 21—Richland Creek, skirmishes on and near.
Oct. 23, 28—Waverly, skirmishes near.
Oct. 24—White Oak Springs, skirmish near.
Nov. 5—Nashville, action at.
Nov. 7—Tyree Springs, skirmish at.

Nov. 7—White Range, skirmish at.
Nov. 7-8—Gallatin, skirmishes at and near.
Nov. 8—Cumberland River, skirmish on the.
Nov. 9—Lebanon, skirmish at.
Nov. 9—Silver Springs, skirmish at.
Nov. 18—Double Bridge, skirmish at.
Nov. 18—Rural Hill, skirmish at.
Nov. 25—Clarksville, skirmish at.
Nov. 26—Somerville, skirmish near.
Nov. 27—Mill Creek, skirmish at.
Nov. 28—Carthage Road, skirmishes on the.
Nov. 28—Hartsville, skirmish near.
Nov. 28—Rome, skirmish near.
Dec. 1, 26, 30—Nolensville, skirmishes at and near.
Dec. 3, 14—Nashville, attacks on forage train near.
Dec. 4—Holly Tree Gap, skirmish near.
Dec. 4—Stewart's Ferry, Stone's River, capture of outpost near.
Dec. 7—Battle of Hartsville.
Dec. 9—Brentwood, skirmish near.
Dec. 9—Dobbins' Ferry, skirmish at.
Dec. 9, 11—La Vergne, skirmishes at and near.
Dec. 10-January 6, 1863—West Tennessee, action in.
Dec. 11, 23, 24—Nashville, skirmishes near.
Dec. 11, 21, 25—Wilson's Creek Pike, skirmishes on the.
Dec. 12—Cherokee Station, skirmish at.
Dec. 12, 26, 27—Franklin, skirmishes at.
Dec. 14—Franklin Pike, skirmish on the.
Dec. 18—Battle of Lexington.
Dec. 19—Carroll Station, affair at.
Dec. 19—Battle of Jackson.
Dec. 19—Spring Creek, affair at.
Dec. 20—Forked Deer River, skirmish at railroad crossing on.
Dec. 20—Humboldt, capture of, by Confederates.
Dec. 20—Humboldt, recapture of, by Union forces.
Dec. 21—Rutherford's Station, affair at.
Dec. 24—Bolivar, skirmishes at and near.
Dec. 24—Middleburg, skirmish at.
Dec. 25—Prim's Blacksmith Shop, skirmish at.
Dec. 26—Knob Gap, skirmish at.
Dec. 26, 27, 30—La Vergne, skirmishes at and near.
Dec. 26, 29—Wilkinson's Cross-Roads, skirmishes at and near.
Dec. 27, 29, 30—Huntingdon, skirmishes at and near.
Dec. 27—Jefferson Pike, skirmish on the.

Dec. 27—Murfreesboro Pike, skirmish on the.
Dec. 27—Stewart's Creek Bridge, Jefferson's Pike, skirmish at.
Dec. 27—Stewart's Creek Bridge, Murfreesboro Pike, skirmish at.
Dec. 27—Triune, skirmish at.
Dec. 28—Perkins' Mill, skirmish at.
Dec. 29—Lizzard's, skirmish at.
Dec. 29-30—Murfreesboro, skirmishes at and near.
Dec. 30—Blountsville, capture of Confederates at.
Dec. 30—Carter's Depot, capture of.
Dec. 30—Clarksburg, skirmish at.
Dec. 30—Jefferson, skirmish at.
Dec. 30—Rock Spring, skirmish at.
Dec. 31-Jan. 3, 1863—Second Battle of Murfreesboro (Yankee name: Battle of Stone's River; see below).
Dec. 31—Overall's Creek, skirmish at.
Dec. 31—Battle of Parker's Cross-Roads.
Dec. 31—Red Mound, engagement at.

1863

Jan. 1—Clifton, skirmishes near.
Jan. 1-5—La Vergne, skirmishes at and near.
Jan. 1—Stewart's Creek, skirmish at.
Jan. 2—Fort Donelson, skirmish near.
Jan. 3—Cox's Hill, skirmish at.
Jan. 3—Somerville, action at.
Jan. 3—Second Battle of Murfreesboro (Yankee name: Battle of Stone's River).
Jan. 4—Manchester Pike, skirmish on the.
Jan. 4—Monterey, skirmish at.
Jan. 5—Franklin, skirmish at.
Jan. 5—Lytle's Creek, skirmish at.
Jan. 5—Nolensville, skirmish near.
Jan. 5—Shelbyville Pike, skirmish on the.
Jan. 5—Wilkinson's Cross-Roads, skirmish near.
Jan. 8—Knob Creek, skirmish at.
Jan. 8—Ripley, skirmish near.
Jan. 10—Clifton, skirmish at.
Jan. 11—Lowry's Ferry, skirmish at.
Jan. 12—Ashland, affair at.
Jan. 13—Chambers' Creek, skirmish at.

Jan. 13—Hamburg, skirmish near.
Jan. 13—Harpeth Shoals, affair at.
Jan. 16—Waverly, expedition to, with skirmish.
Jan. 19—Woodbury, skirmish near.
Jan. 21—Shelbyville Pike, skirmishes on the.
Jan. 23—Bradyville Pike, skirmishes on the.
Jan. 23—Carthage, skirmish at.
Jan. 23—Murfreesboro, skirmishes at and near.
Jan. 24—Woodbury, skirmishes at and near.
Jan. 25—Mill Creek, skirmish near.
Jan. 27—Germantown, affair near.
Jan. 28—Collierville, skirmish near.
Jan. 28—Nashville, skirmish near.
Jan. 28—Yorkville, skirmish near.
Jan. 30—Dyersburg, skirmish at.
Jan. 31—Middleton, skirmish at.
Jan. 31—Rover, skirmish.
Jan. 31—Unionville, skirmish at.
Feb. 3—Cumberland Iron Works, skirmish at.
Feb. 3—Second Battle of Fort Donelson, or Battle of Dover.
Feb. 4-7—Murfreesboro, skirmish.
Feb. 9, 18—Moscow, affairs near.
Feb. 13—Rover, skirmish.
Feb. 15—Auburn, skirmishes near.
Feb. 15—Cainsville, skirmish near.
Feb. 15—Nolensville, skirmish near.
Feb. 16—Bradyville, skirmish.
Feb. 20—Shelbyville Pike, skirmish on the.
Feb. 22—Manchester Pike, skirmish on the.
Feb. 27—Bloomington, skirmish near.
March 1—Bradyville, skirmish.
March 1, 6—Woodbury, skirmishes.
March 2—Eagleville, skirmish near.
March 2—Petersburg, skirmish near.
March 3—Bear Creek, skirmish near.
March 4, 31—Franklin, skirmishes.
March 4, 13, 15—Rover, skirmishes.
March 4—Unionville, skirmishes at.
March 5—Chapel Hill, skirmish.
March 5—Battle of Thompson's Station.
March 6—Christiana, skirmish.
March 6—Middleton, skirmish at.
March 8—Harpeth River, skirmish on the.

March 8, 21—Triune, skirmishes at and near.
March 9-10—Covington, skirmishes near.
March 9, 4-14, 8-12, 23—Thompson's Station, skirmishes at and near.
March 10-22—Murfreesboro, skirmishes.
March 10-11—Rutherford Creek, skirmishes at.
March 10-16—La Fayette and Moscow, scout to, and skirmish.
March 14—Davis' Mill, skirmish at.
March 15—La Fayette Depot, skirmish at.
March 16, 29—Moscow, skirmishes.
March 19—College Grove, skirmish near.
March 10—Liberty, skirmish at.
March 19—Richland Station, skirmish at.
March 19—Spring Hill, skirmish at.
March 20—Milton, action near.
March 20—Battle of Vaught's Hill.
March 21—Salem, skirmish at.
March 24—Davis' Mill Road, skirmish on, near La Grange.
March 24—La Grange, skirmish on Davis' Mill Road, near.
March 25—Battle of Brentwood.
March 25—Little Harpeth River, action at.
March 27—Woodbury Pike, skirmish on the.
March 28—Somerville, skirmish at.
March 29—Belmont, action near.
March 31—Eagleville, skirmish near.
April 1—Columbia Pike, skirmish on the.
April 1—Eagleville, skirmish near.
April 2, 27—Carter Creek Pike, skirmishes on the.
April 2, 3, 6, 7—Liberty, skirmishes at.
April 3—Smith's Ford, skirmish at.
April 3—Snow Hill, skirmish at.
April 4—Lewisburg Pike, skirmish on the.
April 4—Memphis, skirmish on Nonconnah Creek, near.
April 4—Nonconnah Creek, near Memphis, skirmish on.
April 4—Woodbury, skirmish.
April 5—Davis' Mill, skirmish at.
April 6—Green Hill, skirmish near.
April 9—Franklin, skirmish.
April 9—Obion River, skirmish near the.
April 10—Antioch Station, affair at.
April 10—First Battle of Franklin, or Battle of Franklin I.
April 10—La Vergne, skirmish near.
April 12—Stewartsboro, skirmish at.

April 13—Chapel Hill, skirmish.
April 16—Eagleville, skirmish near.
April 18, 22—Hartsville, skirmishes at.
April 19—Trenton, skirmish at.
April 23—Shelbyville Pike, skirmish on the.
April 26—College Grove, affair near.
April 26—Duck River Island, engagement at.
April 26—Little Rock Landing, engagement at.
May 2—Thompson's Station, skirmish.
May 4—Nashville, affair near.
May 5—Rover, skirmish.
May 11—La Fayette, skirmish at.
May 12—Linden, skirmish at.
May 17—Bradyville Pike, skirmish on the.
May 18—Horn Lake Creek, skirmish on.
May 20—Collierville, skirmish at.
May 20—Salem, skirmish at.
May 22—Middleton, skirmish at.
May 22—Yellow Creek, skirmish at.
May 24, 25—Woodbury, skirmishes.
May 29-30—Hamburg Landing, skirmishes at.
May 30—Jordan's Store, skirmish at.
June 3—Murfreesboro, skirmish.
June 4—Triune, action at.
June 4—Franklin, engagement at.
June 4—Liberty, skirmish at.
June 4—Marshall Knob, skirmish near.
June 4—Snow Hill, skirmish at.
June 5—Smithville, skirmish at.
June 6—Shelbyville Pike, skirmish on the.
June 8, 9, 10, 19—Triune, skirmishes at and near.
Juno 11—Battle of Triune.
June 14—Green Hill, skirmish near.
June 15—Trenton, affair near.
June 17—Memphis, attack on Union transports near.
June 17—Montgomery, affair near.
June 17—Wartburg, affair at.
June 19—Lenoir's Station, affair at.
June 19-20—Knoxville, skirmishes at.
June 20—Dixson Springs, skirmish at.
June 20—Rogers' Gap, skirmish at
June 20—Strawberry Plains, skirmish at.
June 21—Powder Springs Gap, skirmish at.

June 22—Powell Valley, skirmish at.
June 23, 28—Rover, skirmishes.
June 23—Uniontown, skirmish at.
June 24—Big Spring Branch, skirmish at.
June 24—Bradyville, skirmish.
June 24—Christiana, skirmish.
June 24-26—Battle of Hoover's Gap.
June 24-27—Liberty Gap, skirmishes at.
June 24—Middleton, skirmish at.
June 25, 27—Fosterville, skirmishes at.
June 25, 27—Guy's Gap, skirmishes at.
June 26—Beech Grove, skirmish at.
June 27—Tullahoma, action at.
June 27—Fairfield, skirmish at.
June 27—Shelbyville, action at.
June 29—Decherd, skirmish at.
June 29—Hillsboro, skirmish near.
June 29—Lexington, skirmish near.
June 29-30—Tullahoma, skirmishes near.
June 30—Cowan Pass, Chattanooga, action at.
July 1—Bobo's Cross-Roads, skirmish near.
July 1, 2—Bethpage Bridge, Elk River, skirmishes at and near.
July 2—Estill Springs, skirmish at.
July 2—Morris' Ford, Elk River, skirmish at.
July 2—Pelham, skirmish at.
July 2—Rock Creek Ford, Elk River, skirmish at.
July 3—Boiling Fork, skirmish at.
July 3—Winchester, skirmish near.
July 4—University Depot, skirmish near.
July 5—Yellow Creek, skirmish at.
July 10—Bolivar, skirmish at.
July 10—Union City, capture of outpost at.
July 13-15—Forked Deer River, skirmishes on.
July 13, 15—Jackson, skirmish at and near.
July 15—Pulaski, skirmish at.
July 17—Stone's River, skirmish on.
July 18—Memphis, skirmish near.
July 29—Fort Donelson, skirmish near.
July 30—Grand Junction, skirmish at.
Aug. 3—Denmark, skirmish near.
Aug. 9—Sparta, skirmish at.
Aug. 17—Calfkiller Creek, near Sparta, skirmish at.
Aug. 19—Weems' Springs, skirmish at.

Aug. 21-Sept. 8—Second Battle of Chattanooga; bombardment of.
Aug. 21—Shellmound, action at.
Aug. 26-27—Harrison's Landing, skirmishes at.
Aug. 27-28—Narrows, near Shellmound, skirmish at the.
Aug. 28—Jacksboro, skirmish at.
Aug. 31—Winter's Gap, skirmish at.
Sept. 5—Paducah, Ky., and Union City, skirmish.
Sept. 5—Tazewell, skirmish at.
Sept. 6—Sweet Water, skirmishes near.
Sept. 6—Wartrace, skirmish at.
Sept. 7—Lookout Valley, skirmish in.
Sept. 8—Limestone Station and Telford's Station, actions at.
Sept. 9—Friar's Island, skirmish at.
Sept, 10, 25—Athens, skirmishes at.
Sept. 12—Rheatown, skirmish at.
Sept. 13—Clark's Creek Church, skirmish at.
Sept. 13—Paris, skirmish at.
Sept. 14—Henderson, skirmish near.
Sept, 16—Montezuma, skirmish at.
Sept. 18, 26—Calhoun, skirmishes at.
Sept. 18—Cleveland, skirmish at.
Sept. 18—Fort Donelson, affair near.
Sept. 18—Kingsport, skirmish at.
Sept. 19—Bristol, skirmish at.
Sept. 19—Como, skirmish at.
Sept. 20-21, 22—Carter's Depot, skirmishes at.
Sept. 20-21—Zollicoffer, action at.
Sept, 21, 28—Jonesboro, skirmishes at.
Sept. 22—Battle of Blountsville.
Sept, 22, 23, 26—Chattanooga, skirmishes.
Sept. 22—Missionary Ridge and Shallow Ford Gap, near Chattanooga, skirmishes at.
Sept. 23—Cumberland Gap, skirmish at.
Sept. 22,—Summertown and Lookout Mountain, skirmishes at.
Sept. 24—Zollicoffer, skirmish at.
Sept. 25—Calhoun and Charleston, skirmishes at.
Sept. 26—Winchester, skirmish near.
Sept. 27—Locke's Mill, near Moscow, skirmish at.
Sept. 27—Philadelphia, skirmish near.
Sept. 28—Buell's Ford, skirmish at.
Sept. 29—Friendship Church, skirmish at.
Sept. 29—Leesburg, skirmish at.
Sept. 30—Cotton Port Ford, Tennessee River, skirmish at.

Sept. 30—Swallow Bluffs, skirmish at.
Oct. 1—Mountain Gap, near Smith's Cross-Roads, skirmish at.
Oct. 2, 8—Chattanooga, skirmishes near.
Oct. 2—Dunlap, skirmish near.
Oct. 2—Greeneville, skirmish at.
Oct. 2—Jasper, skirmish on the Valley Road, near.
Oct. 2—Pitt's Cross-Roads, Sequatchie Valley, skirmish at.
Oct. 3—Bear Creek, skirmish at.
Oct. 3—Beersheba, skirmish at Hill's Gap, near.
Oct. 4—McMinnville, skirmish near.
Oct. 5—Blue Springs, skirmish at.
Oct. 5—Murfreesboro, skirmish at Stone's River Railroad Bridge, near.
Oct. 5, 6—Readyville, skirmishes.
Oct. 6—Christiana, affair at.
Oct. 6—Fosterville, skirmish at Garrison's Creek, near.
Oct. 7—Shelbyville, skirmish at Sims' Farm, near.
Oct. 7—Farmington, action at.
Oct. 9—Cleveland, skirmish at.
Oct. 9—Cowan, affair at the railroad tunnel, near.
Oct. 9—Elk River, skirmish at.
Oct. 9—Sugar Creek, skirmish at.
Oct. 10—Battle of Blue Springs.
Oct. 10—Hartsville, skirmish near.
Oct. 10-11—Sweet Water, skirmishes at.
Oct. 11—Collierville, action at.
Oct. 11—Henderson's Mill and Rheatown, skirmishes at.
Oct. 14—Blountsville, skirmish at.
Oct. 14—Loudon, skirmish near.
Oct. 15—Bristol, skirmish at.
Oct. 15—Philadelphia, skirmish near.
Oct. 16—Island No. 10, skirmish near.
Oct. 19—Spurgeon's Mill, skirmish at.
Oct. 19—Zollicoffer, skirmish at.
Oct. 20, 25-26—Philadelphia, actions at.
Oct. 21—Sulphur Springs, skirmish at.
Oct. 22—New Madrid Bend, skirmish at.
Oct. 26—Jones' Hill, skirmish at.
Oct. 27—Brown's Ferry, skirmish at.
Oct. 27—Clinch Mountain, skirmish at.
Oct. 27—Columbia, scout from, toward Pulaski, and skirmish.
Oct. 28—Clarksville, skirmish at.
Oct. 28, 30—Leiper's Ferry, Holston River, skirmishes at.

Oct. 28-29—Battle of Wauhatchie.
Oct. 29—Centreville, skirmish at.
Oct. 30—Holston River, skirmish at Leiper's Ferry on the.
Nov. 1—Eastport, skirmish at.
Nov. 1—Fayetteville, skirmish at.
Nov. 2—Centreville, skirmish at.
Nov. 3—Battle of Collierville.
Nov. 3—Lawrenceburg, skirmish at.
Nov. 3—Piney Factory, skirmish at.
Nov. 4—Little Tennessee River, skirmish at Motley's Ford, on.
Nov. 5—La Fayette, skirmish at.
Nov. 5—Loudon County, skirmish in.
Nov. 5—Moscow, skirmish at.
Nov. 6—Rogersville, action near.
Nov. 12—Cumberland Gap, skirmish near.
Nov. 13—Blythe's Ferry, Tennessee River, skirmish at.
Nov. 13—Palmyra, skirmish at.
Nov. 14—Maryville, Little River, Rockford, and Huff's Ferry, skirmishes at.
Nov. 15—Lenoir's Station, skirmish at.
Nov. 15—Loudon, skirmish near.
Nov. 15—Pillowville, skirmish at.
Nov. 15—Stock Creek, skirmish at.
Nov. 16—Battle of Campbell's Station.
Nov. 16-23—Kingston, skirmishes at and about.
Nov. 16—Knoxville, skirmish near.
Nov. 17-Dec. 4—Battle of Knoxville; siege of.
Nov. 19—Colwell's Ford, skirmish at.
Nov. 19—Meriwether's Ferry, near Union City, skirmish at.
Nov. 19—Mulberry Gap, skirmish at.
Nov. 20, 24, 26, 27—Sparta, skirmishes at and rear.
Nov. 22—Winchester, skirmish at.
Nov. 23—Knoxville, action at.
Nov. 23—Orchard Knob, or Indian Hill, and Bushy Knob, skirmishes at.
Nov. 23-25—Battles for Chattanooga, also known as the Chattanooga Campaign.
Nov. 24—Kingston, action at.
Nov. 24—Battle of Lookout Mountain.
Nov. 24—Missionary Ridge, skirmish at foot of.
Nov. 25—Battle of Missionary Ridge.
Nov. 25—Yankeetown, skirmish near.
Nov. 26—Charleston, skirmish at.

Nov. 26—Chickamauga Station, skirmish at.
Nov. 26—Pea Vine Valley, skirmish in.
Nov. 26—Pigeon Hills, skirmish at.
Nov. 27—Cleveland, skirmish at.
Nov. 29—Battle of Fort Sanders; Knoxville, assault on.
Nov. 30—Charleston, affair at.
Nov. 30—Yankeetown, skirmish at.
Dec. 1—Maynardville, skirmish near.
Dec. 1-29—West Tennessee, action in.
Dec. 2—Philadelphia, skirmish at.
Dec. 2, 5—Walker's Ford, Clinch River, skirmishes at.
Dec. 3—Log Mountain, skirmish at.
Dec. 3-4—Wolf River Bridge, near Moscow, action at.
Dec. 4—Kingston, skirmish near.
Dec. 4, 27—La Fayette, skirmishes at.
Dec. 4-5—Loudon, skirmishes at and near.
Dec. 5—Crab Gap, skirmish at.
Dec. 6—Clinch Mountain, skirmish at.
Dec. 6—Fayetteville, affair near.
Dec. 7—Eagleville, skirmish at.
Dec. 7, 16, 18—Rutledge, skirmishes at.
Dec. 9-13—Bean's Station, skirmishes at and near.
Dec. 9—Cumberland Mountain, affair at, on road to Crossville.
Dec. 10—Gatlinsburg, skirmish at.
Dec. 10—Long Ford, skirmish at.
Dec. 10, 14—Morristown, skirmishes at and near.
Dec. 10—Russellville, affair at.
Dec. 12—Cheek's Cross-Roads, skirmish at.
Dec. 12-13—Russellville, skirmishes at.
Dec. 12—Shoal Creek, skirmish on.
Dec. 12—Wayland Springs, skirmish near.
Dec. 13—Dandridge's Mill, skirmish at.
Dec. 13—Farley's Mill, Holston River, skirmish at.
Dec. 13—La Grange, skirmish at.
Dec. 14—Battle of Bean's Station.
Dec. 14—Granger's Mill, skirmish at.
Dec. 15, 18—Bean's Station, skirmishes at.
Dec. 15—Livingston, skirmish near.
Dec. 16-19—Blain's Cross-Roads, skirmishes at and near.
Dec. 18, 28—Charleston, skirmishes at.
Dec. 19—Stone's Mill, skirmish at.
Dec. 21—Clinch River, skirmish at.
Dec. 21—McMinnville, skirmish at.

Dec. 22, 29—Cleveland, skirmishes at.
Dec. 23—Mulberry Village, skirmish at.
Dec. 24—Estenaula, skirmish at.
Dec. 24—Hays' Ferry, near Dandridge, action at.
Dec. 24—Jack's Creek, skirmish at.
Dec. 24—Peck's House, near New Market, skirmishes at, and near Mossy Creek Station.
Dec. 26—Mossy Creek, actions at.
Dec. 26—New Castle, skirmish near.
Dec. 26—Somerville, skirmish at.
Dec. 27—Collierville, skirmish at.
Dec. 27—Grisson's Bridge, skirmish at.
Dec. 27—Huntingdon, skirmish at.
Dec. 27—Moscow, skirmish near.
Dec. 27, 29—Talbott's Station, skirmishes at
Dec. 28—Calhoun, action at, and skirmish at Charleston.
Dec. 29—La Vergne, skirmish at.
Dec. 29—Battle of Mossy Creek.

1864

Jan. 1, 14—Dandridge, skirmishes at.
Jan. 2, 25—La Grange, skirmishes at.
Jan. 5—Lawrence's Mill, skirmish at.
Jan. 10, 12—Mossy Creek, skirmishes near.
Jan. 13—Sevierville, affair at.
Jan. 14—Middleton, skirmish at.
Jan. 14—Schultz's Mill, Cosby Creek, skirmish at.
Jan. 16—Kimbrough's Cross-Roads, skirmish at.
Jan. 16—White County, skirmish in.
Jan. 16-17—Bend of Chucky Road, skirmish at.
Jan. 17—Battle of Dandridge.
Jan. 19—Big Springs, near Tazewell, skirmish at.
Jan. 19, 24—Tazewell, skirmishes at and near.
Jan. 20—Tracy City, skirmish at.
Jan. 21-22—Strawberry Plains and Armstrong's Ferry, skirmish at.
Jan. 22—Armstrong's Ferry, skirmish at.
Jan. 23—Newport, skirmish near.
Jan. 26—Flat Creek and Muddy Creek, skirmishes at.
Jan. 26—Sevierville, skirmish at.
Jan. 26, 27—Knoxville, skirmishes near.

Jan. 27—Battle of Fair Garden.
Jan. 27—Kelly's Ford and McNutt's Bridge, skirmishes at.
Jan. 28—Fain's Island, Indian Creek, Island Ford, Kelly's Ford, and Swann's Island, skirmishes at.
Jan. 28—Lee's House, on Cornersville Pike, affair at.
Feb. 6—Bolivar, affair at.
Feb. 9—Hardin County, skirmish in.
Feb. 13—Fentress County, skirmish in.
Feb. 18—Maryville, skirmish near.
Feb. 18—Mifflin, skirmish at.
Feb. 18—Sevierville, skirmish at.
Feb. 20—Flat Creek, skirmish at.
Feb. 20—Knoxville, skirmish near.
Feb. 20—Sevierville Road, near Knoxville, skirmish on.
Feb. 20—Strawberry Plains, skirmish at.
Feb. 22—Calfkiller Creek, skirmish on.
Feb. 22—Powell's Bridge, skirmish at.
Feb. 26—Sulphur Springs, skirmish at.
Feb. 26—Washington, capture of.
Feb. 27—Sequatchie Valley, skirmish in the.
Feb. 28—Dukedom, skirmish at.
March 5—Panther Springs, skirmish at.
March 11—Calfkiller Creek, skirmish on.
March 12—Union City, skirmish near.
March 13—Cheek's Cross-Roads, skirmish at.
March 13—Spring Hill, skirmish at.
March 14—Bent Creek, skirmish at.
March 15-May 5—West Tennessee, action in.
March 15—Flat Creek Valley, skirmish in.
March 17—Manchester, skirmish at.
March 21—Reynoldsburg, skirmish at.
March 24—Murfreesboro, skirmish near.
March 24—Union City, capture of.
March 27—Louisville, affair at.
March 28—Obey's River, skirmish on.
March 29—Bolivar, skirmish near.
April 2—Cleveland, skirmish at.
April 3, 9—Raleigh, skirmishes near.
April 3, 10—Cypress Swamp, skirmishes at.
April 12—Battle of Fort Pillow; capture of.
April 12—Pleasant Hill Landing, skirmish at.
April 13—Mink Springs, near Cleveland, skirmish at.
April 15—Greeneville, skirmish near.

April 16—Rheatown, skirmish at.
April 19-20—Waterhouse's Mill and Boiling Springs, skirmishes at.
April 22—Duck River, skirmish on.
April 29—Berry County, skirmish in.
May 2—Bolivar, skirmish at.
May 10—Winchester, affair with guerrillas at.
May 13—Pulaski, skirmish at.
May 19—Dandridge, skirmish at.
May 24—Nashville, skirmish near.
May 25—Cripple Creek, Woodbury Pike, skirmish near.
May 30—Greeneville, skirmish at.
June 9, 29—La Fayette, skirmishes at.
June 13, 23—Collierville, skirmishes.
June 14—Bean's Station, skirmish at.
June 15—Moscow, skirmish near.
June 20, 26—White's Station, skirmishes at.
June 21—Decatur County, skirmish in.
June 23—La Fayette, attack on train near.
July 2—Byhalia (Miss.) Road, south of Collierville, skirmish at the.
July 2, 24—Collierville, skirmishes near.
July 3—La Grange, skirmish near.
July 20—Blount County, skirmish in.
July 22-23, 30—Clifton, skirmishes at.
July 28—Long's Mills, skirmish at, near Mulberry Gap.
Aug. 1—Athens, skirmish at.
Aug. 2—Morristown, skirmish at.
Aug. 3-4—Triune, skirmishes at.
Aug. 4—Tracy City, skirmish at.
Aug. 8—La Fayette, skirmish at.
Aug. 18—Charleston, skirmish at.
Aug. 20—Pine Bluff, skirmish at.
Aug. 21—Second Battle of Memphis.
Aug. 21, Oct. 8—Rogersville, skirmishes at.
Aug. 23—Blue Springs, skirmish at.
Aug. 31—Clifton, skirmish at.
Sept. 4—Greeneville, skirmish at.
Sept. 4—Park's Gap, skirmish at.
Sept. 6—Readyville, skirmish at.
Sept. 10—Woodbury, skirmish at.
Sept. 12—Memphis, skirmish near.
Sept. 21-Oct. 6—Middle Tennessee, action in.
Sept. 25—Johnsonville, skirmish near.

Sept. 26—Richland Creek, skirmish at, near Pulaski.
Sept. 26—Pulaski, skirmishes.
Sept. 27—Battle of Pulaski.
Sept. 27—Lobelville and Beardstown, skirmishes at.
Sept. 28—Leesburg, skirmish at.
Sept. 28—Rheatown, skirmish near.
Sept. 28—Wells' Hill, skirmish at.
Sept. 29—Centreville, skirmish at.
Sept. 29—Jonesboro, skirmish at.
Sept. 29—Lynchburg, skirmish near.
Sept. 30—Carter's Station, skirmish at.
Sept. 30—Duvall's Ford, skirmish at.
Oct. 1—Carter's Station, skirmish at.
Oct. 1—Clinch River and Laurel Creek Gap, skirmishes at.
Oct. 2—Columbia, skirmish near.
Oct. 4, 20, 25—Memphis, skirmishes near.
Oct. 6—Kingsport, skirmish at.
Oct. 7—Kingston, skirmish at.
Oct. 10—Bean's Station, skirmish near.
Oct. 10—Gallatin, affair near.
Oct. 10—Thorn Hill, near Bean's Station, skirmish at.
Oct. 11—Fort Donelson, skirmish near.
Oct. 12—Greeneville, skirmish at.
Oct. 15—Mossy Creek, skirmish at.
Oct. 16—Bull's Gap, skirmish near.
Oct. 16-Nov. 16—West Tennessee, action in.
Oct. l8—Clinch Mountain, skirmish at.
Oct. 21—Clinch Valley, near Sneedville, skirmish in.
Oct. 27—Fort Randolph, attack on steamer *Belle Saint Louis* at.
Oct. 27—Mossy Creek and Panther Springs, skirmishes at.
Oct. 28—Morristown, action at.
Oct. 28—Russellville, skirmish at.
Oct. 29—Nonconnah Creek, skirmish at.
Oct. 30—Bainbridge, skirmish at.
Nov. 1—Union Station, skirmishes at.
Nov. 2-3—Davidson's Ferry, Tennessee River, attack on gunboats at.
Nov. 3-5—Battle of Johnsonville.
Nov. 11—Russellville, skirmish at.
Nov. 11-13—Battle of Bull's Gap.
Nov. 14—Russellville, action near.
Nov. 15—Collierville, skirmish near.
Nov. 16-17—Strawberry Plains, skirmishes at.

Nov. 17—Flat Creek, skirmish at.
Nov. 22—Lawrenceburg, action at.
Nov. 23—Fouche Springs, skirmish at.
Nov. 22—Henryville, skirmish at.
Nov. 23—Mount Pleasant, action at.
Nov. 24—Campbellsville, action at.
Nov. 24—Lynnville, skirmish at.
Nov. 24-29—Battle of Columbia.
Nov. 28—Duck River, skirmishes at crossings of.
Nov. 28—Shelbyville, skirmish at.
Nov. 29—Columbia Ford, action at.
Nov. 29—Mount Carmel, skirmish at.
Nov. 29—Rally Hill, skirmish near.
Nov. 29—Battle of Spring Hill.
Nov. 29, 30—Thompson's Station, affairs at.
Nov. 30—Second Battle of Franklin, or Battle of Franklin II.
Dec. 1—Owen's Cross-Roads, action at.
Dec. 2-4—Nashville & Chattanooga Railroad, operations against stockade and blockhouses on.
Dec. 4, 6—Bell's Mills, actions at.
Dec. 4—White's Station, skirmish at.
Dec. 5-7—Third Battle of Murfreesboro; demonstrations against.
Dec. 12—Big Creek, near Rogersville, skirmish at.
Dec. 13—Kingsport, action at.
Dec. 13—Murfreesboro, attack on railroad train near.
Dec. 14—Bristol, affair at.
Dec. 14—Memphis, skirmish near, on the Germantown road.
Dec. 15—Murfreesboro, capture of railroad train near.
Dec. 15-16—Battle of Nashville.
Dec. 17—Third Battle of Franklin, or Battle of Franklin III.
Dec. 17—Hollow Tree Gap, action at.
Dec. 17—West Harpeth River, action at.
Dec. 18—Spring Hill, skirmish at.
Dec. 19—Curtis' Creek, skirmish at.
Dec. 19—Rutherford's Creek, skirmish at.
Dec. 20—Columbia, skirmish at.
Dec. 22—Duck River, skirmish at.
Dec. 23—Warfield's, skirmish at, near Columbia.
Dec. 24—Lynnville, skirmish at.
Dec. 24-25—Richland Creek, skirmishes at.
Dec. 25—King's (or Anthony's) Hill, or Devil's Gap, action at.
Dec. 25—White's Station, skirmish near.
Dec. 26—Sugar Creek, action at.

1863

Jan. 28—Athens, action at.
Feb. 1—McLemore's Cove, skirmish in.
Feb. 5—McMinnville, skirmish near.
Feb. 6—Corn's Farm, Franklin County, affair at.
Feb. 9—Memphis, skirmish near.
Feb. 10—Triune, affair near.
Feb. 16—Athens and Sweet Water, attacks upon the garrisons of.
Feb. 21-22—Greeneville, skirmishes near.
March 1—Philadelphia, skirmish near.
March 5—Tazewell, skirmish at.
March 8—Jackson County, skirmish in.
March 18—Livingstone, skirmish at.
March 19, 22—Celina, skirmishes at.
March 25—Brawley Forks, skirmish at.
March 28—Germantown, skirmish at.
March 31—Magnolia, skirmish at.
April 1—White Oak Creek, skirmish at.
April 3, 14—Mount Pleasant, skirmishes at.
April 18—Germantown, skirmish near.

Battle of Chancellorsville, depicting the fatal wounding of Confederate Gen. Stonewall Jackson (right) by friendly fire.

CHAPTER THIRTY-FOUR
TEXAS

1862

Feb. 22—Aransas Bay, engagement in.
April 5-6—San Luis Pass, affair at.
May 14-25—Galveston, blockade of, and operations about.
July 4—Velasco, attack on United States vessels near.
Aug. 10—Nueces River, affair on, near Fort Clark.
Aug. 11—Velasco, affair at.
Aug. 12—*Breaker*, schooner, capture of.
Aug. 16-18—Corpus Christi, bombardment of.
Sept. 13-14—Flour Bluffs, operations at.
Sept. 24-25—First Battle of Sabine Pass.
Sept. 27—Taylor's Bayou, affair on.
Oct. 4—First Battle of Galveston, also known as the Battle of Galveston Harbor.
Oct. 29—Sabine Pass, affair at.
Oct. 31, Nov. 1—Lavaca, bombardment of.
Nov. 20—Matagorda, affair at.
Dec. 7—Padre Island, affair at.

1863

Jan. 1—Second Battle of Galveston; land and naval conflict.
Jan. 21—Sabine Pass, attack on blockading squadron at.
April 18—Sabine Pass, affair at.
May 3—Saint Joseph's Island, affair at.
May 30—Point Isabel, affair at.

Sept. 8—Second Battle of Sabine Pass.
November 2-6—Battle of Brownsville.
Nov. 17—Aransas Pass, capture of Confederate battery at.
Nov. 22-30—Fort Esperanza, Matagorda Island, expedition against and capture of.
Nov. 23—Cedar Bayou, skirmish at.
Dec. 29—Matagorda Peninsula, skirmish on.

1864

Jan, 8-9—Caney Bayou, bombardment of Confederate works at the mouth of.
Feb. 7—Caney Bayou, affair at the mouth of.
Feb. 22—Indianola, affair near.
March 13—Los Patricios, skirmish at.
March 17, 22—Corpus Christi, affairs at.
March 19—Laredo, attack on.
March 21—Velasco, affair at.
June 19—Eagle Pass, affair at.
June 25—Rancho Las Rinas, skirmish at.
Aug. 9—Point Isabel, skirmish at.
Sept. 6—Brazos Santiago, skirmish at the Palmetto Ranch, near.
Oct. 13—Elm Creek, skirmish on.
Oct. 14—Boca Chica Pass, skirmish at.

1865

Jan. 8—Dove Creek, Concho River, action at.
May 12-13—Battle of Palmetto Ranch.
May 13—White's Ranch, skirmish at.

Bird's-eye view of the Battle of Hampton Roads.

CHAPTER THIRTY-FIVE
VERMONT

1864

Oct. 19—St. Albans raid; a group of Confederate soldiers attempt the takeover of the small town in an attempt to disrupt Union war efforts in the South. (Note: This engagement, which Yankees call "the northernmost land action of the War," was not recognized by 19th-Century Southern historians).

Battle of Wild Cat.

Confederate Second Lieutenant Robert Powell Page Burwell, Co. C, Second Virginia Infantry Regiment and Second Co. Stuart Horse Virginia Light Artillery Battery, circa 1862. Burwell passed away on Aug. 31, 1863, due to an infected wound received at the Battle of Brandy Station.

CHAPTER THIRTY-SIX
VIRGINIA

1861

May 9—Gloucester Point, exchange of shots between U.S.S. *Yankee* and batteries at.
May 18-19—Battle of Sewell's Point; engagement with U.S.S. *Monticello* at.
May 23—Hampton, demonstration upon.
May 29-June 1—Battle of Aquia Creek; attack on batteries at.
June 1—Arlington Mills, skirmish at.
June 1—Fairfax Court House, skirmish at.
June 5—Pig Point, attack on Confederate battery at.
June 10—Battle of Big Bethel.
June 17—Vienna, action near.
June 24—Rappahannock River, affair on the.
June 27—Mathias Point, attack on.
July 5—Newport News, skirmish at.
July 12—Newport News, skirmish near.
July 17—Fairfax Court House, skirmish at.
July 18—Blackburn's Ford, action at.
July 18—McLean's Ford, operations at.
July 18—Mitchell's Ford, skirmish at.
July 19—Back River Road, affair on the.
July 21—Battle of First Manassas (Yankee name: First Battle of Bull Run).
Aug. 8—Lovettsville, skirmish at.
Aug. 18—Pohick Church, skirmish at.
Aug. 23—Potomac Creek, engagement between batteries at mouth of, and U.S. steamers *Release* and *Yankee*.
Aug. 27-28—Ball's Cross-Roads, skirmish at.

Aug. 28-30—Bailey's Corners, skirmishes near.
Aug. 31—Munson's Hill, skirmish at.
Sept. 10-11—Lewinsville, action and skirmish at.
Sept. 15—Pritchard's Mill, skirmish at.
Sept. 16—Magruder's Ferry, skirmish at.
Sept. 18—Munson's Hill, affair at.
Sept. 25—Lewinsville, skirmish at.
Sept. 28—Vanderburgh's House, affair at.
Oct. 2-3—Springfield Station, skirmishes at.
Oct. 4—Edwards Ferry, skirmish near.
Oct. 15—Little River Turnpike, skirmish on.
Oct. 21—Battle of Leesburg (Yankee name: Battle of Ball's Bluff).
Oct. 21—New Market Bridge, skirmish near.
Oct. 22—Edwards Ferry, action at.
Nov. 16—Doolan's Farm, capture of Union foraging party at.
Nov. 18-27—Fairfax Court House, skirmishes near.
Nov. 26—Vienna, skirmish near.
Nov. 26-27—Dranesville, expedition to and skirmish at.
Dec. 2—Annandale, skirmish at.
Dec. 4—Burke Station, skirmish at.
Dec. 20—Battle of Dranesville.

1862

Jan. 3—Battle of Cockpit Point, also known as the Battle of Shipping Point, or the Battle of Freestone Point.
Jan. 9—Elk Run, skirmish at.
Jan. 9—Pohick Run, skirmish at.
Jan. 29—Lee's House, affair at.
Feb. 24—Lewis Chapel, affair at.
March 5—Bunker Hill, skirmish at.
March 5—Pohick Church, skirmish near.
March 7—Winchester, skirmish near.
March 8-9—Battle of Hampton Roads, naval engagement in.
March 9—Sangster Station, skirmish at.
March 11—Stephenson Station, skirmish at.
March 18—Middletown, skirmish at.
March 19—Strasburg, skirmish at.
March 22—Kernstown, skirmishes at.
March 23—First Battle of Kernstown.
March 25—Mount Jackson, skirmish at.

March 28—Bealeton Station, affair at.
March 29—Rappahannock Station, affair at.
April 1—Salem, skirmish at.
April 2—Stony Creek, near Edenburg, skirmish at.
April 4—Cockletown, skirmish at.
April 4—Howard's Mill, skirmish at.
April 5—Warwick and Yorktown Roads, skirmish near junction of.
April 5-May 4—Battle of Yorktown; siege of.
April 7, 16—Columbia Furnace, skirmishes at.
April 11, 22, 26—Yorktown, affairs at and skirmishes near.
April 12, 21—Monterey, skirmish at.
April 16—Burnt Chimneys, engagement at.
April 16—Lee's Mill, engagement at.
April 17—Piedmont, skirmish at.
April 17—Rude's Hill, skirmish at.
April 17-19—Falmouth, skirmishes near.
April 19—Shenandoah River, South Fork of, skirmish on, near Luray.
April 22—Luray, skirmish near.
April 24—Harrisonburg, skirmish near.
April 27—McGaheysville, skirmish at.
May 1—Rapidan Station, skirmish at.
May 2—Louisa Court House, skirmish at.
May 2—Trevilian's Depot, skirmish at.
May 5—Columbia Bridge, skirmish at.
May 5—Battle of Williamsburg.
May 6—Harrisonburg, skirmish near.
May 7—Barkhamsville, engagement at.
May 7—Battle of Eltham's Landing.
May 7—Somerville Heights, action at.
May 7—West Point, engagement at.
May 8—Bull Pasture Mountain, engagement near.
May 8—Battle of McDowell.
May 8—Sewell's Point, engagement near.
May 9—McDowell, skirmish near.
May 9—New Kent Court House, skirmishes at and near.
May 9—Slatersville, skirmish at.
May 11—Bowling Green Road, skirmish on.
May 12—Monterey, skirmish at.
May 13—Baltimore Cross-Roads, skirmish near.
May 13—Rappahannock River, affair on.
May 14-15—Gaines' Cross-Roads, Rappahannock County, skirmishes near.

May 15—First Battle of Drewry's Bluff (Yankee name: First Battle of Fort Darling).
May 15, 24—Linden, skirmishes at.
May 18, 21—Woodstock, skirmishes at.
May 19—City Point, James River, skirmish at.
May 23—Antioch Church, skirmish at.
May 23—Buckton Station, skirmish at.
May 23—Ellison's Mill, skirmish at.
May 23—Hogan's, skirmish at.
May 23-24—New Bridge, skirmishes at and near.
May 23—Battle of Front Royal.
May 24—Berryville, skirmish at.
May 24—Middletown, action at.
May 24—Newtown, action at.
May 24—Strasburg, skirmish near.
May 25—First Battle of Winchester.
May 27—Battle of Hanover Court House.
May 27—Kinney's Farm, engagement at.
May 27—Loudoun Heights, skirmish at.
May 30—Fair Oaks, skirmish.
May 30—Zuni, skirmish near.
May 30—Front Royal, action at.
May 31—Front Royal, skirmish near.
May 31-June 1—Battle of Seven Pines (Yankee names: First Battle of Fair Oaks, Battle of Fair Oaks Station).
June 1—Mount Carmel, skirmish at.
June 2—Woodstock, skirmish near.
June 3, 16—Mount Jackson, skirmishes near.
June 3—Tom's Brook, skirmish at.
June 6—Harrisonburg, action near.
June 8—Battle of Cross Keys.
June 8, 18, 27—Fair Oaks, skirmishes at and near.
June 8-9—Battle of Port Republic.
June 13—Garlick's Landing, attack on.
June 13—Hawe's Shop, skirmish at.
June 13—New Market, skirmish at.
June 18—Nine-Mile Road, skirmish on the, near Richmond.
June 18-19—Winchester, skirmishes near.
June 19—Charles City Road, skirmish on, near Richmond.
June 20—Gill's Bluff, James River, affair at.
June 21—Fair Oaks Station, skirmish near.
June 24—Milford, skirmish at.
June 25—Ashland, skirmish near.

June 25-29—Bottom's Bridge, operations about.
June 25—French's Field, engagement at.
June 25—King's School-House, engagement at.
June 25—Battle of Oak Grove.
June 25—Orchard, The, engagement at.
June 26—Atlee's Station, skirmish at.
June 26—Battle of Mechanicsville (Yankee name: Battle of Beaver Dam Creek).
June 26—Battle of Ellison's Mill.
June 26—Hanover Court House, skirmish near.
June 26-27—Hundley's Corner, skirmishes at.
June 26—Meadow Bridge, skirmish at.
June 26—Point of Rocks, Appomattox River, engagement at.
June 27—Battle of Gaines' Mill (Yankee name: Battle of Chickahominy River).
June 27-28—Battle of Garnett's and Golding's Farms.
June 28—Dispatch Station, skirmish at.
June 28—Tunstall's Station, operations about.
June 28—White House, operations about, and destruction of stores at.
June 29—Allen's Farm, engagement at.
June 29—James River Road, skirmish on the.
June 29—Jordon's Ford, White Oak Swamp, skirmish at.
June 29—Peach Orchard, engagement at.
June 29—Battle of Savage's Station.
June 29—Williamsburg Road, skirmish on the.
June 29—Willis Church, skirmish near.
June 30—Brackett's, action at.
June 30—Battle of Frayser's Farm (Yankee names: Battle of Charles City Cross-Roads, Battle of Glendale, Battle of Nelson's Farm, Battle of New Market Cross-Roads, Battle of New Market Road, Battle of White Oak Swamp, Battle of Riddle's Shop).
June 30—Malvern Cliff, engagement at.
June 30—Battle of Willis Church.
July 1—Battle of Crew's Farm.
July 1—Fort Furnace, Powell's Big Fort Valley, skirmish near.
July 1—Battle of Malvern Hill.
July 1—Battle of Poindexter's Farm.
July 2—Malvern Hill, skirmish at.
July 3-4—Harrison's Landing, skirmishes about and near.
July 3-4—Herring Creek, skirmishes near.
July 4—Shirley, capture of arms at, by Confederates.

July 5-7—James River, operations against Union shipping on.
July 13—Rapidan Station, skirmish at.
July 15—Middletown, skirmish near.
July 15—Orange Court House, skirmish at.
July 17—Gordonsville, skirmish near.
July 23—Carmel Church, skirmishes near.
July 31-Aug. 1—Harrison's Landing, attack on camps and shipping between Shirley and.
Aug. 1—Barnett's Ford, skirmish at.
Aug. 2—Orange Court House, skirmish at.
Aug. 3—Sycamore Church, skirmish at.
Aug. 4—White Oak Swamp Bridge, reconnoissance to and skirmish at.
Aug. 5-6—Malvern Hill, skirmishes near.
Aug. 5-6—Massaponax Church, affairs at.
Aug. 5-6—Thornburg, affairs at.
Aug. 6—Malvern Hill, skirmish at.
Aug. 7—Wolftown, skirmish at.
Aug. 8—Madison Court House, action near.
Aug. 8—Slaughter's House, skirmish near.
Aug. 9—Battle of Cedar Mountain.
Aug. 9—Battle of Slaughter's Mountain.
Aug. 10—Cedar Run, skirmish at.
Aug. 18—Clark's Mountain, skirmish at.
Aug. 18—Rapidan Station, skirmish at.
Aug. 18-25—Rappahannock, operations on the.
Aug. 20—Brandy Station, skirmish near.
Aug. 20-21—Kelly's Ford, skirmishes at and near.
Aug. 20—Rappahannock Station, skirmish at.
Aug. 20—Stevensburg, skirmish at.
Aug. 21, 22—Freeman's Ford, action.
Aug. 21, 23—Beverly Ford, action.
Aug. 22—Catlett's Station, skirmish at.
Aug. 22—Hazel River, action at.
Aug. 22-25—First Battle of Rappahannock Station.
Aug. 23—Fant's Ford, skirmish at.
Aug. 23—Smithfield, affair at.
Aug. 23—Winchester, capture of railroad train near.
Aug. 23-24—Sulphur Springs, actions.
Aug. 24-25—Waterloo Bridge, actions at.
Aug. 25-26—Sulphur Springs, skirmishes at and near.
Aug. 25-27—Battle of Manassas Station; capture of.
Aug. 26—Bristoe Station, skirmish at.

Aug. 26, 27—Bull Run Bridge, action.
Aug. 26—Gainesville, skirmish at.
Aug. 26, 28—Hay Market, skirmishes at.
Aug. 26—Manassas Junction, skirmish at.
Aug. 27—Buckland Bridge, skirmish at.
Aug. 27—Kettle Run, engagement at.
Aug. 27—Waterford, skirmish at.
Aug. 28—Centreville, skirmish at.
Aug. 28—Gainesville, engagement near.
Aug. 28—Battle of Thoroughfare Gap.
Aug. 28-30—Lewis' Ford, skirmishes at.
Aug. 28-30—Battle of Second Manassas (Yankee name: Second Battle of Bull Run).
Aug. 29—Battle of Groveton.
Aug. 30—Battle of Groveton Heights.
Aug. 31—Franklin, skirmish.
Aug. 31—Germantown, skirmish at.
Sept. 1—Battle of Ox Hill (Yankee name: Battle of Chantilly).
Sept. 2—Fairfax Court House, skirmish near.
Sept. 2—Falls Church, skirmish near.
Sept. 2—Flint Hill, affair at.
Sept. 2, 14, 17—Leesburg, skirmishes at and near.
Sept. 3-4—Falls Church, skirmishes at.
Sept. 9—Williamsburg, skirmish at.
Sept. 19—Boteler's Ford, skirmish at.
Sept. 20, 22—Ashby's Gap, skirmishes at.
Sept. 26—Catlett's Station, skirmish near.
Oct. 3, 29—Blackwater, skirmishes at and on the.
Oct. 3, 31—Franklin, skirmish.
Oct. 3—Zuni, affair near.
Oct. 10—Kinsell's Ferry, skirmish at.
Oct. 15—Carrsville, skirmish near.
Oct. 19—Catlett's Station, skirmish near.
Oct. 19—Warrenton Junction, skirmish near.
Oct. 21—Lovettsville, skirmishes at.
Oct. 21—Snickersville, skirmish near.
Oct. 24—Bristoe Station, skirmish near.
Oct. 24—Manassas Junction, skirmish at.
Oct. 25—Zuni, skirmish at.
Oct. 31—Aldie, skirmish at.
Oct. 31—Mountville, skirmish at.
Nov. 1—Berry's Ford Gap, skirmish at.
Nov. 1, 9—Philomont, skirmishes at.

Nov. 2-3—Union, skirmishes at.
Nov. 3—Castleman's Ferry, skirmish near.
Nov. 3—Snicker's Gap, skirmish at.
Nov. 4, 10—Markham's Station, skirmishes at.
Nov. 4—Salem, skirmish at.
Nov. 5—Barbee's Cross-Roads, action at.
Nov. 5-6—Manassas Gap, skirmish.
Nov. 7-8—Rappahannock Station, skirmishes at.
Nov. 8—Hazel River, skirmish at.
Nov. 8—Little Washington, skirmish at.
Nov. 9—Fredericksburg, skirmish at.
Nov. 9—Newby's Cross-Roads, skirmish at.
Nov. 10—Amissville, action near.
Nov. 10—Corbin's Cross-Roads, action at.
Nov. 11, 14—Jefferson, skirmishes at.
Nov. 12—Providence Church, skirmish.
Nov. 13-14—Sulphur Springs, skirmishes at.
Nov. 14—Blackwater Bridge, skirmish at.
Nov. 14—Waterloo, skirmish at.
Nov. 14—Zuni, skirmish.
Nov. 15—Sulphur Springs, action at.
Nov. 15—Warrenton Springs, action at.
Nov. 16—Chester Gap, skirmish at.
Nov. 16—Gloucester Point, skirmish at.
Nov. 16—United States Ford, affair at.
Nov. 17—Carrsville, affair near.
Nov. 17—Falmouth, skirmish at.
Nov. 18—Franklin, skirmish.
Nov. 19—Philomont, skirmish at.
Nov. 22—Winchester, skirmish near.
Nov. 24—Newtown, skirmish at.
Nov. 28—Hartwood Church, affair near.
Nov. 29—Berryville, skirmish at.
Dec. 1—Beaver Dam Church, skirmish at.
Dec. 2—Berryville, skirmish at.
Dec. 2—Blackwater, skirmish on the.
Dec. 2—Franklin, skirmish.
Dec. 2—Leeds' Ferry, Rappahannock River, skirmish at.
Dec. 4—Rappahannock River, engagement on the.
Dec. 8-12—Zuni, skirmishes.
Dec. 11-15—First Battle of Fredericksburg.
Dec. 12—Dumfries, skirmish at.
Dec. 12, 13—Leesburg, skirmishes.

Dec. 14—Waterford, skirmish at.
Dec. 19—Occoquan (River), skirmish on the.
Dec. 20, 27, 28—Occoquan, skirmishes at and near.
Dec. 21—Strasburg, skirmish at.
Dec. 22—Joyner's Ferry, skirmish at.
Dec. 22—Windsor, skirmish near.
Dec. 25—Warrenton, skirmish near.
Dec. 27—Dumfries, action at.
Dec. 27-28—Fairfax Court House, skirmishes.
Dec. 27-29—Chantilly, skirmishes near.
Dec. 28—Providence Church, skirmish.
Dec. 28—Suffolk, skirmish near.
Dec. 29—Frying Pan, skirmishes near.

1863

Jan. 2—Jonesville, skirmish at.
Jan. 5—Cub Run, skirmish at.
Jan. 9—Brentsville, skirmish at.
Jan. 9—Fairfax Court House, skirmish.
Jan. 9—Grove Church, skirmish near.
Jan. 9—Providence Church, skirmish.
Jan. 17—Newtown, skirmish near.
Jan. 19—Burnt Ordinary, skirmish at.
Jan. 26—Grove Church, near Morrisville, skirmish at.
Jan. 26-27—Fairfax Court House and Middleburg, skirmishes near and at.
Jan. 30—Deserted House, engagement at.
Jan. 30—Kelly's Store, engagement at.
Jan. 30—Suffolk, engagement near.
Jan. 30—Turner's Mills, skirmish at.
Feb. 5-7—Olive Branch Church, skirmishes at and near.
Feb. 6, 13—Dranesville, skirmishes at.
Feb. 6—Millwood, skirmish at or near.
Feb. 6—Wiggenton's Mills, Aquia Creek, skirmish at.
Feb. 9—Somerville, skirmish near.
Feb. 10—Chantilly, skirmish at.
Feb. 14—Union Mills, affair near.
Feb. 14-16—Hillsboro Road, Loudoun affair on, and scout to.
Feb. 21—Ware's Point, attack on U.S.S. *Dragon* at.
Feb. 24—Strasburg, skirmish near.

Feb. 25, 26—Chantilly, skirmishes at.
Feb. 25—Hartwood Church, skirmish at.
Feb. 26—Germantown, affair near.
March 2—Aldie, skirmish near.
March 4—Independent Hill, Prince William County, skirmish at.
March 9—Fairfax Court House, affair at.
March 9—Windsor, skirmish near.
March 15, 29—Dumfries, affairs near.
March 17—Bealeton Station, skirmish at.
March 17—Franklin, skirmish.
March 17—Herndon Station, affair at.
March 17—Battle of Kelly's Ford, or Battle of Kellyville.
March 19—Winchester, skirmish near.
March 22—Occoquan, affairs near.
March 23—Chantilly, skirmish near.
March 25—Norfolk, affair at.
March 29—Kelly's Ford, skirmish at.
March 29—Williamsburg, skirmish at.
March 30—Zoar Church, skirmish at.
April 1—Broad Run, Loudoun County, skirmish near the mouth of.
April 4—Leesville, skirmish at.
April 8—Millwood Road, near Winchester, skirmish on the.
April 11—South Quay Road, skirmish on.
April 11—Williamsburg, skirmish at.
April 11-May 4—Battle of Suffolk; siege of.
April 12, 15, 24—Edenton Road, skirmishes on the.
April 12—Providence Church Road, skirmish on the.
April 13—Elk Run, skirmish at.
April 13—Snicker's Ferry, skirmish at.
April 13—Somerton Road, skirmish on the.
April 14—West Branch, engagement at mouth of.
April 14-15—Norfleet House, engagements near the.
April 16—Pamunkey River, affair on.
April 16—West Point, affair near.
April 19—Huger, Battery, capture of.
April 22—Fisher's Hill, skirmish at.
April 23—Chuckatuck, affair at.
April 26—Oak Grove, skirmish at.
April 29—Brandy Station, skirmish near.
April 29—Crook's Run and Germanna Ford, skirmishes at.
April 29—Kellysville, skirmish near.
April 29—Stevensburg, skirmish near.

April 30—Chancellorsville, skirmishes at and near.
April 30—Raccoon Ford, skirmish at.
April 30—Spottsylvania Court House, skirmish near.
April 30-May 6—Battle of Chancellorsville.
May 1—Rapidan Station, skirmish at.
May 1—South Quay Bridge, skirmish at.
May 2—Ely's Ford, skirmish at.
May 2—Louisa Court House, skirmish near.
May 3—Ashland, skirmish at.
May 3—Chuckatuck, skirmish at.
May 3—Second Battle of Fredericksburg, also known as the Battle of Marye's Heights.
May 3—Hanover Station, skirmish at.
May 3—Hill's Point, skirmish near.
May 3—Reed's Ferry, skirmish near.
May 3—South Anna Bridge, near Ashland, skirmish at.
May 3—Warrenton Junction, skirmish at.
May 3-4—Battle of Salem Church, also known as the Battle of Salem Heights.
May 4—Ashland Church, skirmish at.
May 4—Banks' Ford, battle near (Battle of Bank's Ford).
May 4—Flemming's (Shannon's) Cross-Roads, skirmish at.
May 4—Hanovertown Ferry, skirmish at.
May 4—Hungary Station, skirmish at.
May 4—Tunstall's Station, skirmish at.
May 5—Aylett's, skirmish at.
May 5—Thompson's Cross-Roads, skirmish at.
May 6, 11, 23, 31—Warrenton, skirmishes at.
May 8—Grove Church, skirmish near.
May 13—Upperville, skirmish at.
May 14—Marsteller's Place, near Warrenton Junction, skirmish at.
May 15-16—Carrsville, skirmish near.
May 16—Piedmont Station, skirmish at.
May 17—Dumfries, skirmish near.
May 17—Providence Church, skirmish.
May 23—Barber's Cross-Roads, skirmish at.
May 30—Greenwich, skirmish near.
June 2—Strasburg, skirmish at.
June 2—Upperville, skirmish at.
June 3—Fayetteville, skirmish near.
June 4—Frying Pan, skirmish at.
June 4—Lawyers' Road, near Fairfax Court House, skirmish at the.

June 5, 13—Franklin's Crossing (or Deep Run), on the Rappahannock, skirmishes at.
June 6—Berryville, skirmish near.
June 9—Battle of Brandy Station, also known as the Battle of Fleetwood, and the Battle of Beverly Ford.
June 9—Stevensburg, skirmish at.
June 11, 20—Diascund Bridge, skirmishes at.
June 11—Suffolk, skirmish near.
June 12—Newtown, Cedarville, and Middletown, skirmishes at.
June 13—Opequon Creek, near Winchester, skirmish at.
June 13—White Post, skirmish at.
June 13-14—Berryville, skirmishes at.
June 13-15—Second Battle of Winchester.
June 14—Nine-Mile Ordinary, skirmish at.
June 17—Battle of Aldie.
June 17—Thoroughfare Gap, skirmish at.
June 17-19—Battle of Middleburg.
June 18, 22—Aldie, skirmishes near.
June 21—Gainesville, skirmish near.
June 21-25—Thoroughfare Gap and Hay Market, skirmishes at and about.
June 21—Battle of Upperville.
June 22—Dover, skirmish near.
June 23-28—South Anna Bridge, expedition from Yorktown to the, and skirmish.
June 27—Fairfax Court House, skirmish near.
June 28-29—Little River Turnpike, affair on the.
July 1—Baltimore Cross-Roads, skirmish at.
July 2—Baltimore, or Crump's, Cross-Roads, and Baltimore Store, skirmishes at.
July 4—South Anna Bridge, skirmish at the.
July 7—Gladesville, skirmish at.
July 12—Ashby's Gap, skirmish at.
July 17—Snicker's Gap, skirmish at.
July 20—Ashby's Gap, skirmish at.
July 20—Berry's Ferry, skirmish near.
July 21-22—Manassas Gap, skirmishes at.
July 21-22, 23—Chester Gap, skirmishes at and near.
July 23—Gaines' Cross-Roads, skirmish near.
July 23—Snicker's Gap, skirmish near.
July 23—Battle of Manassas Gap, also known as the Battle of Wapping Heights.
July 24—Battle Mountain, near Newby's Cross-Roads, skirmish at.

July 25—Barbee's Cross-Roads, skirmish at.
July 31-Aug. 1—Kelly's Ford, skirmishes at.
Aug. 1—Brandy Station, action at.
Aug. 2—Newtown, skirmish at.
Aug. 4—Amissville, skirmish near.
Aug. 4-9—Brandy Station, skirmishes at.
Aug. 5, 27—Little Washington, skirmishes at.
Aug. 5—Muddy Run, near Culpeper Court House, skirmish at.
Aug. 5—Rixeyville Ford, skirmish near.
Aug. 6—Blake's Farm.
Aug. 7—Burke's Station, affair at.
Aug. 8—Waterford, skirmish at.
Aug. 9—Welford's Ford, skirmish near.
Aug. 15—Beverly Ford, skirmish at.
Aug. 15, 25, 28—Hartwood Church, skirmishes at.
Aug. 16—Falls Church, skirmish at.
Aug. 18—Bristoe Station, skirmish at.
Aug. 22—Stafford Court House, skirmish at.
Aug. 24—Coyle's Tavern, near Fairfax Court House, skirmish at.
Aug. 24—King George Court House, skirmish near.
Aug. 25—Lamb's Ferry, Chickahominy River, skirmish near.
Aug. 27—Weaverville, skirmish at.
Sept. 1—Barbee's Cross-Roads, skirmish at.
Sept. 1—Corbin's Cross-Roads, skirmish at.
Sept. 1—Lamb's Creek Church, near Port Conway, skirmish at.
Sept. 1—Leesburg, skirmish at.
Sept. 2—Oak Shade, skirmish near.
Sept. 2—Rixey's Ford, affair near.
Sept. 6—Carter's Run, skirmish at.
Sept. 8-13—Brandy Station, skirmishes at.
Sept. 12—Bristoe Station, skirmish near.
Sept. 12—White Plains, skirmish at.
Sept. 13—Culpeper Court House, skirmish at.
Sept. 13—Muddy Run, near Culpeper Court House, skirmish at.
Sept. 13—Pony Mountain, skirmish at.
Sept. 13—Stevensburg, skirmish at.
Sept. 14—Leesburg, skirmish near.
Sept. 14—Somerville Ford, skirmish at.
Sept. 15—Kempsville, affair near.
Sept. 15—Rapidan Station, skirmish at.
Sept. 15, 17, 19, 22—Raccoon Ford, skirmishes at.
Sept. 15, 23—Robertson's Ford, skirmishes at.
Sept. 16—Smithfield, skirmish at.

Sept. 18—Crooked Run, skirmish at.
Sept. 19—Strasburg, affair at.
Sept. 21—Fisher's Hill, skirmish at.
Sept. 21—Madison Court House, skirmish at.
Sept. 21—Orange Court House, skirmish at.
Sept. 21-22—White's Ford, Rapidan River, skirmishes at.
Sept. 22—Centreville and Warrenton, skirmish between.
Sept. 23—Liberty Mills, skirmish near.
Sept. 24—Bristoe Station, skirmish at.
Sept. 25—Upperville, skirmish near.
Sept. 26—Richard's Ford, skirmish at.
Sept. 30—Neersville, skirmish at.
Sept. 30—Woodville, skirmish at.
Oct. 1—Auburn, skirmish near.
Oct. 1, 11—Culpeper Court House, skirmishes near.
Oct. 1, 3—Lewinsville, skirmishes at.
Oct. 6—Catlett's Station, affair near.
Oct. 7—Hazel River, skirmish at.
Oct. 7, 15—Mitchell's Ford, Bull Run, skirmishes at.
Oct. 7—Utz's Ford, affair at.
Oct. 8—Robertson's River, skirmishes along.
Oct. 8, 9—James City, skirmishes near.
Oct. 10—Bethsaida Church, skirmish at.
Oct. 10—Germanna Ford, skirmish at.
Oct. 10—James City, skirmish at.
Oct. 10—Raccoon Ford, skirmish at.
Oct. 10—Russell's Ford, on Robertson's River, skirmish at.
Oct. 10, 11—Morton's Ford, skirmishes at.
Oct. 11—Brandy Station, skirmish at.
Oct. 11—Culpeper Court House, skirmish at.
Oct. 11—Griffinsburg, skirmish at.
Oct. 1—Kelly's Ford, skirmish at.
Oct. 11—Stevensburg, skirmish at.
Oct. 11-12—Warrenton, or Sulphur Springs, action at.
Oct. 12—Brandy Station, or Fleetwood, skirmish at.
Oct. 12—Gaines' Cross-Roads, skirmish at.
Oct. 12—Jeffersonton, skirmish at.
Oct. 13—First Battle of Auburn.
Oct. 13—Fox's Ford, skirmish at.
Oct. 13—Warrenton, skirmish near.
Oct. 14—Brentsville, skirmishes near.
Oct. 14—Battle of Bristoe Station.
Oct. 14—Second Battle of Auburn, also known as the Battle of

Coffee Hill.
Oct. 14, 19—Catlett's Station, skirmishes at.
Oct. 14—Centreville, skirmish near.
Oct. 14, 19—Gainesville, skirmishes at.
Oct. 14—Grove Church, skirmish at.
Oct. 14—Saint Stephen's Church, skirmish at.
Oct. 15—Blackburn's Ford, Bull Run, skirmish at.
Oct. 15—Manassas, skirmish at.
Oct. 15—McLean's Ford, Bull Run, skirmish at.
Oct. 15—Oak Hill, skirmish at.
Oct. 17—Berryville, skirmish at.
Oct. 17—Chantilly, affair at Stuart's, near.
Oct. 17—Frying Pan Church, near Pohick Church, skirmish at.
Oct. 17-18—Groveton, skirmishes at.
Oct. 17—Manassas Junction, skirmish at.
Oct. 18, 22—Annandale, affairs near.
Oct. 18—Berryville, skirmish near.
Oct. 19—Battle of Buckland Mills, also known as the Battle of Chestnut Hill, and the Battle of Buckland Races.
Oct. 19—Hay Market, skirmish at.
Oct. 19—New Baltimore, skirmish at.
Oct. 22, 24—Bealeton, skirmishes at and near.
Oct. 22—Rappahannock Bridge, skirmish at.
Oct. 23—Fayetteville, skirmish at.
Oct. 23—Rappahannock Station, skirmish near.
Oct. 24—Liberty, skirmish at.
Oct. 25-26—Bealeton, skirmishes at and near.
Oct. 27—Bealeton and Rappahannock Station, skirmishes near.
Oct. 30—Catlett's Station, skirmish near.
Oct. 31—Weaverville, affair near.
Nov. 1—Catlett's Station, skirmish at.
Nov. 6—Falmouth, skirmish near.
Nov. 5—Hartwood Church, skirmish at.
Nov. 6—Falmouth, skirmish near.
Nov. 7—Kelly's Ford, action at.
Nov. 7—Second Battle of Rappahannock Station.
Nov. 8—Brandy Station, skirmish at.
Nov. 8—Jeffersonton, skirmish near.
Nov. 8—Muddy Run, near Culpeper Court House, skirmish at.
Nov. 8—Rixeyville, skirmish at.
Nov. 8—Stevensburg, skirmish at.
Nov. 8—Warrenton, or Sulphur Springs, skirmish at.
Nov. 9—Covington, skirmish near.

Nov. 13—Winchester, skirmish near.
Nov. 14—Tyson's Cross-Roads, skirmish at.
Nov. 14-15—Virginia, eastern shore of, affairs on.
Nov. 16—Edenburg, skirmish at.
Nov. 16—Germantown, affair at.
Nov. 16—Mount Jackson, skirmish at.
Nov. 16—Woodstock, skirmish at.
Nov. 18—Germanna Ford, skirmish near.
Nov. 19—Grove Church, skirmish near.
Nov. 21—Liberty, affair at.
Nov. 24—Little Boston, skirmish near.
Nov. 24—Woodville, skirmish near.
Nov. 25—Sangster's Station, affair near.
Nov. 26, 29—Brentsville, skirmishes at.
Nov. 26—Morton's Ford, skirmish at.
Nov. 26-27, 30—Raccoon Ford, skirmishes at and near.
Nov. 27—Catlett's Station, skirmish at.
Nov. 27—Payne's Farm, engagement at.
Nov. 27—Robertson's Tavern, or Locust Grove, skirmishes at.
Nov. 27-Dec. 2—Battle of Mine Run.
Nov. 28, 30—Mine Run, skirmishes along.
Nov. 29—Jonesville, skirmish near.
Nov. 29—New Hope Church, skirmish at.
Nov. 29—Parker's Store, action at.
Nov. 30—Licking Run Bridge, skirmish at.
Dec. 1—Ely's Ford, skirmish at Jennings' Farm, near.
Dec. 1—Jonesville, skirmish near.
Dec. 3—Ellis' Ford, skirmish at.
Dec. 5—Raccoon Ford, skirmish at.
Dec. 9—Lewinsville, affairs at and near.
Dec. 13—Germantown, affair at.
Dec. 13—Powell's River, skirmish at, near Stickleyville.
Dec. 13—Strasburg, skirmishes near.
Dec. 14—Catlett's Station, affair near.
Dec. 15-17—Sangster's Station, skirmishes at.
Dec. 16—Upperville, skirmish at.
Dec. 18—Culpeper Court House, affair near.
Dec. 19—Barber's Creek, skirmish on.
Dec. 19—Covington, skirmish near.
Dec. 21—Hunter's Mill, affair near.
Dec. 23—Culpeper Court House, skirmish near.
Dec. 24—Germantown, affair near.

1864

Jan. 1—Rectortown, skirmish at.
Jan. 3—Jonesville, action at.
Jan. 6, 18—Flint Hill, affairs at.
Jan. 7—Warrenton, skirmish at.
Jan. 10—Loudoun Heights, skirmish at.
Jan. 12—Accotink, affair near.
Jan. 12—Ellis' Ford, affair near.
Jan. 13, 17—Ely's Ford, affairs near.
Jan. 17—Ellis' and Ely's Fords, affairs near.
Jan. 22—Ellis' Ford, affair at.
Jan. 22—Germantown, skirmish at.
Jan. 27—Thoroughfare Mountain, affair near.
Jan. 28-29—Jonesville, skirmishes near.
Jan. 29—Gloucester Court House, affair near.
Feb. 1—Bristoe Station, skirmish at.
Feb. 2—Strasburg, skirmish near.
Feb. 5—Aldie, skirmish near.
Feb. 5—Winchester, affair at.
Feb. 6—Bottom's Bridge, skirmish at.
Feb. 6-7—Battle of Morton's Ford; Rapidan River, demonstration on the, including skirmishes at Barnett Ford and Culpeper Ford.
Feb. 14—Brentsville, affair near.
Feb. 17-18—Piedmont, skirmish near.
Feb. 20—Upperville and Front Royal, skirmishes at.
Feb. 21-22—Circleville and Dranesville, skirmishes near.
Feb. 22—Gibson's and Wyerman's Mills, skirmishes at, on Indian Creek, and at Powell's Bridge, Tenn.
Feb. 28—Ely's Ford, affair at.
Feb. 29—Beaver Dam Station, skirmish at.
Feb. 29—Charlottesville, skirmish near.
Feb. 29—Stanardsville, skirmish at.
Feb. 29—Taylorsville, skirmish near.
Feb. 29-March 1—Ballahock, on Bear Quarter Road, and Deep Creek, skirmishes at.
Feb. 29-March 1—Deep Creek, skirmish at.
March 1—Ashland, skirmish at.
March 1—Atlee's, skirmish near.
March 1—Brook Turnpike, near Richmond, skirmishes on.
March 1—Burton's Ford, skirmish at.

March 1—Stanardsville, skirmish near.
March 2—Old Church, skirmish near.
March 2—Battle of Walkerton.
March 4-5—Portsmouth, demonstration on.
March 6—Snickersville, skirmish at.
March 9—Greenwich, skirmish near.
March 9—Suffolk, skirmish near.
March 16—Annandale, affair near.
March 16—Bristoe Station, skirmish at.
March 22—Cricket Hill, skirmish at.
April 8—Winchester, skirmish at.
April 11—Greenwich, affair near.
April 13—Nokesville, affair near.
April 13-15—Cherry Grove Landing, skirmish near.
April 15—Bristoe Station and Milford, affairs near.
April 16—Catlett's Station, affair near.
April 17—Ellis' Ford, affair near.
April 19—Leesburg, affair at.
April 23—Hunter's Mills, affair near.
April 24—Middletown, skirmish near.
April 26—Winchester, affair at.
April 27-29—Twelve-Mile Ordinary, skirmish at.
May 4—Chancellorsville, skirmish near.
May 5—Birch Island Bridges, skirmish at.
May 5-7—Battle of the Wilderness.
May 6—Blackwater River, skirmish at.
May 6—Princeton, skirmish at.
May 6-7—Battle of Port Walthall Junction.
May 6-7—Chester Station, engagements at.
May 6-7—Battle of Todd's Tavern.
May 7—Stony Creek Station, skirmish at.
May 8—Alsop's Farm.
May 8—Corbin's Bridge.
May 8—Jarratt's Station, skirmish at.
May 8—Jeffersonville, skirmish at.
May 8—Laurel Hill.
May 8—Todd's Tavern.
May 8—White's Bridge, skirmish at.
May 8-21—Battle of Spotsylvania Court House.
May 9—Brandon (or Brander's) Bridge, skirmish at.
May 9—Battle of Cloyd's Mountain, also known as the Battle of Cloyd's Farm.
May 9—Davenport.

May 9—Fort Clifton, engagement at.
May 9—Battle of Swift Creek, also known as the Battle of Arrowfield Church.
May 9—Ware Bottom Church, skirmishes at.
May 10—Battle of Chester Station.
May 10—Battle of Cove Mountain, also known as the Battle of Grassy Lick; near Wytheville.
May 10—New River Bridge, skirmish at.
May 10—Ny River.
May 10—Po River.
May 10—Wytheville, engagement near.
May 11—Ashland.
May 11—Blacksburg, skirmish at.
May 11—Glen Allen Station.
May 11—Ground Squirrel Bridge, or Church.
May 11—Battle of Yellow Tavern.
May 12—Angle, or the Salient.
May 12—Brook Church, or Richmond Fortifications.
May 12—Battle of Meadow Bridge, or Battle of Meadow Bridges.
May 12—Mechanicsville.
May 12—Strasburg, affair at.
May 12—Strawberry Hill.
May 12-16—Battle of Proctor's Creek.
May 14—Chula Depot, skirmish near.
May 14—Flat Creek Bridge, skirmish at.
May 14—Rude's Hill and New Market, skirmishes at.
May 14-16—Second Battle of Drewry's Bluff (Yankee name: Second Battle of Fort Darling).
May 15—Battle of New Market.
May 15—Piney Branch Church.
May 16—Port Walthall Junction, skirmish at.
May 17—Waterford, skirmish near.
May 18—City Point, skirmish at.
May 18—Foster's Plantation, skirmish at.
May 19—Harris' Farm.
May 20—Battle of Ware Bottom Church.
May 21—Fort Powhatan, skirmish at.
May 21—Guiney's Station.
May 21—Stanard's Mill.
May 21—Quarles Mills.
May 23-26—Battle of North Anna.
May 24—Ox Ford.
May 24—Battle of Wilson's Wharf.

May 25—Jericho Bridge, or Ford, or Mills.
May 27—Dabney's Ferry.
May 27—Hanover Junction.
May 27—Hanovertown.
May 27—Little River.
May 27—Mount Carmel Church.
May 27—Pole Cat Creek.
May 27—Salem Church.
May 27—Sexton's Station.
May 28—Aenon Church.
May 28—Crump's Creek.
May 28—Battle of Hawe's Shop (sometimes spelled Haw's Shop).
May 28—Jones' Farm.
May 28-30—Battle of Totopotomoy Creek.
May 29-30—Newtown, skirmishes at.
May 30—Armstrong's Farm.
May 30—Matadequin Creek.
May 30—Battle of Old Church.
May 30—Shady Grove.
May 31—Totopotomoy River.
May 31—Bethesda Church.
May 31—Mechump's Creek.
May 31—Shallow Creek.
May 31—Turner's Farm.
May 31-June 12—Battle of Cold Harbor.
June 1—Ashland.
June 2—Covington, affair at.
June 3—Hawe's Shop, action at.
June 3—Via's House, skirmish near.
June 4—Harrisonburg, affair at.
June 4—Port Republic, affair at.
June 5—Battle of Piedmont.
June 7-24—Trevilian Raid.
June 9—Loudoun County, affair in.
June 9—First Battle of Petersburg.
June 10—Brownsburg, skirmish at.
June 10—Old Church, skirmish at.
June 10—Middlebrook, skirmish at.
June 10—Waynesboro, skirmish at.
June 11—Lexington, skirmish at.
June 11-12—Battle of Trevilian Station.
June 12—Amherst Court House, skirmish near.
June 12—Long Bridge, action at.

June 12—Newark, or Mallory's Cross-Roads.
June 13—Buchanan, skirmish near.
June 13—Riddle's Shop, skirmish at.
June 13—White Oak Swamp, skirmish at.
June 14—Harrison's Landing, skirmish near.
June 14—New Glasgow, affair at.
June 15—Malvern Hill, skirmish at.
June 15-18—Second Battle of Petersburg.
June 15—Smith's Store, skirmish near.
June 16—Bermuda Hundred Front, action on.
June 16—New London, skirmish at.
June 16—Otter Creek, skirmish on, near Liberty.
June 17—Bermuda Hundred Front, skirmish on.
June 17—Diamond Hill, skirmish at, near Lynchburg.
June 17-18—Battle of Lynchburg.
June 18, 20—King and Queen Court House, skirmishes at.
June 19—Liberty, skirmish at.
June 19-July 31—Petersburg and Richmond, siege of.
June 20—Buford's Gap, skirmish at.
June 20—White House, skirmish at.
June 21—Catawba Mountains, skirmish at.
June 21, 28—Howlett's Bluff, actions at.
June 21—Salem, skirmish at and near.
June 21—White House, or Saint Peter's Church, and Black Creek, or Tunstall's Station, skirmishes at.
June 21-24—Battle of Jerusalem Plank Road, also known as the First Battle of Weldon Railroad.
June 22—Reams Station, skirmish at.
June 23—New Castle, skirmish at.
June 23—Jones' Bridge, skirmish at.
June 23—Nottoway Court House, skirmish near.
June 23-24—Falls Church and Centreville, skirmishes near.
June 24—Hare's Hill, action at.
June 24—Battle of Saint Mary's Church.
June 25—Oak Grove, engagement at.
June 25-29—Bottom's Bridge, operations about.
June 25—Battle of Staunton River Bridge, also known as the Battle of Roanoke Station.
June 28—White House, operations about and destruction of stores at.
June 28-29—Battle of Sappony Church, also known as the Battle of Stony Creek, and the Battle of Stony Creek Depot.
June 29—First Battle of Reams Station (note: while this is the

spelling of the National Park Service, some sources spell the location Ream's Station).
June 30—Malvern Cliff, engagement at.
June 30-July 1—Four-Mile Creek, actions on, at Deep Bottom.
July 1—Battle of Malvern Hill.
July 3—Buckton, skirmish at.
July 6—Mount Zion Church, near Aldie, action at.
July 12—Turkey Creek, skirmish at.
July 12—Warwick Swamp, skirmish at.
July 14, 16—Malvern Hill, actions at.
July 15—Accotink, affair at.
July 15-16—Hillsboro, skirmishes near.
July 16, 28—Four-Mile Creek, actions at.
July 16—Wood Grove, skirmish at.
July 17—Herring Creek, skirmish at.
July 17-18—Battle of Cool Spring, also known as the Battle of Snicker's Ferry, the Battle of Island Ford, the Battle of Castleman's Ferry, and the Battle of Parker's Ford.
July 19—Ashby's Gap, skirmish at.
July 19—Berry's Ford, engagement at.
July 20—Stephenson's Depot, engagement at.
July 20—Battle of Rutherford's Farm, also known as the Battle of Stephenson's Depot, and the Battle of Carter's Farm.
July 22—Berryville, skirmish near.
July 22—Newtown, skirmish at.
July 23—Kernstown, skirmish near.
July 24—Second Battle of Kernstown.
July 27-29—First Battle of Deep Bottom; James River, demonstration on the north bank of; also known as the Battle of Darbytown, the Battle of Strawberry Plains, or the Battle of New Market Road.
July 27, 30—Lee's Mill, skirmishes.
July 30—Battle of the Crater; mine explosion at.
Aug. 1—Deep Bottom, skirmish at.
Aug. 3—Wilcox's Landing, action near.
Aug. 4—Harrison's Landing, action near.
Aug. 4—Jonesville, skirmish near.
Aug. 5—Cabin Point, skirmish at.
Aug. 5—Mine (Confederate), explosion of, in front of Eighteenth Army Corps.
Aug. 8, Nov. 26—Fairfax Station, skirmishes at.
Aug. 9—City Point, explosion at.
Aug. 9—Sycamore Church, affair near.

Aug. 10—Stone Chapel, skirmish near.
Aug. 11—Newtown, action near.
Aug. 11—Toll-Gate, near White Post, action at.
Aug. 11—Winchester, skirmish near.
Aug. 12, 15—Cedar Creek, skirmishes at.
Aug. 13—Berryville, affair at.
Aug. 13—Four-Mile Creek and Dutch Gap, actions at.
Aug. 13, 14, 15—Strasburg, skirmishes at and near.
Aug. 13-20—Bailey's Creek, combat at.
Aug. 13-20—Charles City Road, combat at.
Aug. 13-20—Deep Run (or Creek), combat at.
Aug. 13-20—Second Battle of Deep Bottom, also known as the Battle of Fussell's Mill, the Battle of Gravel Hill, the Battle of Charles City Road, the Battle of White's Tavern, the Battle of Bailey's Creek, and the Battle of New Market Road.
Aug. 16—Cedarville (Front Royal), engagement at.
Aug. 16—Battle of Guard Hill, also known as the Battle of Crooked Run.
Aug. 17—Winchester, action at.
Aug. 18-21—Blick's Station, combat at.
Aug. 18-20—Opequon Creek, skirmishes at.
Aug. 18-21—Second Battle of Weldon Railroad, also known as the Battle of Globe Tavern.
Aug. 18-21—Yellow House, combat at.
Aug. 19, 20, 21—Berryville, skirmishes at and near.
Aug. 21—Loudoun County, skirmish in.
Aug. 22—Vaughan Road, skirmish on.
Aug. 23, 24—Reams Station, actions near.
Aug. 24—Annandale, skirmish at.
Aug. 24—Vaughan Road, near Reams Station, action on.
Aug. 25—Second Battle of Reams Station (note: while this is the spelling of the National Park Service, some sources spell the location Ream's Station).
Aug. 29—Opequon Creek, skirmish on Berryville and Winchester Pike, near.
Aug. 31—Davis House, skirmish near.
Sept. 3-4—Battle of Berryville.
Sept. 3—Sycamore Church, affair near.
Sept. 5—Stephenson's Depot, skirmish near.
Sept. 7—Brucetown, skirmishes near Winchester, and near.
Sept. 9—Currituck Bridge, skirmish at.
Sept. 9—*Fawn*, steamer, capture of, and skirmish at Currituck Bridge.

Sept. 10—Chimneys, assault on Confederate works at.
Sept. 13—Abraham's Creek, near Winchester, skirmish at.
Sept. 13—Berryville, affair near.
Sept. 13, 15—Opequon Creek, skirmishes at.
Sept. 14—Beefsteak Raid, or the Great Cattle Raid, Harrison's Landing.
Sept. 14—Berryville, skirmish at and near.
Sept. 15—Dinwiddie Court House, skirmish at.
Sept. 15—Seivers' Ford, Opequon Creek, skirmish at.
Sept. 16-17—Coggins' Point, affair at (16th) and pursuit of the Confederates.
Sept. 16-17—Snicker's Gap, skirmishes at.
Sept. 17—Limestone Ridge, affair at.
Sept. 19—Culpeper, skirmish at.
Sept. 19—Third Battle of Winchester (Yankee names: Battle of Opequon, Battle of the Opequon, and Battle of Opequon Creek).
Sept. 20—Cedarville, skirmish near.
Sept. 20—Middletown, skirmish at.
Sept. 20, 21—Strasburg, skirmishes at.
Sept. 21-22—Battle of Fisher's Hill.
Sept. 21, 23—Front Royal, skirmishes at.
Sept. 22—Milford, skirmish at.
Sept. 23—Woodstock, skirmish at.
Sept. 23—Edenburg, skirmish near.
Sept. 22, 24—Mount Jackson, skirmishes at.
Sept. 24—Forest Hill (or Timberville), skirmish at.
Sept. 24—Luray, skirmish at.
Sept. 24—New Market, skirmish at.
Sept. 24—Winchester, skirmish near.
Sept. 26—Brown's Gap, skirmish at.
Sept. 26, 27—Weyer's Cave, skirmishes at.
Sept. 26, 28—Port Republic, skirmishes at.
Sept. 28—Rockfish Gap, skirmish at.
Sept. 29—Waynesboro, skirmish at.
Sept. 29-30—Battle of Chaffin's Farm, also known as the Battle of Chaffin's Farm and New Market Heights, and the Battle of New Market Heights.
Sept. 29-Oct. 2—Battle of Poplar Spring Church, also known as the Battle of Poplar Grove Church, the Battle of Poplar Springs Church, and the Battle of Peeble's Farm (the latter also sometimes spelled Peebles Farm or Peebles' Farm).
Oct. 1—Battle of Vaughn Road, also spelled the Battle of Vaughan

Road.
Oct. 2—First Battle of Saltville.
Oct. 2—Bridgewater, skirmish at.
Oct. 2—Mount Crawford, skirmish at.
Oct. 3—Mount Jackson, skirmish at.
Oct. 3—North River, skirmish at.
Oct. 6—Fisher's Hill, skirmish near.
Oct. 6—Brock's Gap, skirmish near.
Oct. 7—Back Road, near Strasburg, skirmish on.
Oct. 7—Columbia Furnace, skirmish near.
Oct. 7—Battle of Darbytown and New Market.
Oct. 8—Luray Valley, skirmish in.
Oct. 9—Piedmont, skirmish near.
Oct. 9—Battle of Tom's Brook.
Oct. 10—Rectortown, skirmish near.
Oct. 11—White Plains, skirmish near.
Oct. 13—Cedar Creek, action at.
Oct. 13—Battle of Darbytown Road.
Oct. 14—Strasburg (or Hupp's Hill), skirmish at.
Oct. l6—Blackwater, skirmish at.
Oct. 17—Cedar Run Church, affair at.
Oct. 19—Battle of Cedar Creek.
Oct. 23—Dry Run, skirmish at.
Oct. 25-26—Milford, skirmishes at.
Oct. 26—Scott County, affair in.
Oct. 27-28—Battle of Boydton Plank Road, also known as the Battle of First Hatcher's Run, and the Battle of Burgess Mill.
Oct. 27—Fort Morton and Fort Sedgwick, skirmish in front of.
Oct. 27-28—Second Battle of Fair Oaks, also known as the Battle of Fair Oaks and Darbytown Road.
Oct. 27-28—Hatcher's Run, engagement at.
Oct. 28—Newtown, skirmish near.
Oct. 29—Johnson's Farm, skirmish at.
Oct. 29—Upperville, skirmish at.
Nov. 5—Fort Haskell and Fort Morton, skirmishes in front of.
Nov. 7—Edenburg, skirmish near.
Nov. 10, 11—Kernstown, skirmishes near.
Nov. 11—Manassas Junction, skirmish at.
Nov. 12—Cedar Creek, action at.
Nov. 12—Newtown (or Middletown), action at.
Nov. 12—Nineveh, action at.
Nov. 16—Lee's Mill, skirmish near.
Nov. 22—Front Royal, skirmish at.

Nov. 22—Mount Jackson, action at Rude's Hill, near.
Nov. 24—Parkins' Mill, skirmish at.
Nov. 24—Prince George Court House, skirmish near.
Nov. 28—Goresville, skirmish at.
Nov. 30—Snicker's Gap, skirmish at.
Dec. 1—Stony Creek Station, expedition to, and skirmish.
Dec. 4—Davenport Church, skirmish near.
Dec. 7-12—Hicksford, expedition to, and skirmishes.
Dec. 8—Belfield, action at.
Dec. 8-9—Jarratt's Station, skirmish.
Dec. 8, 9, 10—Hatcher's Run, skirmishes at.
Dec. 10—Fort Holly, skirmish in front of.
Dec. 15—Abingdon, skirmish near.
Dec. 15—Glade Springs, skirmish near.
Dec. 16—Marion, action at, and capture of Wytheville.
Dec. 17—Lead Mines, capture and destruction of.
Dec. 17—Mount Airy, skirmish near.
Dec. 17-18—Battle of Marion.
Dec. 20-21—Second Battle of Saltville; capture and destruction of salt works at.
Dec. 21—Lacey's Springs, action at.
Dec. 21—Madison Court House, skirmish at.
Dec. 23—Gordonsville, skirmish near.
Dec. 24—Taylortown, skirmish at.

1865

Jan. 9—Disputanta Station, skirmish near.
Jan. 18—Lovettsville, affair near.
Jan. 23-24—Fort Brady, James River, action at.
Jan. 23-25—Battle of Trent's Reach; naval battle.
Jan. 25—Powhatan, skirmish near.
Feb. 5-7—Battle of Hatcher's Run, also known as the Battle of Vaughn Road, the Battle of Armstrong's Mill, the Battle of Rowanty Creek, and the Battle of Dabney's Mill.
Feb. 13-17—Edenburg and Little Fort Valley, expedition from Camp Russell (near Winchester) to, and skirmish at.
March 1—Mount Crawford, skirmish at.
March 2—Swoope's Depot, affair at.
March 2—Battle of Waynesboro.
March 3-8—Bealeton Station, operations about.

March 4—Ball's Bridge, skirmish at.
March 5—Harrisonburg, skirmish at.
March 7—Flint Hill, skirmish near.
March 7—Mount Jackson, skirmish near.
March 7—Rude's Hill, skirmish at.
March 8—Duguidsville, skirmish at.
March 10—South Quay, skirmish at.
March 11—Goochland Court House, skirmish at.
March 12—Peach Grove, skirmish near.
March 12—Warsaw, skirmish near.
March 13—Beaver Dam Station, skirmish near.
March 14—South Anna Bridge, skirmish at.
March 14—Woodstock, skirmish at.
March 15—Ashby's Gap, skirmish near.
March 15—Ashland, skirmish near.
March 15—Hanover Court House, skirmish at.
March 18—Dranesville, skirmish near.
March 21—Fisher's Hill, skirmish near.
March 21—Hamilton, skirmish near.
March 23—Goose Creek, skirmish at.
March 25—Fort Fisher, action at.
March 25—Battle of Fort Stedman.
March 25—Watkins House, action at.
March 29—Battle of Lewis Farm; near Gravelly Run.
March 29—Vaughan Road, skirmish on, near Hatcher's Run.
March 29—Quaker and Boydton Roads, skirmish at junction of.
March 30—Five Forks, skirmish near.
March 30—Hatcher's Run and Gravelly Run, skirmishes on the line of.
March 31—Boydton Road, action at.
March 31—Crow's House, action at.
March 31—Hatcher's Run, or Boydton Road, action at.
March 31—Battle of White Oak Road, also known as the Battle of White Oak Ridge.
March 31—Battle of Dinwiddie Court House.
April 1—Battle of Five Forks.
April 1—White Oak Road, skirmish at.
April 2—Gravelly Ford, on Hatcher's Run, skirmish at.
April 2—Third Battle of Petersburg; assault upon and capture of fortified lines in front of.
April 2—Scott's Cross-Roads, action at.
April 2—Battle of Sutherland's Station; South Side Railroad, engagement at.

April 3—Hillsville, skirmish near.
April 3—Battle of Namozine Church.
April 4—Beaver Pond Creek, skirmish at.
April 4—Tabernacle Church, or Beaver Pond.
April 4-5—Amelia Court House, skirmish at.
April 5—Battle of Amelia Springs.
April 5—Paine's Cross-Roads, skirmish at.
April 6—Amelia Springs, skirmish at Flat Creek, near.
April 6—High Bridge, action near.
April 6—Battle of Rice's Station.
April 6—Battle of Sailor's Creek, also spelled Battle of Sayler's Creek.
April 6—Wytheville, action at.
April 6-7—Battle of High Bridge.
April 7—Farmville, engagement at.
April 7—Battle of Cumberland Church.
April 7—Prince Edward Court House, skirmish at.
April 8—Battle of Appomattox Station.
April 9—Battle of Appomattox Court House (Clover Hill); surrender of Army of Northern Virginia at.
April 10—Arundel's Farm, skirmish at.
April 10—Burke's Station and Arundel's Farm, skirmishes near.

Battle of Atlanta; from the cover of the Sea Raven Press edition of Jefferson Davis' book, *The Rise and Fall of the Confederate Government* (Vol. 1, paperback).

CHAPTER THIRTY-SEVEN
WASHINGTON, D.C.

1864

July 11-12—Battle of Fort Stevens; action near, and skirmishes along the northern defenses of Washington, D.C.

Confederate soldier, name unknown, circa 1862.

Confederate Captain John T. Andrews, Co. A, First South Carolina Infantry Regiment, Sixteenth South Carolina Infantry Regiment, and Twenty-Sixth South Carolina Infantry Regiment, Mobile, AL, 1865.

CHAPTER THIRTY-EIGHT
WEST VIRGINIA

1861

April 18—Harpers Ferry, armory at, destruction of.
June 3—Battle of Philippi.
June 19—New Creek, skirmish at.
June 26—Frankfort, skirmish at.
July 2—Battle of Falling Waters, also known as the Battle of Hoke's Run and the Battle of Hainesville.
July 4—Harpers Ferry, skirmish at.
July 6-7—Middle Fork Bridge, skirmishes at.
July 7—Glenville, skirmish at.
July 7-12—Belington and Laurel Hill, skirmishes at.
July 10—Rich Mountain, skirmish.
July 11—Battle of Rich Mountain.
July 13—Carrick's Ford, action at.
July 13—Red House, skirmish at.
July 16—Barboursville, skirmish at.
July 17—Scary Creek, action at.
July 18—Battle of Blackburn's Ford.

Aug. 20—Hawk's Nest, skirmish at.
Aug. 20—Laurel Fork, skirmish at.
Aug. 25—Grafton, skirmishes near.
Aug. 25—Piggot's Mill, skirmish near.
Aug. 26—Battle of Kessler's Cross Lanes.
Aug. 26-27—Wayne Court House, skirmish at.
Sept. 1—Blue Creek, skirmish at.
Sept. 1—Boone Court House, skirmish at.
Sept. 1—Burlington, skirmish at.
Sept. 2—Beller's Mill, skirmish at.
Sept. 2—Hawk's Nest, skirmish at.
Sept. 2—Worthington, skirmish at.
Sept. 6—Rowell's Run, skirmish at.
Sept. 9—Shepherdstown, skirmish at.
Sept. 10—Battle of Carnifex Ferry, Gauley River.
Sept. 11—Elk Water, action at.
Sept. 12—Petersburg, skirmish at.
Sept. 12—Peytona, skirmish near.
Sept. 12-15—Battle of Cheat Mountain, also known as the Battle of Cheat Summit Fort.
Sept. 16—Princeton, action at.
Sept. 23—Cassville, skirmish at.
Sept. 25—Kanawha Gap, action at.
Oct. 3—Battle of Greenbrier River.
Oct. 11—Harpers Ferry, skirmish at.
Oct. 13—Cotton Hill, skirmish at.
Oct. 16—Bolivar Heights, skirmish at.
Oct. 19-21—New River, skirmishes on.
Oct. 23—Gauley, skirmish at.
Oct. 26—Romney, action at.
Oct. 26—South Branch Bridge, skirmish at.
Oct. 26—Springfield, skirmish at.
Oct. 31—Greenbrier, skirmish at.
Nov. 1-3—Gauley Bridge, skirmishes near.
Nov. 10-11—Blake's Farm, skirmishes at.
Nov. 10—Guyandotte, affair at.
Nov. 12—Laurel Creek, skirmish on.
Nov. 13—Romney, skirmish near.
Nov. 14—Fayetteville, skirmish near.
Nov. 14—McCoy's Mill, skirmish near.
Nov. 30—Little Cacapon River, skirmish near mouth of.
Dec. 8—Romney, skirmish near.
Dec. 12—Greenbrier River, skirmish at.

Dec. 13—Battle of Camp Allegheny, also known as the Battle of Allegheny Mountain.
Dec. 15—Roane County, affair in.
Dec. 25—Cherry Run, skirmish at.
Dec. 29-30—Braxton County, skirmishes in.
Dec. 29-30—Clay County, skirmishes in.
Dec. 29-30—Webster County, skirmishes in.

1862

Jan. 3-4—Bath, skirmishes at.
Jan. 4—Alpine Depot, skirmish at.
Jan. 4—Great Cacapon Bridge, skirmish at.
Jan. 4—Sir John's Run, skirmish at.
Jan. 4—Slane's Cross-Roads, skirmish at.
Jan. 7—Hanging Rock Pass, skirmish at.
Jan. 8—Cheat River, skirmish on Dry Fork of.
Feb. 8—Blue Stone, skirmish at the mouth of the.
Feb. 12—Moorefield, skirmish at.
Feb. 14—Bloomery Gap, affair at.
March 3—Martinsburg, skirmish at.
March 19—Elk Mountain, skirmish at.
March 20—Philippi, skirmish at.
April 18—Chapmanville, skirmish at.
April 23—Grass Lick, skirmish at.
April 26—Gordonsville and Keezletown Cross-Roads, skirmish at.
April 27—Garrett's Mill, skirmish at.
May 1—Camp Creek, skirmish on.
May 1—Clark's Hollow, skirmish at.
May 5, 10, 12, 26—Franklin, skirmishes near.
May 5, 11—Princeton, skirmishes at.
May 6—Arnoldsburg, skirmish at.
May 6—Camp McDonald, skirmish at.
May 7, 29—Wardensville, skirmishes at and near.
May 10-12—Franklin, skirmishes near.
May 12, 30—Lewisburg, skirmishes at.
May 15—Ravenswood, skirmish at.
May 15—Wolf Creek, action at.
May 15-17—Battle of Princeton Court House.
May 23—Lewisburg, action at.
May 28—Charlestown, skirmish at.

June 4-7—Big Bend, skirmishes at.
June 8—Muddy Creek, skirmish at.
June 10—West Fork, skirmish at mouth of.
June 25—Mungo Flata, skirmish at.
June 29—Moorefield, affair at.
July 25—Summerville, affair at.
July 27—Flat Top Mountain, skirmish at.
Aug. 2-8—Wyoming Court House, operations about.
Aug. 6—Beech Creek, skirmish at.
Aug. 6—Pack's Ferry, New River, skirmish at.
Aug. 13-14—Blue Stone, skirmishes at.
Aug. 18—Huttonsville, skirmish at.
Aug. 23—Harpers Ferry, capture of railroad train near.
Aug. 23—Moorefield, skirmish at.
Aug. 30—Buckhannon, skirmish at.
Aug. 31—Weston, capture of.
Sept. 1—Glenville, skirmish at.
Sept. 3, 11—Martinsburg, skirmishes.
Sept. 3—Ravenswood, skirmish at.
Sept. 3—Weston, skirmish at.
Sept. 4—Bunker Hill, skirmish at.
Sept. 7—Darkesville, skirmish at.
Sept. 10—Fayetteville, action at.
Sept. 11—Armstrong's Creek, skirmish at.
Sept. 11—Cannelton, skirmish near.
Sept. 11—Cotton Hill, skirmish at.
Sept. 11—Gauley Ferry, skirmish at.
Sept. 11—Miller's Ferry, skirmish at.
Sept. 12—Hurricane Bridge, skirmish at.
Sept. 12-15—Battle of Harpers Ferry; siege and capture of.
Sept. 13-14—Bolivar Heights, action on.
Sept. 13—Charleston, action at.
Sept. 19—Shepherdstown, Ford, skirmish at.
Sept. 19-20—Battle of Shepherdstown.
Sept. 20—Point Pleasant, skirmish at.
Sept. 26-27—Buffalo, skirmish at.
Sept. 28—Standing Stone, skirmish at.
Sept. 30—Glenville, skirmish near.
Oct. 2—Blue's Gap, affair at.
Oct. 4—Little Cacapon Bridge, capture of Union forces at.
Oct. 4—Paw Paw Tunnel, capture of Union forces at.
Oct. 6—Big Birch, skirmish at.
Oct. 16-17—Kearneysville, skirmishes near.

Oct. 16-17—Shepherdstown, skirmishes near.
Oct. 20—Hedgesville, skirmish at.
Oct. 29—Petersburg, skirmish near.
Oct. 31—Kanawha River, skirmish near the falls of the.
Nov. 6—Martinsburg, skirmish near.
Nov. 9—Saint George, capture of.
Nov. 9—South Fork of the Potomac, skirmish on the.
Nov. 10—Charlestown, skirmish at.
Nov. 15—Guyandotte, skirmish on the.
Nov. 22—Halltown, skirmish near.
Nov. 26—Cockrall's Mill, skirmish at.
Nov. 26—Lewis' Mill, skirmish at.
Dec. 1—Romney, skirmish at.
Dec. 2—Charlestown, skirmish at.
Dec. 3—Moorefield, skirmish at.
Dec. 11—Darkesville, skirmish at.
Dec. 12—Harpers Ferry, skirmish between Leesburg, Va., and.
Dec. 16, 22—Wardensville, skirmishes at.
Dec. 20—Halltown, skirmish near.

1863

Jan. 3-5—Moorefield, skirmishes near.
Jan. 22—Pocahontas County, skirmish in.
Feb. 12—Smithfield and Charlestown, skirmish near.
Feb. 16—Romney, affair near.
March 7—Green Spring Run, skirmish at.
March 28—Hurricane Bridge, skirmish at.
March 30—Point Pleasant, skirmishes at.
April 5—Mud River, skirmish at.
April 6-7—Goings' Ford, skirmish at.
April 6-7—Purgitsville, skirmish at.
April 18—Johnstown, Harrison County, affair near.
April 20—Bridgeport, skirmish at.
April 22—Point Pleasant, skirmish at.
April 24—Beverly, skirmish at.
April 24—Gilmer County, skirmish in.
April 25—Greenland Gap, skirmish at.
April 26—Burlington, skirmish at.
April 26—Portland, skirmish at.
April 26—Rowlesburg, skirmish at.

April 27—Independence, affair at.
April 27—Morgantown, affair at.
April 29—Fairmont, skirmish at.
April 30—Simpson's Creek, skirmish near.
May 2—Lewisburg, skirmish near.
May 5—Janelew, skirmish at.
May 6—West Union, skirmish at.
May 7—Cairo Station, affair at.
May 7—Harrisville (Ritchie Court House), affair at.
May 12—Summerville, skirmish at.
May 16—Charlestown, skirmish at.
May 16—Elizabeth Court House, skirmish at.
May 16—Ravenswood, skirmish at.
May 18-20—Fayetteville, skirmishes at and about.
May 21—West Creek, skirmish at.
June 3—Fayetteville, skirmish near.
June 13—Bunker Hill, skirmish at.
June 14—Martinsburg, skirmish at.
June 26—Loup Creek, skirmish on.
July 4, 28—Fayetteville, skirmishes at.
July 7, 14—Harpers Ferry, skirmishes at and near.
July 15—Halltown, skirmish at.
July 15—Shepherdstown, skirmish at.
July 16—Shanghai, skirmish at.
July 16—Shepherdstown, action at.
July 17—North Mountain Station, skirmish near.
July 18-19—Hedgesville and Martinsburg, skirmishes at and near.
July 31—Morris' Mills, skirmish at.
Aug. 4—Burlington, skirmish at.
Aug. 5—Cold Spring Gap, skirmish at.
Aug. 6—Cacapon Mountain, skirmish at.
Aug. 6—Moorefield, skirmish at.
Aug. 21, 27—Glenville, skirmishes near.
Aug. 22—Huntersville, skirmish at.
Aug. 24—Warm Springs, skirmish near.
Aug. 26—Moorefield, skirmish near.
Aug. 26-27—Rocky Gap, near White Sulphur Springs, engagement at.
Aug. 26-28—Sutton, Elk River and Glenville, skirmishes near.
Aug. 27—Ball's Mill, skirmish at.
Aug. 27—Elk River, skirmish on.
Sept. 4—Moorefield, skirmish at.
Sept. 4—Petersburg Gap, skirmish at.

Sept. 6—Petersburg, skirmish at.
Sept. 7—Bath, skirmish at.
Sept. 8—Beech Fork, Calhoun County, skirmish at.
Sept. 8—Sutton, skirmish at.
Sept. 11, 21—Moorefield, affairs at.
Sept. 12—Roane County, skirmish in.
Sept. 14—Cheat Mountain Pass, skirmish at.
Sept. 15—Smithfield, affair at.
Sept. 20—Shaver Mountain, affair on.
Sept. 24—Greenbrier Bridge, skirmish at.
Sept. 25—Cheat River, skirmish at.
Sept. 25—Seneca Trace Crossing, Cheat River, skirmish at.
Oct. 1—Harpers Ferry, skirmish near.
Oct. 7—Charlestown and Summit Point, skirmishes at.
Oct. 11, 14—Salt Lick Bridge, skirmishes at.
Oct. 13—Bulltown, skirmish at.
Oct. 13—Burlington, skirmish at.
Oct. 15—Hedgesville, affair at.
Oct. 18—Charlestown, attack on, and skirmishes on road to Berryville, Va.
Oct. 26—Ravenswood, skirmish at.
Oct. 27—Elizabeth, skirmish on Sandy River, near.
Nov. 4—Cackleytown, skirmish near.
Nov. 5—Mill Point, skirmish at.
Nov. 6—Battle of Droop Mountain.
Nov. 6—Little Sewell Mountain, skirmish at.
Nov. 7—Lewisburg, capture of.
Nov. 7—Muddy Creek, skirmish near.
Nov. 8—Second Creek, on the road to Union, skirmish at.
Nov. 10—Elk Mountain, near Hillsboro, skirmish on.
Nov. 16—Burlington, skirmish near.
Dec. 4, 11, 14—Meadow Bluff, skirmishes at and near.
Dec. 6—Cheat River, skirmish at.
Dec. 8-25—Kanawha Valley, demonstration from the.
Dec. 11—Big Sewell and Meadow Bluff, skirmish at.
Dec. 11—Marling Bottom Bridge, skirmish at.
Dec. 12—Gatewood's, skirmish at.
Dec. 12—Lewisburg and Greenbrier River, skirmishes at.
Dec. 13—Hurricane Bridge, affair at.
Dec. 14—Blue Sulphur Road, near Meadow Bluff, skirmish on.
Dec. 28—Moorefield, skirmish at.

1864

Jan. 1—Bunker Hill, affair at.
Jan. 10, 15—Petersburg, skirmishes at and near.
Feb. 2—Patterson's Creek, skirmish at.
Feb. 4—Moorefield, skirmish at.
Feb. 15—Laurel Creek, Wayne County, skirmish at.
March 3—Petersburg, skirmish near.
March 10—Charlestown, skirmishes near, and at Kabletown.
March 28—Bloomery Gap, affair at.
April 19—Marling's Bottom, affair at.
May 8—Halltown, affair at.
May 10—Lost River Gap, skirmish at.
May 24—Charlestown, skirmish near.
June 4—Panther Gap, skirmish at.
June 6—Moorefield, skirmish near.
June 19—Petersburg, affair near.
June 23—Cove Gap, skirmish at.
June 23—Sweet Sulphur Springs, skirmish at.
June 26—Wire Bridge and Springfield, skirmishes at.
June 29—Charlestown and Duffield's Station, skirmishes at.
July 3, 19,—Darkesville, skirmishes at.
July 3—Leetown, skirmish at.
July 3, 25—Martinsburg, skirmishes at.
July 3—North Mountain, skirmish at.
July 3—North River Mills, skirmish at.
July 4—Patterson's Creek Bridge, skirmish at.
July 4—South Branch Bridge, skirmish at.
July 6—Big Cacapon Bridge, skirmish at.
July 6—Sir John's Run, skirmish at.
July 10, 18, 19—Kabletown, skirmishes at and near.
July 19, 25—Bunker Hill, skirmishes at.
July 19—Charlestown, skirmish at.
July 24, 26—Falling Waters, skirmishes at.
July 27—Back Creek Bridge, skirmish at.
July 30—Shepherdstown, skirmish near.
Aug. 2—Green Spring Run, skirmish at.
Aug. 4—New Creek, action at.
Aug. 5—Huttonsville, skirmish at.
Aug. 7—Battle of Moorefield.
Aug. 7—Oldfields, engagement at, near Moorefield.
Aug. 15, 21, 26—Charlestown, skirmishes near.

Aug. 19—Franklin, skirmish at.
Aug. 20—Bulltown, skirmish at.
Aug. 21—Middleway, skirmish at.
Aug. 21—Battle of Summit Point, also known as the Battle of Welch's Spring, Battle of Flowing Spring, or Battle of Cameron's Depot.
Aug. 22, 29—Charlestown, skirmishes at.
Aug. 23—Kearneysville, skirmish at.
Aug. 24—Huttonsville, affair at.
Aug. 24—Sutton, skirmish at.
Aug. 24, 25—Halltown, skirmishes at.
Aug. 25—Kearneysville, action near.
Aug. 25—Shepherdstown, action near.
Aug. 25-29—Battle of Smithfield Crossing.
Aug. 26—Halltown, action at.
Aug. 27—Duffield's Station, skirmish at.
Aug. 27—Nutter's Hill, skirmish at.
Aug. 28—Leetown and Smithfield, skirmishes at.
Aug. 29—Opequon Creek, engagement at Smithfield crossing of.
Aug. 30—Smithfield, skirmish near.
Aug. 31—Martinsburg, skirmish at.
Sept. 1—Opequon Creek, skirmish at.
Sept. 2—Bunker Hill, actions at.
Sept. 2, 10—Darkesville, skirmishes at.
Sept. 13—Bunker Hill, skirmish at.
Sept. 14—Centerville, skirmish near.
Sept. 18—Martinsburg, action near.
Sept. 27-28—Buckhannon, skirmishes at.
Sept. 30—Coalsmouth, skirmish at.
Oct. 11—Petersburg, skirmish near.
Oct. 14—Duffield's Station, affair at.
Oct. 26—Winfield, skirmish at.
Oct. 29—Beverly, action at.
Nov. 1—Green Spring Run, affair at.
Nov. 18, 20, 30—Kabletown, skirmishes at.
Nov. 27-28—Moorefield, skirmishes at.
Nov. 28—New Creek, affair at.
Nov. 28—Piedmont, skirmish at.
Nov. 29—Charlestown, skirmish at.
Dec. 22—Liberty Mills, skirmish at.

1865

Jan. 11—Beverly, capture of U.S. forces at.
Feb. 3—Harpers Ferry, affair near.
March 13—Charlestown, skirmish near.
March 22—Patterson's Creek Station, skirmish near.
March 30—Patterson's Creek, affair near.
April 6—Charlestown, affair near.

Confederate General William Lewis Cabell, circa 1861.

CHAPTER THIRTY-NINE
MISCELLANEOUS

1861

Dec. 27—Creeks and Seminoles, skirmish with (location not specified).

1863

Dec. 1—Ponca Indians, affair with (location not specified).

Confederate soldier, name unknown, circa 1863.

Confederate Private James C. Kane, Co. C, First Maryland Infantry Regiment and Co. D, Forty-Third Virginia Cavalry Battalion, and his brother Confederate Private John K. Kane, Co. D, Forty-Third Virginia Cavalry Battalion, Baltimore, MD, 1865.

NOTES

ALL FOOTNOTES, ENDNOTES, & NOTES IN GENERAL ARE MINE, UNLESS OTHERWISE INDICATED. L.S.

1. Seabrook, *Abraham Lincoln Was a Liberal, Jefferson Davis Was a Conservative: The Missing Key to Understanding the American Civil War*, p. 55.
2. Schlüter, p. 23.
3. Woods, p. 47.
4. On Lincoln's socialistic, Marxist, and communist thoughts, ideas, and tendencies, see my books: 1) *Lincoln's War: The Real Cause, The Real Winner, the Real Loser*; 2) *Abraham Lincoln Was a Liberal, Jefferson Davis Was a Conservative: The Missing Key to Understanding the American Civil War*; 3) *Abraham Lincoln: The Southern View*. Also see McCarty, passim; Browder, passim; Benson and Kennedy, passim.
5. See J. W. Jones, TDMV, pp. 144, 200-201, 273.
6. Schlüter, p. 23.
7. Nichols, p. 59. (I have paraphrased this quote. L.S.)
8. *The Independent*, Vol. 102, No. 3724, June 5, 1920, p. 309. For more on this topic see my appendix, "Commies in the White House," in my book *Twelve Years in Hell: Victorian Southerners Expose the Myth of Reconstruction, 1865-1877*.
9. See Seabrook, *The Alexander H. Stephens Reader*, passim. See also, Pollard, LC, p. 178; J. H. Franklin, pp. 101, 111, 130, 149; Nicolay and Hay, ALCW, Vol. 1, p. 627.
10. *Confederate Veteran*, Vol. 12, 1904, p. 442.
11. Seabrook (ed.), *A Short History of the Confederate States of America* (J. Davis), p. 59.
12. Seabrook (ed.), *A Short History of the Confederate States of America* (J. Davis), pp. 55-56.
13. For more on this specific topic, see my book *Everything You Were Taught About the Civil War is Wrong, Ask a Southerner!*, pp. 34-39.
14. BISG (the "Book Industry Study Group"), for example—a Left-wing organization which describes itself as "the leading book trade association for standardized best practices, research and information, and events"—gives its BISAC ("Book Industry Standards and Communications") listing for works on the War for Southern Independence under the heading "Civil War Period, 1850-1877." Nearly all books published in the U.S.A. today are under the categorizational control of this progressive group located in New York City.
15. See e.g., Seabrook, *The Quotable Jefferson Davis*, pp. 30, 38, 76.
16. See e.g., Seabrook (ed.) *The Rise and Fall of the Confederate Government* (J. Davis), Vol. 1, pp. 55, 422; Vol. 2, pp. 4, 161, 454, 610. Besides using the term "Civil War" himself, President Davis cites numerous other individuals who use it as well.
17. See e.g., *Confederate Veteran*, Vol. 20, 1912, p. 122.
18. Minutes of the Eighth Annual Meeting, July 1898, p. 87.
19. For more on the nihilistic, atheistic, anti-life, anti-tradition, anti-American, anti-Constitution, anti-capitalism, anti-South agenda of the Victorian Republican Party (then the Liberal Party) and the modern Democrat Party (now the Liberal Party), otherwise known as "The Communist/Socialist Rules for Revolution," see Hasselberg, pp. 2350-2351; Lenin, passim; Marx and Engels, passim; B. Dodd, passim. Also see my book *What the Confederate Flag Means to Me: Americans Speak Out in Defense of Southern Honor, Heritage, and History*.
20. *Confederate Veteran*, Vol. 9, 1901, p. 318.
21. *Minutes U.C.V.*, Vol. 2. *Proceedings of the Tenth Annual Meeting and Reunion of the United Confederate Veterans*, held at Louisville, Kentucky, May 30-June 3; 1900, New Orleans, LA: United Confederate Veterans, p. 25.
22. Gaslighting, one of the primary weapons of the Left, is defined as "deceiving a person or group of people through repetition of a constructed false narrative." Medically speaking it is defined as "a form of emotional abuse or psychological manipulation involving distorting the truth in order to confuse or create doubt in another person to the point where they begin to question their sanity or reality."
23. I use the term "approximate" for battle-by-state numbers because no one knows, or ever will know, the exact number.

Confederate General Joseph Finegan, circa 1863.

BIBLIOGRAPHY

And Suggested Reading

Alexander, Edward Porter. *Military Memoirs of a Confederate*. New York: Charles Scribner's Sons, 1907.
Anderson, Mabel Washbourne. *Life of General Stand Watie: The Only Indian Brigadier General of the Confederate Army and the Last General to Surrender*. Pryor, OK: self-published, 1915.
Armstrong, J. M. *The Biographical Encyclopedia of Kentucky of the Dead and Living Men of the Nineteenth Century*. Cincinnati, OH: J. M. Armstrong and Co., 1878.
Ashe, Samuel A'Court. *History of North Carolina*. 2 vols. Greensboro, NC: Charles L. Van Noppen, 1908.
Benson, Al, Jr., and Walter Donald Kennedy. *Lincoln's Marxists*. Gretna, LA: Pelican, 2011.
Bond, P. S. (ed.). *Military Science and Tactics: A Text and Reference for the Reserve Officers' Training Corps*. Washington, D.C.: P. S. Bond Publishing Co., 1938.
Boyd, James P. *Parties, Problems, and Leaders of 1896: An Impartial Presentation of Living National Questions*. Chicago, IL: Publishers' Union, 1896.
Brock, Robert Alonzo (ed.). *Southern Historical Society Papers*. 52 vols. Richmond, VA: Southern Historical Society, 1876-1943.
Browder, Earl. *Lincoln and the Communists*. New York, NY: Workers Library Publishers, Inc., 1936.
Bryan, William Jennings. *The First Battle: A Story of the Campaign of 1896*. Chicago, IL: W. B. Conkey Co., 1896.
Burns, James MacGregor. *The Vineyard of Liberty*. New York, NY: Alfred A. Knopf, 1982.
Carpenter, Stephen D. *Logic of History - Five Hundred Political Texts: Being Concentrated Extracts of Abolitionism; Also Results of Slavery Agitation and Emancipation; Together With Sundry Chapters on Despotism, Usurpations and Frauds*. Madison, WI: self-published, 1864.
Christian, George Llewellyn. *Abraham Lincoln: An Address Delivered Before R. E. Lee Camp, No. 1 Confederate Veterans at Richmond, VA, October 29, 1909*. Richmond, VA: L. H. Jenkins, 1909.
——. *A Capitol Disaster: A Chapter of Reconstruction in Virginia*. Richmond, VA: self-published, 1915.
——. *Confederate Memories and Experiences*. Richmond, VA: self-published, 1915.
Commons, John R., David J. Saposs, Helen L. Sumner, E. B. Mittelman, H. E. Hoagland, John B. Andrews, Selig Perlman. *History of Labour in the United States*. New York: Macmillan Co., 1918.
Confederate Veteran (Sumner Archibald Cunningham, ed., 1893-1913; Edith Drake Pope, ed., 1914-1932). 40 vols (original forty year run). Nashville,

TN: Confederate Veteran, 1893-1932.
Curry, Jabez Lamar Monroe. *The Southern States of the American Union Considered in Their Relations to the Constitution of the United States and to the Resulting Union.* New York: G. P. Putnam's Sons, 1894.
Dean, Henry Clay. *Crimes of the Civil War, and Curse of the Funding System.* Baltimore, MD: self-published, 1869.
Dodd, Bella. *School of Darkness.* New York, NY: P. J. Kennedy and Sons, 1954.
Early, Jubal Anderson. *A Memoir of the Last Year of the War for Independence, in the Confederate States of America.* Lynchburg, VA: Charles W. Button, 1867.
Edmonds, George. *Facts and Falsehoods Concerning the War on the South, 1861-1865.* Memphis, TN: self-published, 1904.
Evans, Clement Anselm (ed.). *Confederate Military History.* 12 vols. Atlanta, GA: Confederate Publishing Co., 1899.
Ewing, E. W. R. *Northern Rebellion, Southern Secession.* Philadelphia, PA: The John C. Winston Co., 1904.
Fitzhugh, George. *Cannibals All! Or, Slaves Without Masters.* Richmond, VA: A. Morris, 1857.
Franklin, John Hope. *Reconstruction After the Civil War.* Chicago, IL: University of Chicago Press, 1961.
Gardiner, C. *Acts of the Republican Party as Seen by History.* Washington, D.C.: self-published, 1906.
Hasselberg, P. D. (ed.). *Parliamentary Debates: First Session, Fortieth Parliament, 1982, House of Representatives* (Vol. 445). Wellington, New Zealand: Government Printer, 1982.
Johnson, Robert Underwood, and Clarence Clough Buel (eds.). *Battles and Leaders of the Civil War.* 4 vols. New York, NY: The Century Co., 1884-1888.
Johnstone, Huger William. *Truth of War Conspiracy, 1861.* Idylwild, GA: H. W. Johnstone, 1921.
Jones, John William. *The Davis Memorial Volume; Or Our Dead President, Jefferson Davis and the World's Tribute to His Memory.* Richmond, VA: B. F. Johnson, 1889.
Kamman, William F. *Socialism in German American Literature.* Philadelphia, PA: Americana Germanica Press, 1917.
Lenin, Vladimir. *"Left Wing" Communism: An Infantile Disorder.* Detroit, MI: The Marxian Educational Society, 1921.
Livermore, Thomas L. *Numbers and Losses in the Civil War in America, 1861-65.* 1900. Carlisle, PA: John Kallmann, 1996 ed.
Magliocca, Gerard N. *The Tragedy of William Jennings Bryan: Constitutional Law and the Politics of Backlash.* New Haven, CT: Yale University Press, 2011.
Marx, Karl, and Frederick Engels. *Manifesto of the Communist Party.* Chicago, IL: Charles H. Kerr and Co., 1906.
McCarty, Burke (ed.). *Little Sermons in Socialism by Abraham Lincoln.* Chicago, IL: The Chicago Daily Socialist, 1910.
McPherson, James M. *Abraham Lincoln and the Second American Revolution.* New York, NY: Oxford University Press, 1991.
Meriwether, Elizabeth Avery (pseudonym, "George Edmonds"). *Facts and Falsehoods Concerning the War on the South, 1861-1865.* Memphis, TN: A. R. Taylor and Co., 1904.
Miller, Francis Trevelyan, and Robert S. Lanier (eds.). *The Photographic History of the Civil War.* 10 vols. New York, NY: The Review of Reviews Co.,

1911.
Minutes of the Eighth Annual Meeting and Reunion of the United Confederate Veterans, Atlanta, GA, July 20-23, 1898. New Orleans, LA: United Confederate Veterans, 1907.
Minutes of the Ninth Annual Meeting and Reunion of the United Confederate Veterans, Charleston, SC, May 10-13, 1899. New Orleans, LA: United Confederate Veterans, 1907.
Minutes of the Twelfth Annual Meeting and Reunion of the United Confederate Veterans, Dallas, TX, April 22-25, 1902. New Orleans, LA: United Confederate Veterans, 1907.
Muzzey, David Saville. *The United States of America: Vol. 1, To the Civil War*. Boston, MA: Ginn and Co., 1922.
———. *The American Adventure: Vol. 2, From the Civil War*. 1924. New York, NY: Harper and Brothers, 1927 ed.
Nichols, John. *The "S" Word: A Short History of an American Tradition . . . Socialism*. London, UK: Verso, 2011.
Nicolay, John G., and John Hay (eds.). *Abraham Lincoln: A History*. 10 vols. New York, NY: The Century Co., 1890.
———. *Complete Works of Abraham Lincoln*. 12 vols. 1894. New York, NY: Francis D. Tandy Co., 1905 ed.
———. *Abraham Lincoln: Complete Works*. 12 vols. 1894. New York, NY: The Century Co., 1907 ed.
ORA (full title: *The War of the Rebellion: A Compilation of the Official Records of the Union and Confederate Armies*). 128 vols. Washington, DC: Government Printing Office, 1880.
ORN (full title: *Official Records of the Union and Confederate Navies in the War of the Rebellion*). 30 vols. Washington, DC: Government Printing Office, 1894.
Pollard, Edward Alfred. *The Lost Cause*. New York, NY: E. B. Treat and Co., 1867.
Randall, James Garfield. *Constitutional Problems Under Lincoln*. New York: D. Appleton and Co., 1926.
Rawle, William. *A View of the Constitution of the United States of America*. Philadelphia, PA: self-published, 1825.
Richardson, John Anderson. *Richardson's Defense of the South*. Atlanta, GA: A. B. Caldwell, 1914.
Rogers, William P. *The Three Secession Movements in the United States: Samuel J. Tilden, the Democratic Candidate for Presidency; the Advisor, Aider and Abettor of the Great Secession Movement of 1860; and One of the Authors of the Infamous Resolution of 1864; His Claims as a Statesman and Reformer Considered*. Boston, MA: John Wilson and Son, 1876.
Rove, Karl. *The Triumph of William McKinley: Why the Election of 1896 Still Matters*. New York, NY: Simon and Schuster, 2015.
Rutherford, Mildred Lewis. *Truths of History: A Fair, Unbiased, Impartial, Unprejudiced and Conscientious Study of History*. Athens, GA: n.p., 1920.
Scharf, John Thomas. *History of the Confederate States Navy From its Organization to the Surrender of its Last Vessel*. New York: Rogers and Sherwood, 1887.
Schlüter, Herman. *Lincoln, Labor and Slavery: A Chapter From the Social History of America*. New York: Socialist Literature Co., 1913.
Seabrook, Lochlainn. *Carnton Plantation Ghost Stories: True Tales of the Unexplained from Tennessee's Most Haunted Civil War House!* 2005. Franklin, TN, 2016 ed.
———. *Nathan Bedford Forrest: Southern Hero, American Patriot*. 2007. Franklin, TN,

2010 ed.
——. *Abraham Lincoln: The Southern View*. 2007. Franklin, TN: Sea Raven Press, 2013 ed.
——. *The McGavocks of Carnton Plantation: A Southern History - Celebrating One of Dixie's Most Noble Confederate Families and Their Tennessee Home*. 2008. Franklin, TN, 2011 ed.
——. *A Rebel Born: A Defense of Nathan Bedford Forrest*. 2010. Franklin, TN: Sea Raven Press, 2011 ed.
——. *Everything You Were Taught About the Civil War is Wrong, Ask a Southerner!* 2010. Franklin, TN: Sea Raven Press, revised 2019 ed.
——. *The Quotable Jefferson Davis: Selections From the Writings and Speeches of the Confederacy's First President*. Franklin, TN: Sea Raven Press, 2011.
——. *The Quotable Robert E. Lee: Selections From the Writings and Speeches of the South's Most Beloved Civil War General*. Franklin, TN: Sea Raven Press, 2011 Sesquicentennial Civil War Edition.
——. *Lincolnology: The Real Abraham Lincoln Revealed In His Own Words*. Franklin, TN: Sea Raven Press, 2011.
——. *The Unquotable Abraham Lincoln: The President's Quotes They Don't Want You To Know!* Franklin, TN: Sea Raven Press, 2011.
——. *Honest Jeff and Dishonest Abe: A Southern Children's Guide to the Civil War*. Franklin, TN: Sea Raven Press, 2012.
——. *Encyclopedia of the Battle of Franklin - A Comprehensive Guide to the Conflict that Changed the Civil War*. Franklin, TN: Sea Raven Press, 2012.
——. *The Quotable Nathan Bedford Forrest: Selections From the Writings and Speeches of the Confederacy's Most Brilliant Cavalryman*. Spring Hill, TN: Sea Raven Press, 2012.
——. *Forrest! 99 Reasons to Love Nathan Bedford Forrest*. Spring Hill, TN: Sea Raven Press, 2012.
——. *Give 'Em Hell Boys! The Complete Military Correspondence of Nathan Bedford Forrest*. Spring Hill, TN: Sea Raven Press, 2012.
——. *The Constitution of the Confederate States of America Explained: A Clause-by-Clause Study of the South's Magna Carta*. Spring Hill, TN: Sea Raven Press, 2012 Sesquicentennial Civil War Edition.
——. *The Great Impersonator: 99 Reasons to Dislike Abraham Lincoln*. Spring Hill, TN: Sea Raven Press, 2012.
——. *The Old Rebel: Robert E. Lee As He Was Seen By His Contemporaries*. Spring Hill, TN: Sea Raven Press, 2012 Sesquicentennial Civil War Edition.
——. *The Quotable Stonewall Jackson: Selections From the Writings and Speeches of the South's Most Famous General*. Spring Hill, TN: Sea Raven Press, 2012 Sesquicentennial Civil War Edition.
——. *Saddle, Sword, and Gun: A Biography of Nathan Bedford Forrest for Teens*. Spring Hill, TN: Sea Raven Press, 2013.
——. *The Alexander H. Stephens Reader: Excerpts From the Works of a Confederate Founding Father*. Spring Hill, TN: Sea Raven Press, 2013.
——. *The Quotable Alexander H. Stephens: Selections From the Writings and Speeches of the Confederacy's First Vice President*. Spring Hill, TN: Sea Raven Press, 2013 Sesquicentennial Civil War Edition.
——. *Give This Book to a Yankee! A Southern Guide to the Civil War for Northerners*. Spring Hill, TN: Sea Raven Press, 2014.
——. *The Articles of Confederation Explained: A Clause-by-Clause Study of America's First Constitution*. Spring Hill, TN: Sea Raven Press, 2014.

——. *Confederate Blood and Treasure: An Interview With Lochlainn Seabrook.* Spring Hill, TN: Sea Raven Press, 2015.
——. *Nathan Bedford Forrest and the Battle of Fort Pillow: Yankee Myth, Confederate Fact.* Spring Hill, TN: Sea Raven Press, 2015.
——. *Everything You Were Taught About American Slavery War is Wrong, Ask a Southerner!* Spring Hill, TN: Sea Raven Press, 2015.
——. *Confederacy 101: Amazing Facts You Never Knew About America's Oldest Political Tradition.* Spring Hill, TN: Sea Raven Press, 2015.
——. *The Great Yankee Coverup: What the North Doesn't Want You to Know About Lincoln's War!* Spring Hill, TN: Sea Raven Press, 2015.
——. *Slavery 101: Amazing Facts You Never Knew About America's "Peculiar Institution."* Spring Hill, TN: Sea Raven Press, 2015.
——. *Confederate Flag Facts: What Every American Should Know About Dixie's Southern Cross.* Spring Hill, TN: Sea Raven Press, 2016.
——. *Nathan Bedford Forrest and the Ku Klux Klan: Yankee Myth, Confederate Fact.* Spring Hill, TN: Sea Raven Press, 2016.
——. *Seabrook's Bible Dictionary of Traditional and Mystical Christian Doctrines.* Spring Hill, TN: Sea Raven Press, 2016.
——. *Everything You Were Taught About African-Americans and the Civil War is Wrong, Ask a Southerner!* Spring Hill, TN: Sea Raven Press, 2016.
——. *Nathan Bedford Forrest and African-Americans: Yankee Myth, Confederate Fact.* Spring Hill, TN: Sea Raven Press, 2016.
——. *Women in Gray: A Tribute to the Ladies Who Supported the Southern Confederacy.* Spring Hill, TN: Sea Raven Press, 2016.
——. *Lincoln's War: The Real Cause, the Real Winner, the Real Loser.* Spring Hill, TN: Sea Raven Press, 2016.
——. *The Unholy Crusade: Lincoln's Legacy of Destruction in the American South.* Spring Hill, TN: Sea Raven Press, 2017.
——. *Abraham Lincoln Was a Liberal, Jefferson Davis Was a Conservative: The Missing Key to Understanding the American Civil War.* Spring Hill, TN: Sea Raven Press, 2017.
——. *All We Ask is to be Let Alone: The Southern Secession Fact Book.* Spring Hill, TN: Sea Raven Press, 2017.
——. *The Ultimate Civil War Quiz Book: How Much Do You Really Know About America's Most Misunderstood Conflict?* Spring Hill, TN: Sea Raven Press, 2017.
——. *Rise Up and Call Them Blessed: Victorian Tributes to the Confederate Soldier, 1861-1901.* Spring Hill, TN: Sea Raven Press, 2017.
——. *Victorian Confederate Poetry: The Southern Cause in Verse, 1861-1901.* Spring Hill, TN: Sea Raven Press, 2018.
——. *Confederate Monuments: Why Every American Should Honor Confederate Soldiers and Their Memorials.* Spring Hill, TN: Sea Raven Press, 2018.
——. *The God of War: Nathan Bedford Forrest as He Was Seen by His Contemporaries.* Spring Hill, TN: Sea Raven Press, 2018.
——. *The Battle of Spring Hill: Recollections of Confederate and Union Soldiers.* Spring Hill, TN: Sea Raven Press, 2018.
——. *I Rode With Forrest! Confederate Soldiers Who Served With the World's Greatest Cavalry Leader.* Spring Hill, TN: Sea Raven Press, 2018.
——. *The Battle of Nashville: Recollections of Confederate and Union Soldiers.* Spring Hill, TN: Sea Raven Press, 2018.
——. *The Battle of Franklin: Recollections of Confederate and Union Soldiers.* Spring

Hill, TN: Sea Raven Press, 2018.

———. *A Rebel Born: The Screenplay* (for the film). Written 2011. Franklin, TN: Sea Raven Press, 2020.

———. (ed.) *A Short History of the Confederate States of America* (Jefferson Davis, Belford Company, NY, 1890). A Sea Raven Press Reprint. Spring Hill, TN: Sea Raven Press, 2020.

———. (ed.) *Prison Life of Jefferson Davis: Embracing Details and Incidents in his Captivity, With Conversations on Topics of Public Interest* (John J. Craven, Sampson, Low, Son, and Marston, London, UK, 1866). A Sea Raven Press Reprint. Spring Hill, TN: Sea Raven Press, 2020.

———. *What the Confederate Flag Means to Me: Americans Speak Out in Defense of Southern Honor, Heritage, and History*. Spring Hill, TN: Sea Raven Press, 2021.

———. *Heroes of the Southern Confederacy: The Illustrated Book of Confederate Officials, Soldiers, and Civilians*. Spring Hill, TN: Sea Raven Press, 2021.

———. *Support Your Local Confederate: Wit and Humor in the Southern Confederacy*. Spring Hill, TN: Sea Raven Press, 2021.

———. *America's Three Constitutions: Complete Texts of the Articles of Confederation, Constitution of the United States of America, and Constitution of the Confederate States of America*. Spring Hill, TN: Sea Raven Press, 2021.

———. *Vintage Southern Cookbook: 2,000 Delicious Dishes From Dixie*. Spring Hill, TN: Sea Raven Press, 2021.

———. *The Bittersweet Bond: Race Relations in the Old South as Described by White and Black Southerners*. Spring Hill, TN: Sea Raven Press, 2022.

———. (ed.) *The Rise and Fall of the Confederate Government* (Jefferson Davis, D. Appleton, New York, 1881). 2 vols. A Sea Raven Press Facsimile Reprint. Spring Hill, TN: Sea Raven Press, 2022.

———. *I, Confederate: Why Dixie Seceded and Fought in the Words of Southern Soldiers*. Spring Hill, TN: Sea Raven Press, 2023.

———. *Twelve Years in Hell: Victorian Southerners Expose the Myth of Reconstruction, 1865-1877*. Cody, WY: TN: Sea Raven Press, 2023.

Steel, Samuel Augustus. *The South Was Right*. Columbia, SC: R. L. Bryan Co., 1914.

Stephens, Alexander Hamilton. *Speech of Mr. Stephens, of Georgia, on the War and Taxation*. Washington, D.C.: J & G. Gideon, 1848.

———. *A Constitutional View of the Late War Between the States; Its Causes, Character, Conduct and Results*. 2 vols. Philadelphia, PA: National Publishing, Co., 1870.

———. *Recollections of Alexander H. Stephens: His Diary Kept When a Prisoner at Fort Warren, Boston Harbour, 1865*. New York, NY: Doubleday, Page, and Co., 1910.

Thompson, Holland. *The New South: A Chronicle of Social and Industrial Evolution*. New Haven, CT: Yale University Press, 1920.

Warner, Ezra J. *Generals in Gray: Lives of the Confederate Commanders*. 1959. Baton Rouge, LA: Louisiana State University Press, 1989 ed.

———. *Generals in Blue: Lives of the Union Commanders*. 1964. Baton Rouge, LA: Louisiana State University Press, 2006 ed.

Woods, Thomas E., Jr. *The Politically Incorrect Guide to American History*. Washington, D.C.: Regnery, 2004.

INDEX

INCLUDES TOPICS, PEOPLE, KEYWORDS, SPELLING VARIATIONS, & KEY PHRASES

- Search for a military conflict by proper name, alternate name, nickname, state, town, location, or associated natural feature.
- Many state entries are not actual towns or cities, but simply locations which I have created to facilitate searches within a given state.

A Rebel Born (Seabrook), 23
Abbeville, MS, 124
Aberdeen, MS, 122
Abingdon, VA, 216
abolition, 62
abolitionism, 235
abolitionist, 17
abolitionists, 17
Abraham's Creek, VA, 214
Accotink, VA, 207, 212
action, 23, 25, 33-36, 38, 41-44, 46, 48, 50, 55, 58, 60, 61, 63, 65-68, 79, 80, 84-92, 96-99, 101, 108, 109, 113, 115, 118-124, 127-130, 132-134, 136, 138-141, 147, 150, 153, 155, 156, 159, 164, 165, 167-172, 174-186, 188, 189, 191-199, 203-207, 210-213, 215-219, 221-224, 226, 228, 229
Acworth, GA, 67
Adairsville, GA, 65
Adams (U.S. steamer), 47
Adamstown, MD, 110
Adamsville, TN, 167
Adams' Bluff, AR, 42
Adobe Fort, NM, 150
Aenon Church, VA, 210
affair, 23, 25, 33-37, 41, 43-50, 53, 54, 57, 59, 60, 63, 64, 67-69, 75, 80, 83-93, 95-103, 107-111, 113, 115-117, 119, 121-123, 128-130, 133-142, 149-154, 156, 161-163, 165, 167-175,
177, 178, 180-188, 191-194, 196-200, 202-216, 222-231
African-American Confederate soldiers, 62
African-Americans, Confederate, 62
Aiken, SC, 165
Alabama, 9, 23, 33, 38, 102
Alamo (steamer), 49
Albany, KY, 85, 91
Albany, MO, 141
Albemarle (C.S.S. ironclad ram), 154
Albemarle Sound, NC, 154
Alcorn's Distillery, KY, 90
Aldie, VA, 197, 200, 202, 207, 212
Alexander's Bridge, GA, 64
Alexander's Creek, LA, 102
Allatoona, GA, 67
Allegheny Mountain, WV, 223
Allen, MO, 138
Allen's Farm, VA, 195
Allison, Alexander, 6
Alpine Depot, WV, 223
Alpine, GA, 63
Alsop's Farm, VA, 208
Altamont, MD, 108
Altamont, TN, 169
alternative health, 299
Amelia Court House, VA, 218
Amelia Springs, VA, 218
America, 2, 3, 6, 8, 14, 16, 18, 236-238, 240
American Ranch, CO, 53
American Revolutionary War, 15

American slavery, 2, 239, 301
Americans, 2, 17-19, 62, 158, 239, 240, 295
Amherst Court House, VA, 210
Amissville, VA, 198, 203
Amite River, LA, 95, 96, 101-103
Anderson's Hill, MS, 118
Andracita (British schooner), 33
Andrews, John T., 220
Angle, VA, 209
Angley's Post-Office, SC, 164
Annandale, VA, 192, 205, 208, 213
Antarctica, 299
Anthony's Hill, TN, 185
Antietam Bridge, MD, 109
Antietam Creek, MD, 108
Antietam Ford, MD, 110
Antietam Iron Works, MD, 107
Antietam, MD, 108, 109
Antioch Church, AL, 36
Antioch Church, VA, 194
Antioch Station, TN, 174
Antoine, AR, 46
Apache Canyon, NM, 149
Apache Pass, NM, 150
Appalachia, 299
Appomattox Court House, VA, 218
Appomattox River, VA, 195
Appomattox Station, VA, 218
Aquia Creek, VA, 191, 199
Aransas Bay, TX, 187
Aransas Pass, TX, 188
Arcadia Valley, MO, 140
Arcadia, MO, 140
Arizona, 9, 39
Arkadelphia, AR, 43, 45
Arkansas, 9, 41, 43
Arkansas (C.S.S. ironclad), 116
Arkansas Post, AR, 43
Arlington Mills, VA, 191
armies, 8, 25, 237
armory, 221
Armstrong's Creek, WV, 224
Armstrong's Farm, VA, 210
Armstrong's Ferry, TN, 181
Armstrong's Mill, VA, 216
Armuchee Creek, GA, 65
army, 8, 17, 62, 106, 156, 212, 218, 235

Army of Northern Virginia, 8, 218
Arnoldsburg, WV, 223
Arrow Rock, MO, 132, 133, 138, 139
Arrowfield Church, VA, 209
Articles of Confederation, 2, 238, 240
Arundel's Farm, VA, 218
Ash Creek, KS, 84
Ash Hills, MO, 135
Ashby, Turner, 8
Ashby's Gap, VA, 202
Ashbysburg, KY, 87
Ashby's Gap, VA, 197, 202, 212, 217
Ashepoo River, SC, 163
Ashland Church, VA, 201
Ashland, TN, 172
Ashland, VA, 194, 201, 207, 209, 210, 217
Ashley, MO, 133
Ashley's Mills, AR, 44
Ashley's Station, AR, 48
Ashton, LA, 100
Ashwood Landing, LA, 100
Ashwood, MS, 123
astronomy, 299
Atchafalaya River, LA, 98, 102
Atchafalaya, LA, 97, 98, 101, 102
Athens, AL, 33, 36
Athens, KY, 89
Athens, MO, 127
Athens, OH, 157
Athens, TN, 177, 183, 186
Atkins, Chet, 299
Atkins' Mill, TN, 168
Atlanta, GA, 66, 68
Atlee's Station, VA, 195
Atlee's, VA, 207
attack, 23, 25, 33, 34, 36, 37, 44, 47-49, 51, 54, 61, 63, 65, 69, 83-85, 91, 93, 97, 98, 101, 102, 110, 116, 117, 119, 122-124, 129, 136, 138-141, 145, 147, 152, 162-165, 169, 175, 183-185, 187, 188, 191, 194, 196, 199, 227
Aubrey, KS, 83
Auburn, AL, 36
Auburn, TN, 173
Auburn, VA, 204

Augusta, AR, 46, 48
Augusta, KY, 87
Austin, MS, 116, 119
Auxvasse Creek, MO, 133
Averasboro, NC, 155
Avoyelles Prairie, LA, 101
Aylett's, VA, 201
Back Creek Bridge, WV, 228
Back River Road, VA, 191
Back Road, VA, 215
Backbone Mountain, AR, 44
Bacon Creek, KY, 89
Bailey's Corners, VA, 192
Bailey's Creek, VA, 213
Bainbridge, TN, 184
Baker's Creek, MS, 119, 120, 122
Baker's Springs, AR, 45
Bald Hill, GA, 66
Baldwin County, AL, 23
Baldwin, FL, 60
Baldwin's Ferry, MS, 118, 120
Baldwyn, MS, 115, 116
Ball Town, MO, 135
Ballahock, VA, 207
Ball's Bluff, VA, 192
Ball's Bridge, VA, 217
Ball's Cross-Roads, VA, 191
Ball's Ferry, GA, 68
Ball's Mill, MO, 128
Ball's Mill, WV, 226
Baltimore Cross-Roads, VA, 193, 202
Baltimore Store, VA, 202
Baltimore, MD, 232
Banks' Ford, VA, 201
Barbee's Cross-Roads, VA, 198, 203
Barber's Creek, VA, 206
Barber's Cross-Roads, VA, 201
Barber's Ford, FL, 60
Barboursville, KY, 86, 89, 91
Barboursville, WV, 221
Barbourville, KY, 85
Bardstown Pike, KY, 87
Bardstown Road, KY, 88
Bardstown, KY, 87, 90, 92
Barker's Mill, SC, 164
Barkhamsville, VA, 193
Barnesville, GA, 70
Barnesville, MD, 108
Barnett's Corners, MS, 116

Barnett's Ford, VA, 196, 207
Barnwell Island, SC, 161
Barnwell, SC, 164
Barrancas, FL, 37, 61
Barren Fork, Indian Territory, 80
Barren Mound, KY, 88
Barre's Landing, LA, 97, 99
Barry County, MO, 140, 141
Barry, MO, 132
Barton Station, AL, 34
Barton's Station, AL, 35
Batchelder's Creek, NC, 152-154
Bates County, MO, 135
Batesville, AR, 41-43
Bates' Ferry, SC, 165
Bath County, KY, 90, 91, 93
Bath Springs, MS, 117
Bath, WV, 223, 227
Baton Rouge, LA, 95, 98-101
Battery Huger, VA, 200
Battery Island, SC, 162, 163
Battery Pringle, SC, 164
Battery Simkins, SC, 163, 165
Battery Wagner, SC, 162, 163
battle, 1, 2, 5, 6, 16, 21-31, 34, 39, 41-44, 47, 55, 57, 60, 61, 63, 64, 67, 69, 80, 81, 83-86, 88, 92, 95, 97, 98, 100, 101, 103, 105, 108, 110, 111, 115, 116, 119, 127, 128, 130, 132-134, 136, 140, 141, 143, 145, 154, 155, 157, 161-163, 167, 168, 170, 172-174, 177, 183, 185-192, 194-198, 200-202, 204, 205, 208-218, 221-223, 229, 235, 238, 239, 297, 300
Battle Creek, TN, 168, 169
battle dates, 25
battle designations, 25
Battle Mountain, VA, 202
battle names, modern, 24
battle numbers, total by states, 26, 27
Battle of Adairsville, 65
Battle of Albemarle Sound, 154
Battle of Aldie, 202
Battle of Allatoona, 67
Battle of Allegheny Mountain, 223
Battle of Amelia Springs, 218
Battle of Anderson's Hill, 118

Battle of Antietam, 108
Battle of Appomattox Court House, 218
Battle of Appomattox Station, 218
Battle of Aquia Creek, 191
Battle of Arkansas Post, 43
Battle of Armstrong's Mill, 216
Battle of Arrowfield Church, 209
Battle of Athens (AL), 35
Battle of Athens (IA), 81
Battle of Atlanta, 61, 66, 218
Battle of Auburn (First), 204
Battle of Auburn (Second), 204
Battle of Averasboro, 155
Battle of Backbone Mountain, 44
Battle of Bailey's Creek, 213
Battle of Baker's Creek, 119
Battle of Ball's Bluff, 192
Battle of Bank's Ford, 201
Battle of Barbourville, 85
Battle of Baton Rouge, 95, 297
Battle of Baxter Springs, 83
Battle of Bayou De Glaize, 101
Battle of Bayou Fourche, 98
Battle of Bayou La Fourche, 98
Battle of Bean's Station, 180
Battle of Beaver Dam Creek, 195
Battle of Belle Prairie, 101
Battle of Belmont, 25, 128
Battle of Bentonville, 155
Battle of Berryville, 213
Battle of Beverly Ford, 202
Battle of Big Bethel, 191
Battle of Big Black River Bridge, 119
Battle of Big Blue River, 140
Battle of Blackburn's Ford, 221
Battle of Blair's Landing, 100
Battle of Blountsville, 177
Battle of Blue Springs, 178
Battle of Booneville, 116
Battle of Boonsboro, 109
Battle of Boonsboro Gap, 108
Battle of Boonville (First), 127
Battle of Boonville (Fourth), 140
Battle of Boonville (Second), 128
Battle of Boonville (Third), 136
Battle of Boydton Plank Road, 215
Battle of Brandy Station, 190, 202
Battle of Brentwood, 174
Battle of Brice's Cross-Roads, 23, 123
Battle of Bristoe Station, 204
Battle of Brownsville (AR), 44
Battle of Brownsville (TX), 188
Battle of Buck Head Creek, 68
Battle of Buckland Mills, 205
Battle of Buckland Races, 205
Battle of Buffington Island, 157
Battle of Bull Run (First), 191
Battle of Bull Run (Second), 197
Battle of Bull's Gap, 184
Battle of Burgess Mill, 215
Battle of Burkittsville, 108
Battle of Byram's Ford, 140
Battle of Cabin Creek, 80
Battle of Cameron's Depot, 229
Battle of Camp Allegheny, 223
Battle of Camp Wildcat, 85
Battle of Campbell's Station, 179
Battle of Cane Hill, 43
Battle of Cane River Crossing, 100
Battle of Cape Girardeau, 134
Battle of Carnifex Ferry, 222
Battle of Carter's Farm, 212
Battle of Carthage, 127
Battle of Castleman's Ferry, 212
Battle of Cedar Creek, 215
Battle of Cedar Mountain, 196
Battle of Chaffin's Farm, 214
Battle of Chaffin's Farm and New Market Heights, 214
Battle of Chalk Bluff, 43
Battle of Champion Hill, 119
Battle of Champion's Hill, 119
Battle of Chancellorsville, 186, 201
Battle of Chantilly, 197
Battle of Chaplin Hills, 88
Battle of Charles City Cross-Roads, 195
Battle of Charles City Road, 213
Battle of Charleston Harbor (First), 162
Battle of Charleston Harbor (Second), 163
Battle of Charlotte, 141
Battle of Chattanooga (First), 168
Battle of Chattanooga (Second), 177
Battle of Cheat Mountain, 222
Battle of Cheat Summit Fort, 222

Battle of Chester Station, 209
Battle of Chestnut Hill, 205
Battle of Chickahominy River, 195
Battle of Chickamauga, 64
Battle of Chickasaw Bayou, 117
Battle of Chustenahlah, 79
Battle of Chusto-Talasah, 79
Battle of Clark's Mill, 134
Battle of Cloyd's Farm, 208
Battle of Cloyd's Mountain, 208
Battle of Cockpit Point, 192
Battle of Coffee Hill, 204
Battle of Cold Harbor, 210
Battle of Cole Camp, 127
Battle of Collierville, 179
Battle of Columbia, 185
Battle of Columbus, 69
Battle of Cool Spring, 212
Battle of Corinth (First), 115
Battle of Corinth (Second), 116, 300
Battle of Corydon, 77
Battle of Cotton Plant, 42
Battle of Cove Mountain, 209
Battle of Cox's Plantation, 98
Battle of Crampton's Pass, 108
Battle of Crew's Farm, 195
Battle of Crooked Run, 213
Battle of Cross Keys, 194
Battle of Croton, 81
Battle of Cumberland, 110
Battle of Cumberland Church, 218
Battle of Cynthiana (First), 86
Battle of Cynthiana (Second), 92
Battle of Dabney's Mill, 216
Battle of Dallas, 66
Battle of Dalton (First), 64
Battle of Dalton (Second), 67
Battle of Dandridge, 181
Battle of Darbytown, 212
Battle of Darbytown and New Market, 215
Battle of Darbytown Road, 215
Battle of Davis Bridge, 170
Battle of Davis' Cross Roads, 63
Battle of Day's Gap, 34
Battle of Decatur, 36
Battle of Deep Bottom (First), 212
Battle of Deep Bottom (Second), 213
Battle of Devil's Backbone, 44

Battle of Dinwiddie Court House, 217
Battle of Donaldsonville (First), 95
Battle of Donaldsonville (Second), 98
Battle of Douglas Landing, 50
Battle of Dover, 173
Battle of Dranesville, 192
Battle of Drewry's Bluff (First), 194
Battle of Drewry's Bluff (Second), 209
Battle of Droop Mountain, 227
Battle of Dry Wood Creek, 128
Battle of Elk Creek, 80
Battle of Elkhorn Tavern, 41
Battle of Elkin's Ferry, 46
Battle of Ellison's Mill, 195
Battle of Eltham's Landing, 193
Battle of Ezra Church, 66
Battle of Fair Garden, 182
Battle of Fair Oaks (First), 194
Battle of Fair Oaks (Second), 215
Battle of Fair Oaks and Darbytown Road, 215
Battle of Fair Oaks Station, 194
Battle of Fallen Timbers, 168
Battle of Falling Waters, 221
Battle of First Hatcher's Run, 215
Battle of Fisher's Hill, 214
Battle of Five Forks, 39, 217
Battle of Fleetwood, 202
Battle of Flowing Spring, 229
Battle of Folck's Mill, 110
Battle of Forks Road, 155
Battle of Fort Anderson, 153, 155
Battle of Fort Bisland, 100
Battle of Fort Blair, 83
Battle of Fort Blakely, 38
Battle of Fort Brooke, 60
Battle of Fort Darling (First), 194
Battle of Fort Darling (Second), 209
Battle of Fort Davidson, 140
Battle of Fort De Russy, 99
Battle of Fort Donelson (First), 167
Battle of Fort Donelson (Second), 173
Battle of Fort Fisher (First), 154
Battle of Fort Fisher (Second), 154

Battle of Fort Henry, 111, 167
Battle of Fort Hindman, 43
Battle of Fort Jackson and Fort St. Philip, 26, 95
Battle of Fort Macon, 151
Battle of Fort McAllister (First), 63
Battle of Fort McAllister (Second), 69
Battle of Fort Pillow, 23, 182
Battle of Fort Pulaski, 26, 63, 168
Battle of Fort Sanders, 180
Battle of Fort Stedman, 217
Battle of Fort Stevens, 219
Battle of Fort Sumter (First), 16, 26, 28, 103, 161
Battle of Fort Sumter (Second), 163
Battle of Fort Wagner (First), 162
Battle of Fort Wagner (Second), 163
Battle of Fourche Bayou, 98
Battle of Franklin (First), 174
Battle of Franklin (Second), 185
Battle of Franklin (Third), 185
Battle of Franklin I, 174
Battle of Franklin II, 185
Battle of Franklin III, 185
Battle of Frayser's Farm, 22, 195
Battle of Fredericksburg (First), 30, 198
Battle of Fredericksburg (Second), 201
Battle of Fredericktown, 128
Battle of Freestone Point, 192
Battle of Front Royal, 194
Battle of Fussell's Mill, 213
Battle of Gaines' Mill, 195
Battle of Galveston, 23
Battle of Galveston (First), 187
Battle of Galveston (Second), 187
Battle of Galveston Harbor, 187
Battle of Garnett's and Golding's Farms, 195
Battle of Georgia Landing, 96
Battle of Gettysburg, 159
Battle of Glasgow, 140
Battle of Glendale, 195
Battle of Globe Tavern, 213
Battle of Glorieta Pass, 149
Battle of Goldsboro Bridge, 152

Battle of Goodrich's Landing, 98
Battle of Grand Gulf, 118
Battle of Grassy Lick, 209
Battle of Gravel Hill, 213
Battle of Greenbrier River, 222
Battle of Grimball's Landing, 162
Battle of Griswoldville, 68
Battle of Groveton, 197
Battle of Groveton Heights, 197
Battle of Guard Hill, 213
Battle of Hainesville, 221
Battle of Hampton Roads, 55, 188, 192
Battle of Hancock, 107
Battle of Hanover, 159
Battle of Hanover Court House, 194
Battle of Harpers Ferry, 224
Battle of Hartsville, 171
Battle of Hartville, 134
Battle of Hatcher's Run, 216
Battle of Hatchie Bridge, 170
Battle of Hatchie's Bridge, 170
Battle of Hatteras Inlet Batteries, 151
Battle of Hawe's Shop, 210
Battle of Helena, 43
Battle of High Bridge, 218
Battle of Hill's Plantation, 42
Battle of Hoke's Run, 221
Battle of Honey Hill, 164
Battle of Honey Springs, 80
Battle of Hoover's Gap, 176
Battle of Hurricane Creek, 124
Battle of Independence (First), 132
Battle of Independence (Second), 141
Battle of Irish Bend, 100
Battle of Island Ford, 212
Battle of Island No. 10, 130
Battle of Iuka, 116
Battle of Ivy Mountain, 85
Battle of Jackson, 118, 171
Battle of James Island, 162
Battle of Jenkins' Ferry, 47
Battle of Jerusalem Plank Road, 211
Battle of Johnsonville, 184
Battle of Jonesboro, 67
Battle of Jonesborough, 67
Battle of Kellyville, 200

Battle of Kelly's Ford, 200
Battle of Kennesaw Mountain, 66
Battle of Kernstown (First), 192
Battle of Kernstown (Second), 212
Battle of Kessler's Cross Lanes, 222
Battle of Killdeer Mountain, 57
Battle of Kinston, 152
Battle of Kirksville, 127
Battle of Knoxville, 179
Battle of Kock's Plantation, 98
Battle of Kolb's Farm, 66
Battle of La Fourche, 98
Battle of La Fourche Crossing, 98
Battle of Lake Chicot, 47
Battle of Lebanon (KY), 90
Battle of Lebanon (TN), 168
Battle of Leesburg, 23, 192
Battle of Lewis Farm, 217
Battle of Lexington, 23, 171
Battle of Lexington (First), 128
Battle of Lexington (Second), 128
Battle of Liberty, 128
Battle of Little Blue River, 140
Battle of Little Osage River, 84
Battle of Little Rock, 98
Battle of Logan's Cross-Roads, 86
Battle of Lone Jack, 132
Battle of Lookout Mountain, 179
Battle of Lovejoy's Station, 67
Battle of Lynchburg, 211
Battle of Malvern Hill, 195, 212
Battle of Manassas (First), 21, 191
Battle of Manassas (Second), 197
Battle of Manassas Gap, 202
Battle of Manassas Station, 196
Battle of Mansfield, 100
Battle of Mansura, 101
Battle of Marais des Cygnes, 84
Battle of Marietta, 66
Battle of Marion, 216
Battle of Marks' Mills, 47
Battle of Marmiton River, 141
Battle of Marye's Heights, 201
Battle of McDowell, 193
Battle of Meadow Bridge, 209
Battle of Meadow Bridges, 209
Battle of Mechanicsville, 24, 195
Battle of Memphis (First), 168
Battle of Memphis (Second), 183
Battle of Meridian, 122
Battle of Metamora, 170
Battle of Middle Boggy Depot, 80
Battle of Middle Creek, 86
Battle of Middleburg, 202
Battle of Mill Springs, 86
Battle of Milliken's Bend, 97
Battle of Mine Creek, 84
Battle of Mine Run, 206
Battle of Missionary Ridge, 179
Battle of Mobile Bay, 36
Battle of Monett's Ferry, 100
Battle of Monocacy, 109
Battle of Monroe's Cross-Roads, 155
Battle of Moorefield, 228
Battle of Morrisville, 156
Battle of Morton's Ford, 207
Battle of Mossy Creek, 181
Battle of Mount Zion Church, 129
Battle of Munfordville, 87
Battle of Murfreesboro, 25
Battle of Murfreesboro (First), 25, 168
Battle of Murfreesboro (Second), 25, 145, 172
Battle of Murfreesboro (Third), 185
Battle of Namozine Church, 218
Battle of Nashville, 185
Battle of Natural Bridge, 61
Battle of Nelson's Farm, 195
Battle of New Bern, 29, 151
Battle of New Hope Church, 66
Battle of New Madrid, 130
Battle of New Market, 209
Battle of New Market Cross-Roads, 195
Battle of New Market Heights, 214
Battle of New Market Road, 195, 212, 213
Battle of Newtonia (First), 133
Battle of Newtonia (Second), 141
Battle of North Anna, 209
Battle of Oak Grove, 195
Battle of Oak Hills, 127
Battle of Ocean Pond, 60
Battle of Okolona, 122
Battle of Old Church, 210
Battle of Old Fort Wayne, 79
Battle of Old Oaks, 101
Battle of Old River Lake, 47

Battle of Old Town Creek, 124
Battle of Olustee, 60
Battle of Opequon, 214
Battle of Opequon Creek, 214
Battle of Ox Hill, 197
Battle of Paducah, 91
Battle of Palmetto Ranch, 188
Battle of Parker's Cross-Roads, 172
Battle of Parker's Ford, 212
Battle of Pea Ridge, 41
Battle of Peachtree Creek, 66
Battle of Peeble's Farm, 214
Battle of Perryville, 88
Battle of Petersburg (First), 210
Battle of Petersburg (Second), 211
Battle of Petersburg (Third), 217
Battle of Philippi, 221
Battle of Pickett's Mill, 66
Battle of Piedmont, 210
Battle of Pine Bluff, 44
Battle of Pittsburg Landing, 167
Battle of Plains Store, 97
Battle of Plains Store Road, 97
Battle of Pleasant Hill, 100
Battle of Pleasant Hill Landing, 100
Battle of Plymouth, 154
Battle of Poindexter's Farm, 195
Battle of Poison Spring, 47
Battle of Poplar Grove Church, 214
Battle of Poplar Spring Church, 214
Battle of Poplar Springs Church, 214
Battle of Port Gibson, 118
Battle of Port Hudson, 97
Battle of Port Republic, 194
Battle of Port Royal, 161
Battle of Port Walthall Junction, 208
Battle of Portland Harbor, 105
Battle of Prairie D'Ane, 46
Battle of Prairie Grove, 43
Battle of Princeton Court House, 223
Battle of Proctor's Creek, 209
Battle of Pulaski, 184
Battle of Rappahannock Station (First), 196

Battle of Rappahannock Station (Second), 205
Battle of Raymond, 118
Battle of Reams Station (First), 211
Battle of Reams Station (Second), 213
Battle of Resaca, 65
Battle of Rice's Station, 218
Battle of Rich Mountain, 221
Battle of Richmond, 86
Battle of Riddle's Shop, 195
Battle of Ringgold Gap, 64
Battle of Ripley, 123
Battle of Rivers' Bridge, 164
Battle of Roanoke Island, 151
Battle of Roanoke Station, 211
Battle of Roan's Tan-Yard, 129
Battle of Rocky Face Ridge, 65
Battle of Round Mountain, 79
Battle of Rowanty Creek, 216
Battle of Rowlett's Station, 85
Battle of Rutherford's Farm, 212
Battle of Sabine Cross-Roads, 100
Battle of Sabine Pass (First), 187
Battle of Sabine Pass (Second), 188
Battle of Sacramento, 85
Battle of Sailor's Creek, 218
Battle of Saint Charles, 42
Battle of Saint John's Bluff, 59
Battle of Saint Mary's Church, 211
Battle of Salem Church, 201
Battle of Salem Heights, 201
Battle of Saltville (First), 215
Battle of Saltville (Second), 216
Battle of Sand Mountain, 34
Battle of Santa Rosa Island, 59
Battle of Sappony Church, 211
Battle of Savage's Station, 195, 300
Battle of Sayler's Creek, 218
Battle of Secessionville, 162
Battle of Selma, 38
Battle of Seven Pines, 194
Battle of Sewell's Point, 191
Battle of Sharpsburg, 73, 108
Battle of Shepherdstown, 224
Battle of Shiloh, 167
Battle of Shipping Point, 192
Battle of Simmon's Bluff, 162
Battle of Slaughter's Mountain,

196
Battle of Smithfield Crossing, 229
Battle of Smith's Plantation, 101
Battle of Snicker's Ferry, 212
Battle of Snyder's Bluff, 118
Battle of South Mills, 151
Battle of South Mountain, 108
Battle of Southwest Creek, 155
Battle of Spanish Fort, 23, 38
Battle of Spotsylvania Court House, 23, 208
Battle of Spring Hill, 23, 185
Battle of Springfield (First), 128
Battle of Springfield (Second), 134
Battle of Springfield Road, 97
Battle of Staunton River Bridge, 211
Battle of Stephenson's Depot, 212
Battle of Stirling's Plantation, 98
Battle of Stone's River, 25, 172
Battle of Stony Creek, 211
Battle of Stony Creek Depot, 211
Battle of Strawberry Plains, 212
Battle of Suffolk, 200
Battle of Sugar Loaf Hill, 155
Battle of Sulphur Branch Trestle, 36
Battle of Summit Point, 229
Battle of Sutherland's Station, 217
Battle of Swift Creek, 209
Battle of Tahkahokuty Mountain, 57
Battle of Tallahatchie, 123
Battle of Tampa, 59
Battle of Taylor's Hole Creek, 155
Battle of the Crater, 212
Battle of the Hemp Bales, 128
Battle of the Opequon, 214
Battle of the Wilderness, 208
Battle of Thompson's Station, 173
Battle of Thoroughfare Gap, 197
Battle of Todd's Tavern, 208
Battle of Tom's Brook, 215
Battle of Totopotomoy Creek, 210
Battle of Town Creek, 155
Battle of Tranter's Creek, 152
Battle of Trent's Reach, 216
Battle of Trevilian Station, 210
Battle of Triune, 175
Battle of Tupelo, 124
Battle of Turner's Pass, 108
Battle of Tuscaloosa, 38
Battle of Upperville, 202
Battle of Utoy Creek, 67
Battle of Valverde, 149
Battle of Vaughan Road, 214
Battle of Vaughn Road, 214, 216
Battle of Vaught's Hill, 174
Battle of Vermillion Bayou, 100
Battle of Vicksburg, 119
Battle of Walkerton, 208
Battle of Wapping Heights, 202
Battle of Ware Bottom Church, 209
Battle of Washington, 153
Battle of Wauhatchie, 179
Battle of Waynesboro (GA), 69
Battle of Waynesboro (VA), 216
Battle of Welch's Spring, 229
Battle of Weldon Railroad (First), 211
Battle of Weldon Railroad (Second), 213
Battle of West Point (GA), 69
Battle of West Point (MS), 122
Battle of Westport, 141
Battle of White Hall, 152
Battle of White Oak Ridge, 217
Battle of White Oak Road, 217
Battle of White Oak Swamp, 195
Battle of White's Tavern, 213
Battle of Wild Cat, 85, 189
Battle of Williamsburg, 193
Battle of Williamsport, 109
Battle of Willis Church, 195
Battle of Wilmington, 155
Battle of Wilson's Creek, 127
Battle of Wilson's Wharf, 209
Battle of Winchester (First), 194
Battle of Winchester (Second), 202
Battle of Winchester (Third), 214
Battle of Woodsonville, 87
Battle of Wyse Fork, 155
Battle of Yellow Bayou, 101
Battle of Yellow Tavern, 209
Battle of Yorktown, 193
battle statistics, 22
Battles for Chattanooga, 179
Baxter Springs, KS, 83
Bay Saint Louis, MS, 121
Bay Springs, MS, 121

Bayou Alabama, LA, 102
Bayou Boeuf Crossing, LA, 98
Bayou Boeuf, LA, 101
Bayou Bonfouca, LA, 103
Bayou Bourbeau, LA, 99
Bayou Courtableau, LA, 97
Bayou De Glaize, LA, 101
Bayou De Large, LA, 103
Bayou De Paul, LA, 100
Bayou des Arc, AR, 48
Bayou Fordoche Road, LA, 101
Bayou Fourche, AR, 98
Bayou Goula, LA, 103
Bayou Grand Caillou, LA, 102
Bayou Grossetete, LA, 100, 101
Bayou La Fourche, LA, 98
Bayou Lamourie, LA, 101
Bayou Liddell, LA, 102
Bayou Macon, LA, 98
Bayou Maringouin, LA, 102
Bayou Meto, AR, 44
Bayou Pierre, LA, 100
Bayou Pierre, MS, 118
Bayou Portage, LA, 99
Bayou Rapides Bridge, LA, 100
Bayou Rapides, LA, 99
Bayou Robert, LA, 101
Bayou Saline, LA, 100
Bayou Sara, 102
Bayou Sara, LA, 95, 99, 102
Bayou Teche, LA, 103
Bayou Tensas, LA, 97, 98, 101, 102
Bayou Tunica, LA, 99
Bayou Vidal, LA, 96
Beach Fork, KY, 87
Bealer's Ferry, AR, 47
Bealeton Station, VA, 193, 200, 216
Bealeton, VA, 205
Beall, William N. R., 74
Bean's Station, TN, 180, 183, 184
Bear Creek Station, GA, 68
Bear Creek, MS, 119, 120
Bear Creek, TN, 173
Bear Quarter Road, VA, 207
Bear Wallow, KY, 87, 89
Beardstown, TN, 184
Beattie's Prairie, Indian Territory, 79
Beatty's Mill, AR, 49

Beauregard, Pierre G. T., 8
Beaver Creek, MD, 109
Beaver Creek, NC, 154
Beaver Dam Church, VA, 198
Beaver Dam Creek, VA, 195
Beaver Dam Station, VA, 207, 217
Beaver Pond Creek, VA, 218
Beaver Pond, VA, 218
Bee Creek, MO, 137
Beech Creek, SC, 165
Beech Creek, WV, 224
Beech Fork, WV, 227
Beech Grove, TN, 176
Beefsteak Raid, 214
Beersheba, TN, 178
Belfield, VA, 216
Belington, WV, 221
Bell Mines, KY, 92
Belle Prairie, LA, 101
Belle Saint Louis (steamer), 184
Beller's Mill, WV, 222
Bell's Mills, TN, 185
Belmont, MO, 128
Belmont, MS, 119
Belmont, TN, 174
Benevola, MD, 109
Benjamin, Judah P., 77
Bennett's Bayou, AR, 45
Bennett's Bayou, MO, 135
Bennett's House, NC, 156
Benson's Bridge, KY, 92
Bent Creek, TN, 182
Benton County, AR, 49
Benton Road, AR, 46, 48, 50
Benton, AL, 38
Benton, AR, 44, 48
Benton, MS, 120, 123
Bentonville, AR, 41, 43, 50
Bentonville, NC, 155
Benton's Cross-Roads, NC, 155
Benton's Ferry, LA, 101
Berlin, MD, 107
Berlin, OH, 157
Bermuda Hundred Front, VA, 211
Bernard Bayou, Indian Territory, 79
Berry County, TN, 183
Berryville and Winchester Pike, VA, 213
Berryville, VA, 194, 198, 202, 205, 212-214, 227

Berry's Ferry, VA, 202
Berry's Ford Gap, VA, 197
Berry's Ford, VA, 212
Bertrand, MO, 129
Berwick Bay (C.S.S. steamer), 117
Berwick Bay, LA, 96, 98
Berwick, LA, 97, 100
Bethel, TN, 168
Bethesda Church, VA, 210
Bethpage Bridge, TN, 176
Bethsaida Church, VA, 204
Beulah, NC, 156
Beverly Ford, VA, 196, 202, 203
Beverly, WV, 225, 229, 230
Bible, 3, 239, 299
Big Bend, WV, 224
Big Bethel, VA, 191
Big Birch, WV, 224
Big Black Bridge, MS, 124
Big Black Creek, SC, 165
Big Black River Bridge, MS, 119, 120
Big Black River, MS, 118-120
Big Blue River, MO, 140
Big Bushes, KS, 84
Big Cacapon Bridge, WV, 228
Big Cove Valley, AL, 36
Big Creek Bluffs, MO, 131
Big Creek Gap, TN, 168
Big Creek, AR, 48
Big Creek, MO, 130, 133, 135, 138
Big Creek, TN, 185
big government, 14, 16
Big Gravois, MO, 142
Big Hatchie, TN, 170
Big Hill, KY, 86, 88
Big Hill, TN, 170
Big Hurricane Creek, MO, 128
Big Indian Creek, AR, 41
Big Laramie, Dakota Territory, 58
Big Mound, MO, 55
Big North Fork, MO, 138
Big Pigeon River, KY, 93
Big Piney, MO, 141
Big River, MO, 140
Big Rock Castle Creek, KY, 88
Big Sandy Creek, MS, 118
Big Sewell, WV, 227
Big Shanty, GA, 66, 67
Big Spring Branch, TN, 176

Big Springs, TN, 181
Big Swift Creek, NC, 153
Big Warrior River, AL, 34
Biloxi, MS, 115
Binnaker's Bridge, SC, 165
biography, 2, 238, 299
Birch Cooley, MN, 113
Birch Island Bridges, VA, 208
Birdsong Ferry, MS, 119
Bird's Point, MO, 128
Birmingham, MS, 118
Black Bayou, LA, 99
black Confederate, 62
black Confederates, 62
Black Creek, 60, 165, 211
Black Creek, AL, 34
Black Creek, FL, 60
Black Creek, NC, 155
Black Creek, VA, 211
Black Dog, 158
black enlistment, 62
Black Fork Hills, MO, 135
Black Jack Church, NC, 154
Black River, LA, 97
Black River, MO, 133
Black River, NC, 155
Black Run, MO, 131
Blackburn's Ford, VA, 191, 205
Blackburn's Ford, WV, 221
Blackland, MS, 115, 118
blacks, 62
Blacksburg, VA, 209
blacksmith, 171
Blackville, SC, 164
Blackwater Bridge, VA, 198
Blackwater Creek, MO, 129, 130
Blackwater River, KY, 93
Blackwater River, MO, 138, 142
Blackwater River, VA, 197, 198, 208
Blackwater, MO, 131
Blackwater, VA, 215
Blackwell's Station, MO, 128
Black's Mill, AR, 45
Blain's Cross-Roads, TN, 180
Blair's Landing, LA, 100
Blakely, AL, 38
Blakeny's, SC, 165
Blake's Farm, VA, 203
Blake's Farm, WV, 222
Blick's Station, VA, 213

blockade, 25, 187
blockhouses, 185
Bloomery Gap, WV, 223, 228
Bloomfield, KY, 88, 93
Bloomfield, MO, 130, 132-138, 142
Bloomington, TN, 173
Blount County, TN, 183
Blountsville, AL, 34
Blountsville, TN, 172, 177, 178
Blount's Creek, NC, 153, 154
Blount's Plantation, AL, 34
Blue Bird Gap, GA, 64
Blue Creek, WV, 222
Blue Earth River, MN, 113
Blue Hills, MO, 127
Blue Mills Landing, MO, 128
Blue Mountains, AR, 42
Blue Pond, AL, 36
Blue Ridge Mountains, NC, 156
Blue River, MO, 137
Blue Springs, MO, 134
Blue Springs, TN, 178, 183
Blue Stone, WV, 223, 224
Blue Sulphur Road, WV, 227
Blue's Gap, WV, 224
Bluff Springs, FL, 61
Blythe's Ferry, TN, 179
Bobo's Cross-Roads, TN, 176
Bob's Creek, MO, 130
Boca Chica Pass, TX, 188
Boeuf Bayou, LA, 96
Boggs' Mills, AR, 50
Boggy Depot, Indian Territory, 80
Bogue Chitto Creek, MS, 121
Bogue Sound Blockhouse, NC, 154
Boiling Fork, TN, 176
Boiling Springs, TN, 183
Boles' Farm, MO, 131
Bolivar Heights, WV, 222, 224
Bolivar, AL, 33
Bolivar, MO, 129
Bolivar, MS, 116, 123
Bolivar, TN, 169, 171, 176, 182, 183
Bolling, Edith, 299
Bollinger County, MO, 137
Bollinger's Mill, MO, 132
Bolton Depot, MS, 122
Bolton Station, MS, 118, 120

Bonfouca Bayou, LA, 96
Bonito Rio, NM, 150
Bonnet Carré, LA, 96
Boone County, MO, 139
Boone Court House, WV, 222
Boone, NC, 156
Boone, Pat, 299
Booneville, KY, 92
Booneville, MS, 115
Boonsboro Gap, MD, 108
Boonsboro, AR, 43
Boonsboro, MD, 109
Boonville, MO, 127, 128, 136, 140, 142
Boonville, NC, 156
Boston Mountains, AR, 43, 44
Boston, KY, 89
Boteler's Ford, VA, 197
Bottom's Bridge, VA, 195, 207, 211
Boutte Station, LA, 96
Bowers' Mill, MO, 136
Bowling Green Road, KY, 87
Bowling Green Road, VA, 193
Box Ford, MS, 116
Boyce's Bridge, LA, 97
Boyce's Plantation, LA, 101
Boydton Plank Road, VA, 215
Boydton Road, VA, 217
Boyd's Landing, SC, 164
Boyd's Station, AL, 37
Boykins' Mill, SC, 165
Brackett's, VA, 195
Braddock's Farm, FL, 61
Bradfordsville, KY, 93
Bradyville Pike, TN, 173, 175
Bradyville, TN, 173, 176
Bragg, Braxton, 8
Bragg's Farm, MO, 133
Branchville, AR, 45, 46
Brandenburg, KY, 87, 90
Brander's Bridge, VA, 208
Brandon Bridge, VA, 208
Brandon, MS, 120, 122
Brandy Station, VA, 196, 200, 202-205
Brashear City, LA, 98
Brawley Forks, TN, 186
Braxton County, WV, 223
Brazos Santiago, TX, 188
Breaker (schooner), 187

Breckinridge, MO, 137
Brentsville, VA, 199, 204, 206, 207
Brentwood, TN, 170, 171, 174
Brewer's Lane, AR, 49
Brice's Cross-Roads, MS, 123
Bridgeport, AL, 33, 34
Bridgeport, MS, 119
Bridgeport, WV, 225
bridges, 64, 70, 164, 208, 209
Bridgewater, VA, 215
Brier Fork, MO, 127
Brimstone Creek, KY, 91
Bristoe Station and Milford, VA, 208
Bristoe Station, VA, 196, 197, 203, 204, 207, 208
Bristol, TN, 177, 178, 185
Britain, 15
British Empire, 15
Britton's Lane, TN, 169
Broad Run, VA, 200
Brock's Gap, VA, 215
Brodie, Alexander O., 52
Brook Church, VA, 209
Brook Turnpike, VA, 207
Brookhaven, MS, 118, 120, 124
Brooklyn, KS, 83
Brooks' Mill, AR, 46
Brookville, KY, 87
Brown Hill, KY, 88
Brown, Henry A., 52
Brownsburg, VA, 210
Brownsville, AR, 44, 48, 49
Brownsville, KY, 85
Brownsville, MD, 109
Brownsville, MS, 120, 121, 123, 124
Brown's Ferry, TN, 178
Brown's Gap, VA, 214
Brown's Plantation, LA, 103
Brown's Plantation, MS, 116
Brown's Spring, MO, 132
Broxton's Bridge, SC, 164
Brucetown, VA, 213
Brunswick, GA, 63
Brunswick, MO, 128, 139, 140
Bryan Court House, GA, 69
Bryant's Plantation, FL, 61
Buchanan, Franklin, 104
Buchanan, Patrick J., 299

Buchanan, VA, 211
Buck Creek, GA, 69
Buck Head Church, GA, 68
Buck Head Creek, GA, 68, 69
Buck Head Station, GA, 68
Buck Head, GA, 66
Buck Horn, AR, 47
Buckhannon, WV, 224, 229
Buckhorn Tavern, AL, 35
Buckingham, SC, 161
Buckland Bridge, VA, 197
Buckland Mills, VA, 205
Buckland Races, VA, 205
Buckskull, AR, 49
Buckton Station, VA, 194
Buckton, VA, 212
Budd's Ferry, MD, 107
Buell's Ford, TN, 177
Buffalo City, AR, 45
Buffalo Creek, MO, 139
Buffalo Mountains, AR, 44
Buffalo River, AR, 44
Buffalo, WV, 224
Buffington Island, OH, 157
Buford's Bridge, SC, 164
Buford's Gap, VA, 211
Bugbee Bridge, SC, 163
Bull Bayou, AR, 48
Bull Creek, MO, 142
Bull Island, SC, 162
Bull Pasture Mountain, VA, 193
Bull Run Bridge, VA, 197
Bull Run, VA, 197, 204, 205
Bullitt's Bayou, LA, 102
Bulltown, WV, 227, 229
Bull's Gap, TN, 184
Bunker Hill, VA, 192
Bunker Hill, WV, 224, 226, 228, 229
Burden's Causeway, SC, 164
Burgess Mill, VA, 215
Burke Station, VA, 192
Burkesville Road, KY, 89
Burkesville, KY, 88
Burke's Station, VA, 203, 218
Burkittsville, MD, 108
Burlington, WV, 222, 225-227
Burnsville, AL, 34
Burnsville, MS, 116, 117, 119
Burnt Bridge, TN, 170
Burnt Chimneys, VA, 193

Burnt Cross-Roads, KY, 87
Burnt Hickory, GA, 65
Burnt Ordinary, VA, 199
Burrowsville, AR, 45
Burton's Ford, VA, 207
Burwell, Robert P. P., 190
Bushy Creek, KY, 92
Bushy Knob, TN, 179
Bushy Swamp, NC, 155
Butler, MO, 129, 131
Buzzard Roost Gap, GA, 68
Buzzard Roost, GA, 65, 70
Byhalia Road, TN, 183
Byhalia, MS, 121, 122
Byram's Ford, MO, 141
C.S. navy, 56, 78, 104
C.S.A., 15, 21, 40, 158
Cabell, William L., 230
Cabin Creek, Indian Territory, 80
Cabin Point, VA, 212
Cacapon Mountain, WV, 226
Cache Bayou, AR, 42
Cache River Bridge, AR, 41
Cache River, AR, 42, 47
Cackleytown, WV, 227
Caddo Gap, AR, 44, 45
Caddo Mill, AR, 44
Cahawba River, AL, 38
Cainsville, TN, 173
cairns, 29
Cairo Station, WV, 226
Cajoude Arivaypo, NM, 150
Caledonia Iron Works, PA, 160
Caledonia, LA, 97
Caledonia, MO, 139
Calfkiller Creek, TN, 176, 182
Calhoun County, WV, 227
Calhoun, GA, 65
Calhoun, KY, 89
Calhoun, TN, 177, 181
Calico Rock, AR, 41
California House, MO, 133, 134, 137
California, MO, 140
Callaway County, MO, 133
Camargo Cross-Roads, MS, 123
Camden County, NC, 151
Camden Court House, NC, 153
Camden Point Mill, MO, 138
Camden Point, MO, 138
Camden, AR, 46, 47

Camden, SC, 165
Cameron's Depot, WV, 229
Camp Allegheny, WV, 223
Camp Cooper, FL, 60
Camp Creek, GA, 67
Camp Creek, WV, 223
Camp Davies, MS, 121
Camp Dennison, Cincinnati, OH, 113
Camp Dennison, OH, 157
Camp Finegan, FL, 60
Camp Goggin, KY, 85
Camp Gonzales, FL, 60
Camp Jackson, TN, 167
Camp Joe Underwood, KY, 85
Camp McDonald, WV, 223
Camp Pratt, LA, 99
Camp Russell, VA, 216
Camp Vance, NC, 154
Camp Wildcat, KY, 85
Campbell, Joseph, 299
Campbellsville, TN, 185
Campbellton, GA, 66, 67
Campbell's Station, TN, 179
camps, 196
Campti, LA, 100
Canada Alamosa, NM, 149
Cane Creek, AL, 35
Cane Hill, AR, 43, 49
Cane River Crossing, LA, 100
Cane River, LA, 100
Caney Bayou, TX, 188
Cannelton, WV, 224
Cannon's Bridge, SC, 164
Canoe Creek, FL, 61
Canton Road, MS, 121
Canton, KY, 92
Canton, MS, 120, 122, 123
Cape Girardeau, MO, 134, 137, 141
Caperton's Ferry, AL, 34, 35
capitalism, 18
Carlisle, PA, 159
Carmel Church, VA, 196
Carnifex Ferry, WV, 222
Carnton, 3, 237, 238
Carnton Plantation, 3, 237, 238
Carrick's Ford, WV, 221
Carrion Crow Bayou, LA, 99
Carroll County, MO, 142
Carroll Station, TN, 171

Carrollton, AR, 45, 48
Carrollton, MO, 132, 140
Carroll's Mill, LA, 100
Carrsville, VA, 197, 198, 201
Carson, Martha, 299
Carter County, KY, 91
Carter Creek Pike, TN, 174
Cartersville, GA, 65-67
Carter's Depot, TN, 172, 177
Carter's Farm, VA, 212
Carter's Run, VA, 203
Carter's Station, TN, 184
Carthage Road, TN, 171
Carthage, MO, 83, 127, 135, 136, 138, 139
Carthage, TN, 173
Caruthersville, MO, 141
Cash, Johnny, 299
Cass County, MO, 134
Cass Station, GA, 66
Cassville, GA, 65, 66
Cassville, MO, 131, 133, 135
Cassville, WV, 222
Castleman's Ferry, VA, 198, 212
Caston's Plantation, SC, 162
Castor River, MO, 135
Catawba Mountains, VA, 211
Catawba River, NC, 156
Catlett's Gap, GA, 64
Catlett's Station, VA, 196, 197, 204-206, 208
Cato, KS, 83
Catoctin Creek, MD, 108
Catoctin Mountain, MD, 108, 109
Catoosa Platform, GA, 65
Catoosa Springs, GA, 65
cattle, 214
cavalry, 2, 8, 106, 232, 239
Cave City, KY, 86, 87
Cedar Bayou, TX, 188
Cedar Bluff, AL, 34
Cedar Bluffs, CO, 51
Cedar Church, KY, 87
Cedar County, MO, 136
Cedar Creek, FL, 60
Cedar Creek, VA, 213, 215
Cedar Glade, AR, 45
Cedar Keys, FL, 61
Cedar Mountain, VA, 196
Cedar Point, NC, 154
Cedar Run Church, VA, 215

Cedar Run, VA, 196
Cedarville, VA, 202, 213, 214
Celeste (steamer), 49
Celina, KY, 89
Celina, TN, 186
Center Creek, MO, 142
Center Star, AL, 35
Centerville, AL, 38
Centerville, WV, 229
central government, 14
Centralia, MO, 139, 140
centralists, 13
centralization, 18
Centre Creek, MO, 135
Centre, AL, 34
Centreville, LA, 96, 97
Centreville, MO, 136, 141
Centreville, TN, 179, 184
Centreville, VA, 197, 204, 205, 211
Chacahoula Station, LA, 98
Chacahoula, LA, 103
Chaffin's Farm, VA, 214
Chalk Bluff, AR, 41, 43
Chambersburg, PA, 159, 160
Chambers' Creek, TN, 172
Champion Hill, MS, 119
Champion's Hill, MS, 122
Chancellorsville, VA, 201, 208
Chantilly, VA, 197, 199, 205
Chapel Hill, MO, 138
Chapel Hill, NC, 156
Chapel Hill, TN, 173, 175
Chaplin Hills, KY, 88
Chaplintown, KY, 93
Chapmanville, WV, 223
Chariton Bridge, MO, 132
Chariton County, MO, 132, 135, 137, 142
Chariton River, MO, 132
Chariton Road, MO, 138
Charles City Cross-Roads, VA, 195
Charles City Road, VA, 194, 213
Charleston & Savannah Railroad, SC, 164
Charleston Harbor, SC, 162, 163
Charleston, MO, 128, 129, 137, 141
Charleston, SC, 162, 163
Charleston, TN, 177, 179-181,

183
Charleston, WV, 224
Charlestown, AR, 46
Charlestown, WV, 223, 225-230
Charlotte, MO, 141
Charlottesville, VA, 207
Chattahoochee River, GA, 66
Chattanooga Campaign, 179
Chattanooga River, GA, 64
Chattanooga, TN, 168, 176-179
Chavis Creek, KS, 84
Cheat Mountain Pass, WV, 227
Cheat Mountain, WV, 222
Cheat River, WV, 223, 227
Cheat Summit Fort, WV, 222
Cheek's Cross-Roads, TN, 180, 182
Chehaw, AL, 36
Cheraw, SC, 165
Cherokee Bay, AR, 47
Cherokee County, NC, 153
Cherokee Station, AL, 34, 35
Cherokee Station, TN, 171
Cherry Creek, MS, 123
Cherry Grove Landing, VA, 208
Cherry Grove, MO, 131
Cherry Run, WV, 223
Cheshire, OH, 157
Chesser's Store, KY, 88
Chester Gap, VA, 198, 202
Chester Station, VA, 208, 209
Chesterfield (steamer), 163
Chesterfield, SC, 165
Chestnut Hill, VA, 205
Chewalla, TN, 170
Chicamacomico, NC, 151
Chickahominy River, VA, 195, 203
Chickamauga Creek, GA, 64, 65
Chickamauga Station, TN, 180
Chickamauga, GA, 64
Chickasaw, 117
Chickasaw Bayou, MS, 117
Chickasaw Bluffs, MS, 117
Chickasaw Bridge, MS, 124
children, 2
Chimneys, VA, 214
Chisolm's Island, SC, 161
Choctaw Bayou, LA, 97
Christ, 3
Christian, 3, 18, 115, 142, 160, 235, 239
Christian County, MO, 142
Christiana, TN, 173, 176, 178
Christianity, 3
Christiansburg, KY, 90
Christmas, 3
Chuckatuck, VA, 200, 201
Chucky Road, TN, 181
Chula Depot, VA, 209
Chulahoma, MS, 117
Chunky Creek, MS, 122
church, 36, 47, 64-69, 86, 87, 108, 118, 124, 129, 138, 154, 177, 191, 192, 194-201, 203-206, 208-216, 218
Chustenahlah, Indian Territory, 79
Chusto-Talasah, Indian Territory, 79
Cincinnati (U.S.S. ironclad), 119
Cincinnati, AR, 49
Cincinnati, OH, 113
Circleville, VA, 207
citizens, 15
Citronelle, AL, 38
City of Alton (steamboat), 129
City Point, VA, 194, 209, 212
Civil War, 2, 3, 13-18, 22, 236-239, 299, 301
Clapper's Saw-Mill, AR, 43
Clara Bell (steamer), 48
Clara Eames (U.S.S. steamer), 47
Clarendon, AR, 42, 45, 46, 49
Clarke, James, 148
Clarksburg, TN, 172
Clarkston, MO, 134
Clarksville, AR, 46, 47, 49, 50
Clarksville, TN, 171, 178
Clark's Bayou, LA, 97
Clark's Creek Church, TN, 177
Clark's Hollow, WV, 223
Clark's Mill, MO, 132, 134
Clark's Mountain, VA, 196
Clark's Neck, KY, 91
clay, 65, 135, 236
Clay County, MO, 135, 138
Clay County, WV, 223
Clay Village, KY, 87
Claysville, AL, 35
Clear Creek, AR, 45, 50
Clear Creek, GA, 66
Clear Creek, MO, 132, 135

Clear Creek, MS, 116
Clear Fork, MO, 135, 138
Clear Lake, AR, 50
Clear Spring, MD, 109
Cleveland, TN, 177, 178, 180-182
Clifton, TN, 172, 183
Clinch Mountain, TN, 178, 180, 184
Clinch River, TN, 180, 184
Clinch Valley, TN, 184
Clinton, GA, 66, 68
Clinton, KY, 92
Clinton, LA, 100, 102
Clinton, MO, 130, 141
Clinton, MS, 120, 122, 123
Clinton's Ferry, TN, 168
Cloud's House, SC, 165
Cloutierville, LA, 100
Clover Hill, VA, 218
Cloyd's Farm, VA, 208
Cloyd's Mountain, VA, 208
Coahoma County, MS, 116
Coal Hill, OH, 157
Coal Run, KY, 90
Coalsmouth, WV, 229
Cockletown, VA, 193
Cockpit Point, VA, 192
Cockrall's Mill, WV, 225
Cockrum's Cross-Roads, MS, 116
Coffee Hill, VA, 205
Coffeeville, MS, 117
Coggins' Point, VA, 214
Cold Harbor, VA, 210
Cold Spring Gap, WV, 226
Coldwater Bridge, MS, 119
Coldwater Ferry, MS, 122
Coldwater Railroad Bridge, MS, 116
Coldwater River, MS, 117, 118, 120, 121, 124
Coldwater Station, MS, 116
Coldwater, MS, 117, 121
Cole Camp, MO, 127, 133, 136
Cole County, MO, 140
Colesburg, KY, 93
Cole's Island, SC, 162
College Grove, TN, 174, 175
Collierville, TN, 173, 175, 178, 179, 181, 183, 184
Colorado, 9, 27, 51, 53, 54, 84, 150

Colorado Territory, 9, 53, 54
Columbia, 185, 240
Columbia Bridge, VA, 193
Columbia Ford, TN, 185
Columbia Furnace, VA, 193, 215
Columbia Pike, TN, 174
Columbia, KY, 90
Columbia, LA, 99
Columbia, MO, 133, 134, 138, 139, 142
Columbia, SC, 165
Columbia, TN, 168, 170, 178, 184, 185
Columbus Road, AL, 38
Columbus, GA, 69
Columbus, KY, 85, 91, 92
Columbus, MO, 129, 132, 138, 142
Colwell's Ford, TN, 179
Combahee Ferry, SC, 164
Combahee River, SC, 164
combat, 22, 23, 25, 65-68, 213
Combs, Bertram T., 299
Comite River, LA, 97, 102
Commerce, MO, 129
Commerce, MS, 119
Commercial (steamer), 49
communism, 14, 236
communist, 13, 17, 18, 236, 297
communists, 15, 235
Como Landing, LA, 101
Como, TN, 177
Compton's Ferry, MO, 132
Conchas Springs, NM, 150
Concho River, TX, 188
Concord Church, MS, 124
Concordia Bayou, LA, 101
Concordia, LA, 101
Confederacy, 2, 3, 8, 29, 81, 239, 240
Confederate, 2, 3, 8, 13, 14, 16-19, 22-24, 26, 28-30, 38, 40, 47, 52, 56, 58, 59, 62, 70-72, 74-78, 81, 82, 94, 97, 104-106, 112, 114, 125, 126, 144, 146, 148, 151, 153, 156, 158, 163, 166, 186, 188-191, 212, 214, 218-220, 230-232, 234-240, 295, 298-301
Confederate ancestors, 23

Confederate army, 62, 156, 235
Confederate Army Intelligence Office, 106
Confederate battery, 188, 191
Confederate flag, 2, 18, 239, 240, 301
Confederate forces, 38, 153
Confederate generals, 16, 300
Confederate government, 3, 17, 218, 240
Confederate military, 22, 62, 236
Confederate Military History (Evans), 22
Confederate ordnance officers, 105
Confederate outposts, 97
Confederate perspective, 22
Confederate rifle-pits, 163
Confederate Secret Service, 106
Confederate Soldier Monument, 82
Confederate States, 2, 3, 8, 14, 236-238, 240, 295, 298
Confederate States Infantry Regiment, 295, 298
Confederate States of America, 2, 3, 8, 14, 236, 238, 240
Confederate steamers, 97
Confederate Stockade Cemetery, 82
Confederate veteran reunions, 62
Confederate veterans, 16, 17, 19, 22, 23, 26, 29, 62, 114, 235, 237, 299
Confederate viewpoint, 22
Confederate works, 23, 188, 214
Confederates, 16, 25, 62, 155, 171, 172, 195, 214
confederation, 2, 238, 240
Congaree Creek, SC, 165
Congaree River, SC, 165
Congress, 6
Conrad, Thomas N., 106
Conrad's Ferry, MD, 107
conservatism, 14
Conservatives, 13, 14
consolidation, 14
Constitution, 2, 16, 18, 19, 21, 28, 236-238, 240
Constitution of the Confederate States, 2, 238, 240

constitutional law, 236
constitutional rights, 29
conventions, 6, 29
cooks, 62
Cook's Canyon, NM, 150
Cool Spring, VA, 212
Coombs' Ferry, KY, 89
Coon Creek, MO, 133
Coosa River, AL, 36
Coosaville Road, GA, 68
Coosawattee River, GA, 69
Corbin's Bridge, VA, 208
Corbin's Cross-Roads, VA, 198, 203
Core Creek, NC, 152, 153
Corinth Road, MS, 115
Corinth, MS, 115, 116, 119-121, 125
Cornersville Pike, TN, 182
Corn's Farm, TN, 186
Corpus Christi, TX, 187, 188
Corydon, IN, 77
Cosby Creek, TN, 181
Cotile Bayou, LA, 97
Cotile Landing, LA, 100
cotton, 42
Cotton Creek, FL, 61
Cotton Hill, WV, 222, 224
Cotton Plant, AR, 41, 42, 47
Cotton Port Ford, TN, 177
Cotton River Bridge, GA, 68
Council Grove, KS, 84
Courtland, AL, 35, 36
Courtney's Plantation, MS, 118
Couteau, MN, 113
Cove Creek, AR, 43
Cove Gap, WV, 228
Cove Mountain, VA, 209
Cove Point, MD, 110
Covington (U.S.S. gunboat), 101
Covington, KY, 86
Covington, LA, 95
Covington, TN, 174
Covington, VA, 205, 206, 210
Cow Creek Station, KS, 84
Cow Creek, KS, 84
Cow Ford Creek, FL, 60
Cowan Pass, TN, 176
Cowan, TN, 178
Cowpen Ford, SC, 164
Cowskin Bottom, MO, 137

Cox's Bridge, NC, 155
Cox's Hill, TN, 172
Cox's Plantation, LA, 98
Coyle's Tavern, VA, 203
Crab Gap, TN, 180
Crab Orchard Road, KY, 88
Crab Orchard, KY, 88, 91
Crampton's Pass, MD, 108
Cranberry Summit, MD, 108
Crane Creek, MO, 129
Crater, the, VA, 212
Cravensville, MO, 132
Craven's Plantation, MS, 120
Crawford, AL, 38
Crawford, Cindy, 299
Creek, 34, 35, 37-39, 41-43, 45-51, 53, 54, 57, 58, 60, 61, 63-70, 73, 80, 84-92, 97, 99, 102, 107-110, 115-124, 127-140, 142, 145, 147, 152-156, 163-165, 168-186, 188, 191, 193, 195, 199, 202, 203, 206-218, 221-224, 226-230
Creeks (tribe), 231
Creelsboro, KY, 89, 90
Crew's Farm, VA, 195
Cricket Hill, VA, 208
Cripple Creek, TN, 183
Crittenden, KY, 92
Crooked Creek, 43
Crooked Creek, AL, 34
Crooked Creek, AR, 43, 45
Crooked Creek, MO, 133
Crooked River, FL, 59
Crooked Run, VA, 204, 213
Crook's Run, VA, 200
Cross Bayou, LA, 101
Cross Hollow, AR, 42
Cross Keys, VA, 194
Cross Timbers, MO, 132, 136
Cross-Roads, KY, 88
Crossville, TN, 180
Crowley's Ridge, AR, 43
Crow's House, VA, 217
Crow's Station, MO, 131
Crow's Valley, GA, 65
Cruise, Tom, 299
Crump's Creek, VA, 210
Crump's Cross-Roads, VA, 202
Crump's Hill, LA, 100
Cub Run, VA, 199
Cuba, 146
Cuba, MO, 137, 140
Cubero, NM, 149
Culpeper Court House, VA, 203-206
Culpeper Ford, VA, 207
Culpeper, VA, 214
Cumberland Church, VA, 218
Cumberland Gap, TN, 167-169, 177, 179
Cumberland Iron Works, TN, 169, 173
Cumberland Mountain, TN, 180
Cumberland River, 85, 90, 91, 170
Cumberland River, KY, 85, 90, 91
Cumberland River, TN, 170, 171
Cumberland, MD, 110
Cummings Point, SC, 163
Cumming's Ferry, KY, 90
Cunningham's Bluff, SC, 163
Cunningham's Cross-Roads, PA, 159
Curlew (U.S.S. steamer), 47
Currituck Bridge, VA, 213
Curtis' Creek, TN, 185
Curtis' Wells, AL, 36
Cuyler's Plantation, GA, 69
Cynthiana, KY, 86, 92
Cypress Bend, AR, 43
Cypress Creek, AR, 47, 49
Cypress Creek, LA, 99
Cypress Swamp, GA, 69
Cypress Swamp, TN, 182
Cyrus, Miley, 299
Dabney's Ferry, VA, 210
Dabney's Mill, VA, 216
Dade County, MO, 135
Dakota Territory, 9, 57, 58
Dallas, AR, 45
Dallas, GA, 66, 67
Dallas, MO, 128, 133
Dalton, GA, 64, 65, 67-69
Dan Smith's Ranch, CO, 54
Dandridge, TN, 181, 183
Dandridge's Mill, TN, 180
Dannelly's Mills, AL, 37
Danville Cross-Roads, KY, 88
Danville Road, AL, 36

Danville, AR, 46
Danville, KY, 88, 89, 93
Danville, MO, 140
Danville, MS, 121
Darbytown Road, VA, 215
Darbytown, VA, 212, 215
Dardanelle, AR, 44, 47, 49
Darien, GA, 63
Darkesville, WV, 224, 225, 228, 229
Dauphin Island, AL, 37
Davenport Church, VA, 216
Davenport, VA, 208
Davidson's Ferry, TN, 184
David's Ferry, LA, 101
Davis Bridge, TN, 170
Davis Gap, AL, 33
Davis House, VA, 213
Davis, Jefferson, 13, 14, 16, 54, 77, 114, 160, 218, 300
Davisboro, GA, 68
Davis' Bend, LA, 101
Davis' Bridge, TN, 170
Davis' Cross Roads, GA, 63
Davis' Gap, AL, 35
Davis' House, GA, 64
Davis' Mill Road, TN, 174
Davis' Mill, MS, 117
Davis' Mill, TN, 174
Davis' Mills, MS, 123
Dayton, MO, 129, 135, 137
Day's Gap, 34
Day's Gap, AL, 34
De Kalb County, AL, 37
De View Bayou, AR, 42
Dead Buffalo Lake, ND, 55
Dead Man's Fork, Dakota Territory, 58
death, 3
Debs, Eugene V., 13
debunk, 2
Decatur County, TN, 183
Decatur, AL, 33, 35-37
Decatur, GA, 67
Decherd, TN, 176
Declaration of Independence, 15
Deep Bottom, VA, 212, 213
Deep Creek, VA, 207, 213
Deep Gully, NC, 151, 153
Deep Run, VA, 202, 213
Deep Water, MO, 131

Deepwater Township, MO, 137
deer, 120, 171, 176
Deer Creek, 120
Deer Creek, Dakota Territory, 57
Deer Creek, MO, 136
Deer Creek, MS, 117, 118
Deer Park Road, AL, 37
Deloach's Bluff, LA, 100
Delta (steamer), 122
Democratic Party, 13, 14
demonstration, 23, 25, 36, 44, 47, 65, 80, 85, 92, 96, 97, 118, 152, 153, 162-164, 167, 191, 207, 208, 212, 227
Denkins' Mill, SC, 165
Denmark, TN, 169, 176
Department of Alabama, Mississippi, and East Louisiana (CSA), 38
Des Allemands Bayou, LA, 95, 96
Des Allemands, LA, 98
Desert Station, LA, 96
Deserted House, VA, 199
despotism, 235
Devall's Bluff, AR, 42, 44, 47-50
Devil's Backbone, AR, 44
Devil's Gap, TN, 185
Diamond Grove Prairie, MO, 138
Diamond Grove, MO, 130, 139
Diamond Hill, VA, 211
Diascund Bridge, VA, 202
Dickson Station, AL, 34
Dickson's Station, AL, 35
Dick's Ford, KY, 88
Dillingham's Cross-Roads, SC, 164
Dingle's Mill, SC, 165
Dinwiddie Court House, VA, 214, 217
Dirt Town, GA, 64
disaster, 235
disorder, 24, 236
Dispatch Station, VA, 195
Disputanta Station, VA, 216
Dixie, 3, 40, 75, 78, 144, 158, 240
Dixon's Island, SC, 162
Dixson Springs, TN, 175
Dobbins' Ferry, TN, 171
Doboy River, GA, 63
Donaldsonville, LA, 95, 96, 98,

99
Doniphan, MO, 130, 135, 139
Doolan's Farm, VA, 192
Double Bridge, TN, 171
Double Bridges, GA, 70
Doubtful Canyon, NM, 150
Douglas County, MO, 134
Douglas Landing, AR, 50
Douglass, Frederick, 62
Dove Creek, TX, 188
Dover, AR, 46
Dover, MO, 139, 140
Dover, NC, 153
Dover, TN, 173
Dover, VA, 202
Downsville, MD, 109
Doyal's Plantation, LA, 102
Dragon (U.S.S. steamer), 199
Drake's Creek, TN, 169
Dranesville, VA, 192, 199, 207, 217
Drewry's Bluff, VA, 194, 209
Dripping Spring, MO, 139
Dripping Springs, AR, 43
Droop Mountain, WV, 227
Drumgould's Bluff, MS, 118
Dry Creek, Dakota Territory, 57
Dry Fork, MO, 127
Dry Fork, WV, 223
Dry Run, VA, 215
Dry Valley, GA, 64
Dry Wood Creek, MO, 128
Drywood Creek, MO, 137
Drywood, MO, 134, 135
duck, 164
Duck Branch, SC, 164
Duck River Island, TN, 175
Duck River, TN, 183, 185
Duckett's Plantation, AL, 37
Ducktown Road, GA, 65
Duffield's Station, WV, 228, 229
Dug Ford, MO, 136
Dug Gap, GA, 64
Duguidsville, VA, 217
Dukedom, TN, 182
Dumfries, VA, 198, 200, 201
Dunbar's Plantation, LA, 96
Duncanville, SC, 164
Dunklin County, MO, 142
Dunksburg, MO, 138
Dunlap, TN, 178

Dunn, George, 52
Dunn's Bayou, LA, 101
Durham Station, NC, 156
Dutch, 213
Dutch Gap, VA, 213
Dutch Mills, AR, 46
Dutton's Hill, KY, 89
Duvall, Robert, 299
Duvall's Ford, TN, 184
Dyersburg, TN, 169, 173
Dyer's Ford, GA, 64
Eagle Island, NC, 155
Eagle Pass, TX, 188
Eagleport, OH, 157
Eagleville, TN, 173-175, 180
Earl of Oxford, 299
Earl, Van Dorn, 8
East Macon, GA, 68
East Point, GA, 67, 68
East River Bridge, FL, 61
eastern shore of, VA, 206
Eastport (steamer), 100
Eastport, MS, 124
Eastport, TN, 179
Eatonton, GA, 68
Ebenezer Creek, GA, 69
Eddyville, KY, 93
Eden Station, GA, 69
Edenburg, VA, 193, 206, 214-216
Edenton Road, VA, 200
Edenton, NC, 152
Edgefield Junction, TN, 169
Edina, MO, 127
Edisto Island, SC, 161, 162
Edisto Railroad Bridge, SC, 164
Edisto River, SC, 164
Edmonton, KY, 90
education, 19, 29
educators, 28, 299
Edwards Ferry, VA, 192
Edwards Station, MS, 119, 120
Edwards' Ferry, MS, 122
Edward's Ferry, MD, 107, 109
Egypt Station, MS, 122
Egypt, MS, 124
Eight-Mile Creek Bridge, AL, 38
Eight-Mile Post, MS, 124
Eighteenth Army Corps, 212
election of 1896, 14
Eleven Points River, MO, 134
Eleven Points, MO, 131

Elizabeth City, NC, 152
Elizabeth Court House, WV, 226
Elizabeth, WV, 227
Elizabethtown Road, KY, 87
Elizabethtown, KY, 89
Elk Chute, MO, 139
Elk Creek, Indian Territory, 80
Elk Mountain, WV, 223, 227
Elk River, TN, 168, 176, 178
Elk River, WV, 226
Elk Run, VA, 192, 200
Elk Water, WV, 222
Elkhorn Tavern, AR, 41, 42
Elkin's Ferry, AR, 46
Elkmont, AL, 36
Ellison's Mill, VA, 194, 195
Ellistown, MS, 124
Ellisville, MS, 119
Ellis' Bridge, MS, 122
Ellis' Ford, VA, 206-208
Elm Creek, TX, 188
Elm Springs, AR, 43
Elrod's Tan-yard, AL, 37
Eltham's Landing, VA, 193
Elyton, AL, 37, 38
Ely's Ford, VA, 201, 206, 207
Eminence, MO, 131
Emmitsburg, MD, 109, 110
empire, 15
engagement, 22, 23, 25-28, 44, 47, 48, 53, 60, 64, 66, 85, 86, 90, 95-97, 99-101, 105, 115, 117-119, 123, 124, 149-154, 156, 161-163, 167, 168, 170, 172, 175, 187, 189, 191-195, 197-200, 206, 209, 211-213, 215, 217, 218, 226, 228, 229
Engagements, by state, 9
English, 13, 15, 17
Ennis Cross-Roads, SC, 164
Enterprise, MO, 136, 139
Escambia River, FL, 61
Estenaula, TN, 181
Estill Springs, TN, 176
Etna, MO, 127
Etowah River, GA, 65
Euchee Anna Court House, FL, 60
Eudora Church, AR, 47
European royalty, 299
European socialist revolution
(1848), 297
Evans, Clement A., 22
Evergreen, AL, 37
Everhart, Steve, 62
Exchange (U.S.S. steamer), 47
Ezra Church, GA, 66
Fain's Island, TN, 182
Fair Garden, TN, 182
Fair Grounds, KY, 87
Fair Oaks Station, VA, 194
Fair Oaks, VA, 194, 215
Fair Play (steamer), 95
Fairburn, GA, 67
Fairfax Court House, VA, 191, 192, 197, 199-203
Fairfax Station, VA, 212
Fairfield Gap, PA, 159
Fairfield, NC, 152, 154
Fairfield, PA, 159
Fairfield, TN, 176
Fairmont, WV, 226
Fairview Heights, MD, 108
Fairview, AR, 41
fake history, mainstream, 27
Fallen Timbers, TN, 168
Falling Creek, NC, 155
Falling Waters, MD, 109
Falling Waters, WV, 221, 228
Falls Church, VA, 197, 203, 211
Falmouth, KY, 87
Falmouth, VA, 193, 198, 205
Fancy Farms, KY, 91
Fant's Ford, VA, 196
Farley's Mill, TN, 180
Farmington Heights, MS, 115
Farmington, MO, 127, 140
Farmington, MS, 115
Farmington, TN, 178
farms, 91, 195
Farmville, VA, 218
Fawn (steamer), 213
Fayette Road, MO, 138
Fayette, MO, 138-141
Fayette, MS, 121, 124
Fayetteville, AR, 42-44, 47-50
Fayetteville, NC, 93, 155
Fayetteville, TN, 179, 180
Fayetteville, VA, 201, 205
Fayetteville, WV, 222, 224, 226
federal government, 14
Fender's Mill, MO, 139

Fentress County, TN, 182
Fern Creek, KY, 87
Fernandina, FL, 59
Ferry Landing, AR, 44
Fike's Ferry, AL, 38
Finegan, Joseph, 234
First Maryland Infantry Regiment, 232
First Osage Battalion, 158
First South Carolina Infantry Regiment, 220
Fish Lake Bridge, MS, 117
Fish Lake, MO, 128
Fishburn's Plantation, SC, 164
Fisher's Hill, VA, 200, 204, 214, 215, 217
Fishing Creek, KY, 85, 86
Fitzhugh's Woods, AR, 46
Five Forks, VA, 217
Flat Creek Bridge, VA, 209
Flat Creek Valley, TN, 182
Flat Creek, GA, 68
Flat Creek, MO, 129
Flat Creek, TN, 181, 182, 185
Flat Creek, VA, 218
Flat Lick, 86
Flat Rock Bridge, GA, 66
Flat Rock Road, GA, 67
Flat Top Mountain, WV, 224
Fleetwood, VA, 202, 204
Flemming's Cross-Roads, VA, 201
Fletcher's Ferry, AL, 36
Flint Creek, AR, 45
Flint Hill, VA, 197, 207, 217
Flint River Bridge, GA, 67
Flint River, AL, 35
Flint River, GA, 67, 70
Flintstone Creek, MD, 110
Florence, AL, 34-36
Florence, KY, 87
Florence, SC, 165
Florida, 9, 52, 59
Florida, MO, 131
Flour Bluffs, TX, 187
Flowing Spring, WV, 229
Floyd County, KY, 89
Floyd, LA, 98
Floyd's Spring, GA, 65
Folck's Mill, MD, 110
Folly Island, SC, 162
Foote, Shelby, 299

forage train, 171
Fordoche, LA, 98
Ford's Mill, NC, 153
Forest Hill, VA, 214
Forked Deer Creek, MS, 120
Forked Deer River, TN, 171, 176
Forks of Beaver, KY, 92
Forks Road, NC, 155
Forrest, Nathan B., 8, 16
Forsyth, MO, 127, 132
Fort Abercrombie, ND, 55
Fort Adams, MS, 125
Fort Anderson, NC, 153, 155
Fort Arbuckle, 51
Fort Barrancas, LA, 95
Fort Beaulieu, GA, 69
Fort Beauregard, LA, 97, 98
Fort Beauregard, SC, 161
Fort Bisland, LA, 95, 100
Fort Blair, KS, 83
Fort Blakely, AL, 38
Fort Brady, VA, 216
Fort Bragg, NC, 155
Fort Brooke, FL, 60
Fort Caswell, NC, 152, 155
Fort Clark, TX, 187
Fort Clifton, VA, 209
Fort Collins, CO, 54
Fort Cottonwood, NE, 147
Fort Craig, NM, 149, 150
Fort Darling, VA, 194, 209
Fort Davidson, MO, 140
Fort De Russy, LA, 97, 99
Fort Dodge, KS, 84
Fort Donelson, TN, 167, 169, 170, 172, 173, 176, 177, 184
Fort Esperanza, TX, 188
Fort Fisher, VA, 217
Fort Frederick, MD, 107
Fort Furnace, VA, 195
Fort Gaines, AL, 36
Fort Garland, CO, 54
Fort Gibson, Indian Territory, 79, 80
Fort Halleck, WY, 55
Fort Haskell, VA, 215
Fort Heiman, KY, 86, 93
Fort Henry, TN, 167
Fort Hindman, AR, 43
Fort Holly, VA, 216
Fort Holt, KY, 85

Fort Jackson, LA, 95
Fort Johnson, SC, 163
Fort Jones, KY, 93
Fort Kearny, NE, 147
Fort Lancaster, 80
Fort Larned, KS, 84
Fort Lawrence, MO, 134
Fort Lincoln, KS, 84
Fort Livingston, LA, 95
Fort Lyon, CO, 53
Fort Macon, NC, 151
Fort McAllister, GA, 63, 69
Fort McCook, TN, 169
Fort McRee, FL, 59
Fort Mitchel, KY, 87
Fort Morgan, AL, 36
Fort Morton, VA, 215
Fort Moultrie, SC, 147
Fort Myers, FL, 61
Fort Pemberton, MS, 117, 118
Fort Pillow, TN, 23, 182
Fort Powhatan, VA, 209
Fort Pulaski, 44
Fort Pulaski, GA, 63
Fort Pulaski, TN, 168
Fort Randolph, TN, 184
Fort Rice, Dakota Territory, 57
Fort Ridgely, MN, 113
Fort Riley, KS, 84
Fort Riley, TN, 170
Fort Rosedew, GA, 69
Fort Sanders, TN, 180
Fort Scott, KS, 83
Fort Sedgwick, VA, 215
Fort Smith, AR, 48-50
Fort St. Philip, LA, 95
Fort Stedman, VA, 217
Fort Stevens, Washington, D.C., 219
Fort Strong, NC, 155
Fort Sumter, SC, 105, 162, 163
Fort Thorn, NM, 149
Fort Tyler, GA, 69
Fort Wagner, SC, 162
Fort Walker, SC, 161
Fort Wayne, OK, 79
Fort Zarah, KS, 84
Forty Hills, MS, 118
Forty-Third Virginia Cavalry Battalion, 232
Fosterville, TN, 176, 178
Foster's Plantation, VA, 209
Fouche Springs, TN, 185
Founding Fathers, 14, 29
Fountain Dale, PA, 159
Four Locks, MD, 108
Four Mile, MO, 133
Four-Mile Creek, VA, 212, 213
Fourche Bayou, AR, 44, 98
Fourteen-Mile Creek, MS, 118
Fowl River Narrows, AL, 37
Fox Creek, MO, 130
Fox Springs, KY, 90
Fox's Ford, VA, 204
Foy's Plantation, NC, 151
Frampton's Plantation, SC, 162
Frankfort and Louisville Road, KY, 87
Frankfort, KY, 92
Frankfort, WV, 221
Franklin County, AR, 44
Franklin County, TN, 186
Franklin Creek, MS, 124
Franklin Pike, TN, 171
Franklin Road, KY, 86
Franklin, KY, 90
Franklin, MO, 140, 141
Franklin, TN, 171-175, 185
Franklin, VA, 197, 198, 200
Franklin, WV, 223, 229
Franklin's Crossing, VA, 202
Frayser's Farm, VA, 195
Frederick City, MD, 108
Frederick, MD, 108, 109
Fredericksburg, MO, 138, 139
Fredericksburg, VA, 30, 198, 201
Fredericktown, MO, 128, 134
Free Bridge, MS, 117
Free Bridge, NC, 153, 154
Freeman's Ford, VA, 196
Freestone Point, VA, 192
Frémont, John C., 13
Fremont's Orchard, CO, 51
French's Field, VA, 195
Friar's Island, TN, 177
Friar's Point, MS, 116
Friendship Church, TN, 177
Frog Bayou, AR, 43, 44
Front Royal, VA, 194, 207, 213-215
Frying Pan Church, VA, 205
Frying Pan, VA, 199, 201

Fulton Road, MS, 116
Fulton, MO, 127, 131, 132, 141
Funkstown, MD, 109
Fussell's Mill, VA, 213
Gadsden Road, AL, 36
Gadsden, AL, 34
Gainesville, FL, 60
Gainesville, VA, 197, 202, 205
Gaines' Cross-Roads, VA, 193, 202, 204
Gaines' Landing, AR, 42, 43
Gaines' Mill, VA, 195
Gales' Creek, NC, 154
Gallatin Pike, TN, 170
Gallatin, TN, 169, 171, 184
Galloway's Farm, AR, 41
Galveston, TX, 187
Garden Hollow, MO, 135
Garlick's Landing, VA, 194
Garnett's Farm, VA, 195
Garrettsburg, KY, 88
Garrett's Mill, WV, 223
garrisons, 186
Garrison's Creek, TN, 178
gaslighting, 19
gastronomy, 299
Gatewood's, WV, 227
Gatlinburg, TN, 180
Gauley Bridge, WV, 222
Gauley Ferry, WV, 224
Gauley River, WV, 222
Gauley, WV, 222
Gayheart, Rebecca, 299
Gayoso, MO, 132, 139
Geiger's Lake, KY, 86, 92
genealogy, 299
Gentilly's Plantation, LA, 102
George III, King, 15
Georgia, 9, 62, 63, 68, 69, 96, 240
Georgia Central Railroad Bridge, GA, 68
Georgia Landing, LA, 96
Gerald Mountain, AR, 49
Germanna Ford, VA, 200, 204, 206
Germantown road, TN, 185
Germantown, TN, 173, 186
Germantown, VA, 197, 200, 206, 207
Gettysburg, PA, 159

Ghent, KY, 92
Gibson's Mills, VA, 207
Gilgal Church, GA, 66
Gillett's Farm, NC, 151
Gill's Bluff, VA, 194
Gilmer County, WV, 225
Girard, AL, 38
Gittrell's Ranch, CO, 54
Glade Springs, VA, 216
Gladesville, VA, 202
Glasgow, KY, 87, 89, 91, 93
Glasgow, MO, 140, 141
Glass Village, AR, 49
Glen Allen Station, VA, 209
Glendale, MS, 115, 120
Glendale, VA, 195
Glenville, WV, 221, 224, 226
Globe Tavern, VA, 213
Glorieta Pass, NM, 149
Glorieta, NM, 149
Gloucester Court House, VA, 207
Gloucester Point, VA, 191, 198
God, 2, 3, 239
Godfrey's Ranch, CO, 53
Goings' Ford, WV, 225
gold, 2, 5, 299
Golding's Farm, VA, 195
Goldsboro Bridge, NC, 152
Goldsboro, NC, 155, 156
Gonzales, Ambrosio J., 295
Goochland Court House, VA, 217
Goodlettsville, TN, 170
Goodrich's Landing, LA, 98, 99
Goose Creek, VA, 217
Gordon, GA, 68
Gordon, John B., 16, 19
Gordonsville, VA, 196, 216
Gordonsville, WV, 223
Gordon's Mill, GA, 64
Goresville, VA, 216
Goshen Swamp, NC, 152
Goshen, AL, 36
Gouge's Mill, MO, 130
government, 3, 14-18, 62, 218, 236, 237, 240
Governor Moore's Plantation, LA, 100
Gradyville, KY, 85
Grafton, WV, 222
Grahamville, SC, 164
Graham's Plantation, LA, 101

Granby, MO, 133
Grand Bayou, LA, 103
Grand Coteau, LA, 99
Grand Ecore, LA, 100
Grand Gulf, MS, 115, 116, 118, 122, 124
Grand Junction, TN, 170, 176
Grand Lake, LA, 99
Grand Pass, ID, 71
Grand Prairie, AR, 42
Grand River, Indian Territory, 79
Grand River, LA, 102
Grand River, MO, 129, 132
Granger's Mill, TN, 180
Granny White's Pike, TN, 167
Grant's Creek, NC, 156
Grant's Ferry, MS, 120
grass, 49
Grass Lick, WV, 223
Grassy Lick, VA, 209
Grassy Mound, KY, 88
Gravel Hill, VA, 213
Gravelly Ford, VA, 217
Gravelly Run, VA, 217
graves, 299
Graves, Robert, 299
gravestones, 29
Graysville, GA, 63, 64
Great Bear Creek, AL, 34
Great Britain, 15
Great Cacapon Bridge, WV, 223
Great Cattle Raid, 214
Great Falls, MD, 107
Green Hill, TN, 174, 175
Green Oak, PA, 159
Green River Bridge, KY, 90
Green River, KY, 85
Green Spring Furnace, MD, 108
Green Spring Run, WV, 225, 228, 229
Green, John S., 112
Greenbrier Bridge, WV, 227
Greenbrier River, WV, 222, 227
Greenbrier, WV, 222
Greencastle, PA, 159
Greeneville, TN, 178, 182-184, 186
Greenfield, MO, 136
Greenland Gap, WV, 225
Greenleaf Prairie, Indian Territory, 80

Greenpoint, AL, 36
Greensburg, LA, 97
Greenton Valley, MO, 136
Greenton, MO, 137, 141, 142
Greenville, KY, 91
Greenville, MO, 131
Greenville, MS, 116, 118, 119, 123
Greenville, NC, 154
Greenwell Springs Road, LA, 98
Greenwich, VA, 201, 208
Greenwood, MS, 119
Green's Chapel, KY, 89
Green's Farm, AR, 44
Gregory's Landing, AR, 49
Grenada, MS, 120
Grider's Ferry, KY, 85
Griffinsburg, VA, 204
Griffith, Andy, 299
Grimball, John, 56
Grimball's Landing, SC, 162
Grisson's Bridge, TN, 181
Griswoldville, GA, 68
Grossetete, LA, 99
Ground Squirrel Bridge, VA, 209
Ground Squirrel Church, VA, 209
Grove Church, VA, 199, 201, 205, 206
Groveton Heights, VA, 197
Groveton, VA, 197, 205
Grubb's Cross-Roads, KY, 92
Grundy County, MO, 138
Guard Hill, VA, 213
guerrillas, 183
Guiney's Station, VA, 209
Gulley's, NC, 156
Gum Swamp, NC, 153
gunboats, 34, 85, 101, 119, 184
Guntersville, AL, 33
Gunter's Bridge, SC, 165
Gunter's Landing, AL, 34
Gunter's Prairie, Indian Territory, 80
Guntown, MS, 123
Gurley's Tank, AL, 37
Guyandotte, WV, 222, 225
Guy's Gap, TN, 176
Hagerstown, MD, 108-110
Hager's Mountain, MD, 109
Hahn's Farm, AR, 48
Hainesville, WV, 221

Halcolm Island, MO, 137
Half Mountain, KY, 92
Half-Moon Battery, NC, 155
Hallowell's Landing, AL, 35
Hallsville, MO, 129
Halltown, WV, 225, 226, 228, 229
Hall's Ferry, MS, 118
Hambright's Station, MO, 131
Hamburg Landing, TN, 175
Hamburg, MO, 128
Hamburg, TN, 173
Hamden, OH, 157
Hamilton, NC, 152
Hamilton, VA, 217
Hamilton's Ford, KY, 89
Hamilton's Plantation, MS, 116
Hampton Bridge, VA, 142
Hampton Roads, 55, 188, 192
Hampton Roads, VA, 192
Hampton, VA, 191
Hampton, Wade, 8
Hancock, MD, 107, 110
Hanging Rock Pass, WV, 223
Hankinson's Ferry, MS, 118, 120
Hannah's Creek, NC, 155
Hanover Court House, VA, 194, 195, 217
Hanover Junction, VA, 210
Hanover Station, VA, 201
Hanover, PA, 159
Hanovertown Ferry, VA, 201
Hanovertown, VA, 210
happiness, 3
Hard Times Landing, LA, 97
Hardeeville, SC, 164
Hardin County, TN, 182
Harding, William G., 299
Hare's Hill, VA, 211
Harpers Ferry, WV, 221, 222, 224-227, 230
Harpeth River, TN, 173
Harpeth Shoals, TN, 173
Harrisburg, PA, 159
Harrison County, WV, 225
Harrison, MO, 140
Harrisonburg, LA, 98, 99
Harrisonburg, VA, 193, 194, 210, 217
Harrisonville, MO, 127, 134, 136
Harrison's Gap, AL, 35

Harrison's Landing, AR, 44
Harrison's Landing, TN, 177
Harrison's Landing, VA, 195, 196, 211, 212, 214
Harrisville, WV, 226
Harris' Farm, VA, 209
Harrodsburg, KY, 93
Hartford (U.S.S. sloop-of-war steamer), 117
Hartsville Road, TN, 169
Hartsville, TN, 171, 175, 178
Hartville, MO, 139
Hartwood Church, VA, 198, 200, 203, 205
Hassayampa Creek, AZ, 39
Hatcher's Run, VA, 215-217
Hatchie Bottom, MS, 116
Hatchie Bottom, TN, 169
Hatchie River, MS, 116
Hatchie River, TN, 170
Hatchie's Bridge, TN, 170
Hatch's Ferry, AR, 48
Hatteras Inlet Batteries, NC, 151
Hatteras Inlet, NC, 151
Haughton's Mill, NC, 152
Hawe's Shop, VA, 194, 210
Hawk's Nest, WV, 222
Haw's Shop, VA, 210
hay, 14, 202, 237
Hay Market, VA, 197, 202, 205
Hay Station No. 3, AR, 48
Hay Station, Indian Territory, 80
Haynes' Bluff, MS, 118, 119
Hays' Ferry, TN, 181
Hazel Bottom, MO, 133
Hazel River, VA, 196, 198, 204
Hazen's Farm, AR, 49
Hazle Green, KY, 89
Hedgesville, WV, 225-227
Helena, AR, 42, 43, 48
Henderson County, KY, 88
Henderson, KY, 93
Henderson, TN, 177
Hendersonville, NC, 156
Henderson's Gap, GA, 64
Henderson's Hill, LA, 99
Henderson's Mill, TN, 178
Henryville, TN, 185
Hermann, MO, 140
Hermitage Ford, TN, 170
Hernando, MS, 117-119, 121, 124

Herndon Station, VA, 200
Heroes of the Southern Confederacy (Seabrook), 81
Herring Creek, VA, 195, 212
Hertford, NC, 154
Hickman, KY, 85
Hickman's Bridge, KY, 89
Hickory Grove, MO, 133
Hickory Hill, SC, 164
Hickory Plains, AR, 48
Hickory Station, AR, 50
Hicksford, VA, 216
High Bridge, VA, 218
Highland Stockade, LA, 101
Hillsboro Road, VA, 199
Hillsboro, AL, 37
Hillsboro, GA, 67
Hillsboro, MS, 122
Hillsboro, TN, 176
Hillsboro, VA, 212
Hillsboro, WV, 227
Hillsville, VA, 218
Hill's Gap, TN, 178
Hill's Plantation, AR, 42
Hill's Point, NC, 153
Hill's Point, VA, 201
Hilton Head, SC, 162
Hinesville, GA, 69
historians, conventional, 28
history, 2, 3, 6, 14, 15, 17-19, 21-24, 27-29, 160, 235-238, 240, 299
Hockingport, OH, 157
Hodge's Plantation, LA, 102
Hoe Mountain, AL, 34
Hog Island, MO, 135
Hog Jaw Valley, AL, 37
Hogan's, VA, 194
Hoke's Run, WV, 221
Holden, MO, 139
Hollow Tree Gap, TN, 185
Holly Creek, GA, 69
Holly Springs, MS, 116, 117, 119-123
Holly Tree Gap, TN, 171
Holman's Bridge, SC, 165
Holmes County, OH, 157
Holston River, TN, 178-180
honey, 80, 137, 164
Honey Creek, MO, 136, 137
Honey Hill, SC, 164

Honey Springs, Indian Territory, 80
Hood, John B., 8
Hookerton, NC, 156
Hoover's Gap, TN, 176
Hopefield, AR, 45
Hopewell, MO, 135, 136
Hopkinsville, KY, 85
Horn Lake Creek, MS, 116
Horn Lake Creek, TN, 175
Hornersville, MO, 139
Hornsboro, SC, 165
Horse Cave, KY, 87
Horse Creek, Dakota Territory, 58
Horse Creek, MO, 130
Horse Head Creek, AR, 45
Horseshoe Bottom, KY, 90
Hot Springs, AR, 45
Houlka Swamp, MS, 122
House of Representatives, 236
Houston, MS, 122
Howard County, MO, 133
Howard, David R., 40
Howard, James M., 40
Howard's Gap, NC, 156
Howard's Mill, VA, 193
Howard's Mills, KY, 90, 93
Howell's Ferry, GA, 68
Howlett's Bluff, VA, 211
Hudsonville, MS, 117, 119
Hudson's Crossing, Indian Territory, 80
Huff's Ferry, TN, 179
Huger Battery, AL, 38
Humansville, MO, 130, 132, 136
Humboldt, TN, 169-171
humor, 3, 240, 299
Hundley's Corner, VA, 195
Hungary Station, VA, 201
Hunnewell, MO, 128, 129, 137
Hunterstown, PA, 159
Huntersville, AR, 48
Huntersville, WV, 226
Hunter's Mill, VA, 206
Hunter's Mills, VA, 208
Hunting Island, SC, 161
Huntingdon, TN, 171, 181
Huntsville, AL, 33, 36
Huntsville, AR, 42, 44, 49, 50
Huntsville, GA, 65, 66

Huntsville, MO, 134, 138-140
Huntsville, TN, 169
Hunt's Mill, AL, 35
Hupp's Hill, VA, 215
Hurricane Bridge, WV, 224, 225, 227
Hurricane Creek, 124, 128
Hurricane Creek, MS, 124
Hustonville, KY, 93
Hutchinson, MN, 113
Huttonsville, WV, 224, 228, 229
I, Confederate (Seabrook), 40, 75, 78, 158
Iberia, MO, 133
Ida (C.S.S. steamer), 69
Idaho, 9, 27, 71, 73
Idaho Territory, 9
ignorance, 19, 20
Illinois, 9, 75
Independence Station, LA, 97
Independence, MO, 129, 131, 132, 134, 135, 137, 139, 141
Independence, MS, 121
Independence, WV, 226
Independent Hill, VA, 200
Indian Bay, AR, 45, 46
Indian Bayou, LA, 99
Indian Bayou, MS, 123
Indian Bend, LA, 96
Indian Creek, TN, 182
Indian Creek, VA, 207
Indian Hill, TN, 179
Indian Territory, 9, 51, 79
Indian Village, LA, 96, 102
Indiana, 9, 77
Indianola, TX, 188
Indians, 22, 51, 53, 54, 57, 58, 71, 84, 113, 147, 150, 231
Indiantown, NC, 154
industry, 15, 16
Ingraham Heights, MS, 118
Ingraham's Plantation, MS, 121
Ingram's Mill, MS, 121
Inman Hollow, MO, 131
intelligence, 106
Iowa, 9, 81
Ireland, 3
Irish, 100
Irish Bend, LA, 96, 100
iron, 107, 133, 160, 169, 173
Iron Bridge, Indian Territory, 80

Iron County, MO, 133
ironclads, 55
Ironton, MO, 140
Irvine, KY, 91
Island Ford, TN, 182
Island Ford, VA, 212
Island Mound, MO, 134
Island No. 10, KY, 91
Island No. 10, TN, 170, 178
Island No. 82, MS, 119
Issaquena County, MS, 123
Iuka, MS, 116, 120
Ivey's Farm, MS, 122
Ivey's Ford, AR, 50
Ivey's Hill, MS, 122
Ivy Mountain, KY, 85
J. D. Perry (steamer), 49
Jacinto, MS, 120
Jacksboro, TN, 167, 177
Jackson (C.S. gunboat), 70
Jackson County, MO, 136, 138
Jackson County, TN, 186
Jackson, AR, 42
Jackson, KY, 91
Jackson, LA, 98, 99, 102
Jackson, MO, 127, 130, 134, 140
Jackson, MS, 118, 120, 123
Jackson, Stonewall, 8, 62, 186
Jackson, TN, 168, 171, 176
Jacksonport, AR, 41, 44, 47
Jacksonville, FL, 60
Jacksonville, NC, 152
Jackson's Bridge, FL, 60
Jackson's Ferry, AL, 35
Jackson's Mill, MS, 121
Jack's Creek, TN, 181
Jack's Ford, MO, 135
James City, VA, 204
James Creek, MO, 142
James Island, SC, 162, 163, 165
James River Road, VA, 195
James River, VA, 194, 196, 212, 216
Jamestown, KY, 90
James' Plantation, LA, 96
Janelew, WV, 226
Jarratt's Station, VA, 208, 216
Jasper, TN, 168, 178
Jeanerette, LA, 96
Jefferson City, MO, 83, 140
Jefferson Davis Historical Gold

Medal, 2, 5, 299
Jefferson Pike, TN, 171
Jefferson, MD, 108
Jefferson, Thomas, 13
Jefferson, TN, 172
Jefferson, VA, 198
Jeffersonton, VA, 204, 205
Jeffersonville, VA, 208
Jenkins' Ferry, AR, 47
Jenks' Bridge, GA, 69
Jennie's Creek, KY, 86
Jennings' Farm, VA, 206
Jenny Lind, AR, 44
Jericho Bridge, VA, 210
Jericho Ford, VA, 210
Jericho Mills, VA, 210
Jerusalem Plank Road, VA, 211
Jesus, 3
Johnson County, AR, 44, 50
Johnson County, MO, 137
Johnsonville, TN, 183, 184
Johnson's Crook, GA, 69
Johnson's Farm, VA, 215
Johnson's Ferry, KY, 89
Johnson's Island, OH, 82
Johnson's Station, SC, 165
Johnston, Albert S., 8
Johnston, Joseph E., 8, 16
Johnstown, MO, 129, 136
Johnstown, WV, 225
John's Island, SC, 163, 164
Jollification, MO, 133
Jones, John, 236
Jonesboro, AL, 33
Jonesboro, AR, 42
Jonesboro, GA, 67, 68
Jonesboro, MO, 128, 136
Jonesboro, TN, 177, 184
Jonesville, VA, 199, 206, 207, 212
Jones' Bridge, VA, 211
Jones' Cross-Roads, MD, 109
Jones' Cross-Roads, MS, 118
Jones' Farm, VA, 210
Jones' Ferry, MS, 120
Jones' Hill, TN, 178
Jones' Plantation, MS, 119
Jones' Station, AR, 48
Jordan's Store, TN, 175
Jordon's Ford, VA, 195
Jornada del Muerto, NM, 150

Joyner's Ferry, VA, 199
Judd, Ashley, 299
Judd, Naomi, 299
Judd, Wynonna, 299
Jug Tavern, GA, 67
Julesburg, CO, 53, 54
Jumpertown, MS, 117
Juniper Creek, SC, 165
Kabletown, WV, 228, 229
Kanawha Gap, WV, 222
Kanawha River, WV, 225
Kanawha Valley, WV, 227
Kane, James C., 232
Kane, John K., 232
Kansas, 9, 51, 83, 84
Kearneysville, WV, 224, 229
Keedysville, MD, 109, 110
Keezletown Cross-Roads, WV, 223
Keller's Bridge, KY, 92
Kellysville, VA, 200
Kellyville, VA, 200
Kelly's Ford, TN, 182
Kelly's Ford, VA, 196, 200, 203-205
Kelly's Mill, MS, 123
Kelly's Plantation, AL, 35
Kelly's Store, VA, 199
Kempsville, VA, 203
Kenansville, NC, 153
Kendal's Grist-Mill, AR, 49
Kenesaw Water Tank, GA, 67
Kennesaw Mountain, GA, 66
Kentucky, 9, 19, 85, 235, 299
Kentucky Line, KY, 86
Kentucky River, KY, 86
Keough, Riley, 299
Kernstown, VA, 192, 212, 215
Kessler's Cross Lanes, WV, 222
Kettle Creek, KY, 90
Kettle Run, VA, 197
Keytesville, MO, 129, 134, 138, 139
Kickapoo Bottom, AR, 41
Kilkenny River, SC, 162
Killdeer Mountain, ND, 57
Kimbrough's Cross-Roads, TN, 181
Kinderhook, TN, 169
King and Queen Court House, VA, 211

King George Court House, VA, 203
Kingsport, TN, 177, 184, 185
Kingston, AR, 44
Kingston, GA, 65
Kingston, TN, 179, 180, 184
Kingsville, MO, 137
King's Creek, MS, 118
King's Creek, SC, 163
King's Hill, TN, 185
King's House, MO, 136
King's River, AR, 45-47
King's School-House, VA, 195
King's Store, AL, 38
Kinney's Farm, VA, 194
Kinsell's Ferry, VA, 197
Kinston Road, NC, 152
Kinston, NC, 152, 153
Kirksville, MO, 127, 128, 132
Kirk's Bluff, SC, 162
Kittredge's Sugar House, LA, 103
Klapsford, MO, 128
Knight's Cove, AR, 42
Knob Creek, TN, 172
Knob Gap, TN, 171
Knobnoster, MO, 129
Knoxville, TN, 175, 179, 181, 182
Kock's Plantation, LA, 98
Kolb's Farm, GA, 66
Kossuth, MS, 116
Ku Klux Klan, 2, 239
Kurz, Louis, 6
La Fayette County, MO, 130, 134, 136, 142
La Fayette Depot, TN, 174
La Fayette Landing, TN, 170
La Fayette Road, GA, 64
La Fayette Station, TN, 168
La Fayette, GA, 64, 66, 68
La Fayette, KY, 91
La Fayette, TN, 174, 175, 179, 180, 183
La Fourche Crossing, LA, 98
La Fourche, LA, 98
La Grange, AR, 42, 43
La Grange, TN, 180, 181, 183
La Mine Bridge, MO, 136
La Vergne, TN, 170-172, 174, 181
Labadieville, LA, 102
labor, 237, 297
Lacey's Springs, VA, 216
Ladd's House, AL, 37
Ladiga, AL, 36
Lake Borgne, LA, 99
Lake Bruin, LA, 97
Lake Chicot, AR, 47
Lake City, FL, 60
Lake Fausse Pointe, LA, 102
Lake Providence, LA, 97, 98
Lake Saint Joseph, LA, 97
Lake Springs, MO, 140
Lake Verret, LA, 103
Lake Village, AR, 45
Lamar, MO, 133, 134, 137
Lamar, MS, 124
Lamb's Creek Church, VA, 203
Lamb's Ferry, VA, 203
Lamb's Plantation, AR, 48
Lancaster Road, KY, 88
Lancaster, KY, 88, 91
Lancaster, MO, 129, 133
Lane's Bridge, SC, 164
Lane's Prairie, MO, 137
Langley's Plantation, MS, 123
Lanier's Mills, AL, 38
Laredo, TX, 188
Larkinsville, AL, 34, 35
Latin-Americans, Confederate, 295
Latin-Americans, 295
Lauderdale Springs, MS, 122
Laurel Creek Gap, TN, 184
Laurel Creek, WV, 222, 228
Laurel Fork, WV, 222
Laurel Hill, VA, 208
Laurel Hill, WV, 221
Lavaca, TX, 187
law, 3, 6, 236
Lawrence County, KY, 91
Lawrence, KS, 83
Lawrenceburg, KY, 88
Lawrenceburg, TN, 167, 179, 185
Lawrenceville, AR, 44
Lawrenceville, GA, 68
Lawrence's Mill, TN, 181
Lawtonville, SC, 164
Lawyers' Road, VA, 201
Law's Landing, AL, 33
Lead Mines, VA, 216
Leasburg, MO, 140

Lebanon (U.S.S. steamer), 47
Lebanon Junction, KY, 87
Lebanon Road, TN, 170
Lebanon, AL, 35
Lebanon, KY, 86, 90
Lebanon, MO, 141
Lebanon, TN, 168, 171
Lee, Fitzhugh, 8
Lee, Robert E., 8
Lee, Stephen D., 8
Lee's Mill, GA, 64
Lee's Mills, GA, 64
Leeds' Ferry, VA, 198
Leesburg, AL, 36
Leesburg, TN, 177, 184
Leesburg, VA, 192, 197, 198, 203, 208
Leesburg, WV, 225
Leesville, MO, 130
Leesville, VA, 200
Leetown, WV, 228, 229
Leet's Tan-yard, GA, 64, 65
Lee's Creek, AR, 47
Lee's Cross-Roads, GA, 65
Lee's House, TN, 182
Lee's House, VA, 192
Lee's Mill, VA, 193, 212, 215
Left-wing Civil War mythology, 62
Left-wing, 14, 16, 18, 19, 62
Legare's Point, SC, 163
Leggett's Hill, GA, 66
Leighton, AL, 34, 37
Leiper's Ferry, TN, 178
Leitersburg, MD, 109
Lenoir's Station, TN, 175, 179
Leo's Mill, GA, 64
Lewinsville, VA, 192, 204, 206
Lewis Chapel, VA, 192
Lewis Farm, VA, 217
Lewisburg Pike, TN, 174
Lewisburg, AR, 45, 48-50
Lewisburg, WV, 223, 226, 227
Lewis' Ford, VA, 197
Lewis' Mill, WV, 225
Lexington, KY, 88, 92
Lexington, MO, 128, 134-137, 139-142
Lexington, MS, 124
Lexington, SC, 165
Lexington, TN, 171, 176

Lexington, VA, 210
Libby Prison, 297
Libby Prison, VA, 297
liberalism, 14
liberalization, 18
liberals, 13-16
libertarian, 13
liberty, 87, 91, 124, 128, 211, 235
Liberty Gap, TN, 176
Liberty Mills, VA, 204
Liberty Mills, WV, 229
Liberty Post-Office, AR, 46
Liberty, MO, 128, 133, 138
Liberty, TN, 174, 175
Liberty, VA, 205, 206, 211
Lick Creek, AR, 43
Lick Creek, TN, 168
Licking River, KY, 92
Licking Run Bridge, VA, 206
Licking, MO, 131, 141
Lillian Springs Ranch, CO, 54
Limestone Ridge, VA, 214
Limestone Station, TN, 177
Limestone Valley, AR, 46
Lincoln, Abraham, 13, 15-19, 73, 297
Lincoln's War, 2, 3, 13, 15, 18, 19, 23, 239, 297, 301
Lincoln's War (Seabrook), 18
Linden, TN, 175
Linden, VA, 194
Lindley, MO, 138
Linn Creek, MO, 128, 132, 142
Lisbon, MD, 108
Litchfield, AR, 41
Lithonia, GA, 66
Little Bear Creek, AL, 34, 35
Little Black River, MO, 139
Little Blue River, MO, 128, 131, 135, 138, 140, 142
Little Boston, VA, 206
Little Cacapon Bridge, WV, 224
Little Cacapon River, WV, 222
Little Cohera Creek, NC, 155
Little Compton, MO, 132
Little Creek, NC, 152
Little Fort Valley, VA, 216
Little Harpeth River, TN, 174
Little Laramie, 58
Little Laramie, Dakota Territory,

58
Little Missouri River, AR, 46
Little Missouri River, MO, 139
Little Ogeechee River, GA, 69
Little Osage River, KS, 84
Little Piney, MO, 142
Little Pond, TN, 169
Little Red River, AR, 41, 47
Little River Bridge, MO, 133
Little River Turnpike, VA, 192, 202
Little River, AL, 36
Little River, AR, 46
Little River, MO, 141
Little River, TN, 179
Little River, VA, 210
Little Rock Landing, TN, 175
Little Rock, AR, 47-50, 98
Little Rockcastle River, KY, 88
Little Salkehatchie River, SC, 164
Little Santa Fe, MO, 128, 130
Little Sewell Mountain, WV, 227
Little Sni, MO, 130
Little Tennessee River, TN, 179
Little Washington, VA, 198, 203
Liverpool Heights, MS, 122
Liverpool Landing, MS, 119
Liverpool, MS, 123
Livingston, MS, 121, 123
Livingston, TN, 180
Livingstone, TN, 186
Lizzard's, TN, 172
Lobelville, TN, 184
Locke's Mill, TN, 177
Lockhart's Mill, MS, 121
Lockridge's Mill, TN, 168
Lockwood's Folly Inlet, NC, 154
Locust Grove, Indian Territory, 79
Locust Grove, VA, 206
Log Church, KY, 87
Log Mountain, TN, 180
Logan's Cross-Roads, KY, 86
London, KY, 86, 90
Lone Jack, MO, 132, 139, 142
Long Bridge, VA, 210
Long Ford, TN, 180
Long View, AR, 46
Longstreet, James, 16
Longwood, MO, 139, 142
Long's Mills, TN, 183
Lookout Church, GA, 64
Lookout Mountain, GA, 63
Lookout Mountain, TN, 177, 179
Lookout Valley, TN, 177
Loper's Cross-Roads, SC, 164
Los Patricios, TX, 188
Lost Cause, 237
Lost Creek, MO, 130
Lost Mountain, GA, 66, 67
Lost River Gap, WV, 228
Lotspeich Farm, MO, 131
Loudon County, TN, 179
Loudon, TN, 178-180
Loudoun County, VA, 200, 210, 213
Loudoun Heights, VA, 194, 207
Loudoun, VA, 199
Louisa Court House, VA, 193, 201
Louisa, KY, 89
Louisiana, 9, 38, 95, 97, 148, 156, 240
Louisiana (C.S.S. ironclad), 156
Louisiana Belle (steamer), 97
Louisiana State University, 240
Louisville, GA, 68
Louisville, KY, 87
Louisville, TN, 182
Loup Creek, WV, 226
Lovejoy's Station, GA, 66-68
Loveless, Patty, 299
Lovettsville, VA, 191, 197, 216
Lower Post Ferry, TN, 168
Lowndesboro, AL, 38
Lowry's Ferry, TN, 172
Lucas Bend, MO, 128
Luce's Plantation, MS, 123
Lumpkin County, GA, 67
Lumpkin's Mill, MS, 117
Lumpkin's Station, GA, 69
Luna Landing, AR, 45
Lundy's Lane, AL, 34
Luray Valley, VA, 215
Luray, VA, 193, 214
Lusby's Mill, KY, 86
Lynchburg, TN, 184
Lynchburg, VA, 211
Lynch's Creek, SC, 165
Lynnville, TN, 185
Lyon County, KY, 93
Lytle's Creek, TN, 172
L'Anguille Ferry, AR, 42

Mackville, KY, 86
Macon Bayou, LA, 97
Macon County, MO, 132
Macon Ford, MS, 119
Macon, GA, 66, 68, 70
Macon, MO, 137, 142
Madison County, AR, 50
Madison Court House, VA, 196, 204, 216
Madison Station, AL, 35
Madison, AR, 50
Madisonville, KY, 86
Madisonville, LA, 95, 99
Madisonville, MS, 123
Magna Carta, 2, 238
Magnolia Landing, LA, 101
Magnolia, FL, 60
Magnolia, TN, 186
Magruder's Ferry, VA, 192
Mahone, William, 298
Maine, 9, 105
malice, 19
Mallory, Stephen R., 77, 126
Mallory's Cross-Roads, VA, 211
Malvern Cliff, VA, 195, 212
Malvern Hill, VA, 195, 196, 211, 212
Mammoth Cave, KY, 86
Manassas Gap, VA, 198, 202
Manassas Junction, VA, 197, 205, 215
Manassas Station, VA, 196
Manassas, VA, 191, 197, 205
Manchester Pike, TN, 172, 173
Manchester, KY, 88
Manchester, TN, 182
Manscoe Creek, TN, 169
Mansfield, LA, 100
Mansura, LA, 101
Man's Creek, MO, 136
Maplesville, AL, 38
Marais des Cygnes, KS, 84
Marblehead (U.S.S. gunboat), 163
Marianna, AR, 43
Marianna, FL, 60
Maries County, MO, 137
Marietta, GA, 66
Marietta, MS, 116
Marion Station, MS, 122
Marion, VA, 216
markers, 29

Markham's Station, VA, 198
Marksville Prairie, LA, 99, 101
Marks' Mills, AR, 46, 47
Marling Bottom Bridge, WV, 227
Marling's Bottom, WV, 228
Marmaduke, John S., 72
Marmiton River, MO, 141
Marmiton, MO, 141
Marrowbone Creek, KY, 91
Marrowbone, KY, 90
Marshall Knob, TN, 175
Marshall, KY, 91
Marshall, MO, 130, 136
Marshfield, MO, 129, 134
Marsteller's Place, VA, 201
Martin Creek, KY, 90
Martinsburg, MO, 127
Martinsburg, WV, 223-226, 228, 229
Martinsville, NC, 156
Martin's Creek, AR, 45
Martin's House, Indian Territory, 80
Martin's Lane, LA, 103
Marvin, Lee, 299
Marx, Karl, 17, 297
Marye's Heights, VA, 201
Maryland, 9, 40, 107, 232
Maryland Heights, MD, 108
Maryville, TN, 179, 182
Masonboro Inlet, NC, 154
Massaponax Church, VA, 196
Massard Prairie, AR, 48
Matadequin Creek, VA, 210
Matagorda Island, TX, 188
Matagorda Peninsula, TX, 188
Matagorda, TX, 187
Matamoras, Mexico, 111
Mathias Point, VA, 191
Mattawoman Creek, MD, 107
Matthews' Ferry, MS, 119
Mayfield Creek, KY, 85
Mayfield, KY, 92
Maynardville, TN, 180
Mayport Mills, FL, 59
Maysville, AL, 34, 35, 37
Maysville, AR, 44, 47, 48
Maysville, KY, 90
McAfee's Cross-Roads, GA, 66
McBlair, William, Jr., 78
McClellarsville, SC, 163

McConnellsburg, PA, 159, 160
McCormick's Gap, KY, 93
McCoy's Ferry, MD, 108
McCoy's Mill, WV, 222
McCulla's Store, MO, 127
McDonough Road, GA, 67, 68
McDowell, VA, 193
McGaheysville, VA, 193
McGavocks, 3, 238
McGirt's Creek, FL, 60
McGraw, Tim, 299
McGuire's Ferry, AR, 42
McGuire's, AR, 42
McKay's Farm, MO, 130
McKenzie's Creek, MO, 142
McLean's Ford, VA, 191, 205
McLemore's Cove, TN, 186
McMinnville, TN, 178, 180, 186
McNutt's Bridge, TN, 182
McNutt's Hill, LA, 100
McWilliams' Plantation, LA, 96
Meadow Bluff, WV, 227
Meadow Bridge, VA, 195, 209
Meadow Bridges, VA, 209
Mechanicsburg, MS, 119, 123, 124
Mechanicsville, VA, 195, 209
Mechump's Creek, VA, 210
medicine, 113
Medicine Creek, MO, 130
Medoc, MO, 128
Medon Station, TN, 169, 170
Medon, TN, 169
Meffleton Lodge, AR, 48
Memminger, Christopher G., 77
memorial, 236
memories, 17, 19, 21, 235
Memphis, MO, 131
Memphis, TN, 168, 169, 174-176, 183-186
men, 8, 22, 24, 62, 114, 235
Mercersburg, PA, 160
Meridian, MS, 122
Meriwether's Ferry, TN, 169, 179
Merrill's Crossing, MO, 136
Merry Oaks, KY, 87
Mesilla, NM, 149
Messinger's Ferry, MS, 120
Metamora, TN, 170
Meto Bayou, AR, 44
Mexico, 10, 111, 149

Mexico, MO, 127
Miami, MO, 131, 142
Middle Boggy Depot, Indian Territory, 80
Middle Creek, KY, 86
Middle Fork Bridge, WV, 221
Middlebrook, VA, 210
Middleburg, TN, 171
Middleburg, VA, 199, 202
Middleton, TN, 170, 173, 175, 176, 181
Middletown, MD, 108, 109
Middletown, VA, 192, 194, 196, 202, 208, 214, 215
Middleway, WV, 229
Mier, Mexico, 111
Mifflin, TN, 182
Milford, MO, 129
Milford, VA, 194, 214, 215
military, 2, 16, 19, 21-23, 25, 29, 62, 154, 158, 235, 236, 238, 241, 295, 299
Military Order of Stars and Bars, 29
military terms defined, 25
Mill Creek Bridge, MO, 134
Mill Creek, MO, 137
Mill Creek, NC, 152, 155
Mill Creek, TN, 171, 173
Mill Point, WV, 227
Mill Springs, KY, 86, 90
Millen's Grove, GA, 69
Miller's Ferry, WV, 224
Milliken's Bend, LA, 95, 97, 98
mills, 37, 38, 44, 46, 47, 50, 59, 64, 70, 90-93, 107, 108, 119, 121, 123, 128, 129, 135, 138, 140, 151, 153, 155, 183, 185, 191, 199, 204, 205, 207-210, 226, 228, 229
Millwood Road, VA, 200
Millwood, VA, 199
Milton, FL, 60
Milton, TN, 174
Mimm's Mills, GA, 70
Mine Creek, KS, 84
Mine Run, VA, 206
Mineral Point, MO, 140
Mingo Creek, NC, 155
Mingo Swamp, MO, 134
Mink Springs, TN, 182

Minnesota, 10, 113
Missionary Ridge, 179
Missionary Ridge, TN, 177, 179
Mississippi, 10, 38, 91, 115, 119, 122
Mississippi County, MO, 142
Mississippi River, 91, 119, 122
Mississippi River, KY, 91
Mississippi River, LA, 95
Mississippi Springs, MS, 118
Missouri, 10, 46, 127, 138, 139, 142
Missouri River, 46, 139, 142
Missouri River, MO, 142
Mitchell's Cross-Roads, MS, 117
Mitchell's Ford, VA, 191, 204
Mobile & Ohio Railroad, 116
Mobile & Ohio Railroad, MS, 116
Mobile Bay, AL, 36, 37
Mobile, AL, 38
Moccasin Creek, NC, 155
Moccasin Swamp, NC, 156
Mocksville, NC, 156
Moffat's Station, AR, 44
Molino, MS, 121
Monagan Springs, MO, 130, 131
Monarch (U.S. steamer), 47
monarchy, 15
Monett's Ferry, LA, 100
Moniteau County, MO, 130
Monitor (U.S.S. ironclad), 163
Monocacy Aqueduct, MD, 107
Monocacy Church, MD, 108
Monocacy Junction, MD, 110
Monocacy, MD, 109
Monongahela (U.S.S. sloop-of-war), 117
Monroe Station, MO, 127
Monroe's Cross-Roads, NC, 155
Montana, 10, 26, 27, 143
Montana Territory, 10, 143
Monteith Swamp, GA, 69
Monterey Gap, PA, 159
Monterey, KY, 86
Monterey, TN, 167, 172
Monterey, VA, 193
Montevallo, AL, 38
Montevallo, MO, 130, 132, 137, 140
Montezuma, TN, 177
Montgomery, AL, 38

Montgomery, TN, 175
Monticello, 48, 90, 191
Monticello (U.S.S. wooden steamer), 191
Monticello Bridge, MO, 128
Monticello Road, AR, 48, 50
Monticello, AR, 45, 49, 50
Monticello, KY, 90, 91
Montpelier Springs, AL, 38
Moon's Station, GA, 67
Moore, Thomas O., 100
Moorefield, WV, 223-229
Moore's Bluff, MS, 124
Moore's Ford, MS, 120
Moore's Mill, MO, 131, 132
Moore's Ranch, CO, 54
Moreau Creek, MO, 140
Moreauville, LA, 101
Morgan County, KY, 91
Morgan County, TN, 167
Morgan, John H., 8
Morganfield, KY, 86, 92
Morganton, NC, 156
Morgantown, KY, 85
Morgantown, WV, 226
Morganza Bend, LA, 103
Morganza, LA, 98, 101-103
Morgan's Ferry Road, LA, 101
Morgan's Ferry, AL, 36
Morgan's Ferry, LA, 98, 102
Morgan's Mill, AR, 45
Moro Bottom, AR, 47
Morris Island, SC, 162, 163
Morrison's Ranch, CO, 53
Morristown, MO, 128
Morristown, TN, 180, 183, 184
Morrisville, NC, 156
Morrisville, VA, 199
Morris' Ford, TN, 176
Morris' Mills, WV, 226
Morse's Mills, MO, 128
Morton, MS, 122
Morton's Ford, VA, 204, 206, 207
MOSB (Military Order of Stars and Bars), 29
Mosby, John S., 299
Moscow, AR, 46
Moscow, TN, 173, 174, 177, 179-181, 183
Moseley Hall, NC, 156
Moselle Bridge, MO, 141

Mossy Creek Station, TN, 181
Mossy Creek, TN, 181, 184
Motley's Ford, TN, 179
Moulton, AL, 35, 36
Mound City, KS, 84
Mound Plantation, LA, 98
Mount Airy, VA, 216
Mount Carmel Church, VA, 210
Mount Carmel, KY, 90
Mount Carmel, TN, 185
Mount Carmel, VA, 194
Mount Crawford, VA, 215, 216
Mount Elba, AR, 46
Mount Elon, SC, 165
Mount Ida, AR, 44
Mount Jackson, VA, 192, 194, 206, 214-217
Mount Olive Station, NC, 152
Mount Pleasant Landing, LA, 101
Mount Pleasant, AL, 38
Mount Pleasant, MS, 120, 121, 123
Mount Pleasant, TN, 168, 169, 185, 186
Mount Sterling, KY, 89, 91, 92
Mount Vernon, KY, 88
Mount Vernon, MO, 133, 139
Mount Washington, KY, 87
Mount Zion Church, KY, 86
Mount Zion Church, MO, 129
Mount Zion Church, VA, 212
Mountain Fork, AR, 45
Mountain Gap, KY, 88
Mountain Gap, TN, 178
Mountain Grove, MO, 130
Mountain Home, AR, 42
Mountain Side, KY, 88
Mountain Store, MO, 131
Mountville, VA, 197
Mud Creek, MS, 119
Mud Lick Springs, KY, 90
Mud River, WV, 225
Mud Springs, NE, 147
Mud Town, AR, 49
Muddy Branch, MD, 108
Muddy Creek, AL, 37
Muddy Creek, TN, 181
Muddy Creek, WV, 224, 227
Muddy River, KY, 85
Muddy Run, VA, 203, 205
Mulberry Creek, GA, 67

Mulberry Gap, TN, 179, 183
Mulberry River, AR, 43
Mulberry Village, TN, 181
Muldraugh's Hill, KY, 89
Mullahla's Station, NE, 147
Munfordville, KY, 87, 89
Munford's Station, AL, 38
Mungo Flata, WV, 224
Munson's Hill, VA, 192
Murfreesboro Pike, TN, 172
Murfreesboro, TN, 145, 168-170, 172-175, 178, 182, 185
Murphy, NC, 154
Murray's Inlet, SC, 162
Murrell's Inlet, SC, 163
Muscle Fork, MO, 132
Muscogee (C.S. gunboat), 69
music, 299
musicians, 62, 299
Nahunta Station, NC, 156
Namozine Church, VA, 218
Napoleonville, LA, 101, 103
Nashville & Chattanooga Railroad, TN, 185
Nashville, TN, 167, 168, 170, 171, 173, 175, 183, 185
Natchez and Liberty Road, MS, 124
Natchez, MS, 120, 121, 123, 124
Natchitoches, LA, 100, 101
national government, 18
National Park Service, 22, 212, 213
National Statuary Hall, Washington, D.C., 114
nationalism, 14
Native-Americans, Confederate, 158
Native-Americans, 158
Natural Bridge, FL, 61
nature, 3, 299
Naumkeag (U.S.S. steamer), 48
naval engagement, 168, 192
navies, 237
navy, 56, 62, 77, 78, 104, 126, 237
Neal Dow Station, GA, 66
Neal's Gap, AL, 35
Nebraska, 10, 27, 145, 147
Nebraska Territory, 10, 147
Neely's Bend, TN, 170

Neersville, VA, 204
Negro Head Cut, KY, 89
Nelson's Bridge, LA, 98
Nelson's Cross-Roads, KY, 88
Nelson's Farm, VA, 195
Neosho River, Indian Territory, 80
Neosho, MO, 130-133, 136, 137, 141
Neuse River Bridge, NC, 155
Neuse River, NC, 155, 156
New Albany, MS, 118-120, 122
New Baltimore, VA, 205
New Bern, NC, 151-153
New Bridge, VA, 194
New Carthage, LA, 96
New Castle, TN, 181
New Castle, VA, 211
New Creek, WV, 221, 228, 229
New Franklin, MO, 133
New Glasgow, VA, 211
New Haven, KY, 89, 92
New Hope Church, GA, 66, 67
New Hope Church, VA, 206
New Hope Station, KY, 90
New Hope, KY, 91
New Iberia, LA, 98
New Kent Court House, VA, 193
New London, VA, 211
New Madrid Bend, TN, 178
New Madrid County, MO, 141
New Madrid, MO, 130, 141
New Market Bridge, VA, 192
New Market Cross-Roads, VA, 195
New Market Heights, VA, 214
New Market Road, VA, 195, 212, 213, 215
New Market, AL, 33, 35, 37
New Market, KY, 89, 93
New Market, TN, 181
New Market, VA, 194, 209, 214, 215
New Mexico, 10
New Orleans, LA, 95, 148
New Providence, TN, 170
New River Bridge, VA, 209
New River, LA, 99
New River, WV, 222, 224
New South, 240
New Testament, 3

New Texas Road, LA, 102
New York, 16, 235-237, 240
Newark Cross-Roads, VA, 211
Newark, MO, 131
Newby's Cross-Roads, VA, 198, 202
Newnan, GA, 67
Newport Barracks, NC, 154
Newport Bridge, FL, 61
Newport Cross-Roads, LA, 101
Newport News, VA, 191
Newport, NC, 151
Newport, TN, 181
Newton County, MO, 137
Newtonia, MO, 132, 133, 141
Newtown, LA, 96
Newtown, VA, 194, 198, 199, 202, 203, 210, 212, 213, 215
Nickajack Creek, GA, 66
Nickajack Gap, GA, 65
Nickajack Trace, GA, 65
Nine-Mile Ordinary, VA, 202
Nine-Mile Ridge, KS, 84
Nine-Mile Road, VA, 194
Nineveh, VA, 215
Nixonton, NC, 153
Nokesville, VA, 208
Noland's Ferry, MD, 109
Nolensville, TN, 171-173
Nolin, KY, 89
Nonconnah Creek, TN, 169, 174, 184
Noonday Creek, GA, 66
Norfleet House, VA, 200
Norfolk, MO, 128
Norfolk, VA, 200
Norris Creek, MO, 139
Norristown, AR, 47, 49
North, 2, 3, 10, 19, 27, 138, 146, 147, 151, 156, 165, 209, 212, 235, 239, 299
North Anna, VA, 209
North Carolina, 10, 151, 156, 235, 299
North Edisto River, SC, 165
North Mountain Station, WV, 226
North Mountain, WV, 228
North Platte River, 147
North Platte River, NE, 147
North River Mills, WV, 228
North River, VA, 215

Northeast Ferry, NC, 155
Northern battle names, 24
Northern historians, 24
Northern propagandists, 21
Northerners, 2, 24, 238
Northernization, 18
Northport, AL, 38
Nose's Creek, GA, 66
Nottoway Court House, VA, 211
Noyes' Creek, GA, 66
Nueces River, TX, 187
nurses, 62
Nutter's Hill, WV, 229
Ny River, VA, 209
Oak Grove, VA, 195, 200, 211
Oak Hill, VA, 205
Oak Hills, MO, 127
Oak Ridge, MS, 122
Oak Shade, VA, 203
Oakland Station, KY, 87
Oakland, MD, 108
Oakland, MS, 117
obelisks, 29
Obey's River, TN, 182
Obion River, MS, 119
Obion River, TN, 169, 174
Occoquan River, VA, 199
Occoquan, VA, 199, 200
Ocean Pond, FL, 60
Ocklocknee Bay, FL, 60
Oconee River, GA, 68
OCR (Order of Confederate Rose), 29
Octorara (U.S. steamer), 37
Official Records, 237
Offutt's Cross-Roads, MD, 108
Ogeechee Canal, GA, 69
Ogeechee River, GA, 69
Ohio, 10, 116, 157
Oil Trough Bottom, AR, 46
Okolona, AR, 46
Okolona, MS, 121-124
Old Antietam Forge, MD, 109
Old Church, VA, 208, 210
Old Deposit Ferry, AL, 33
Old Fort Wayne, OK, 79
Old Lamar, MS, 117
Old Oaks, LA, 101
Old Randolph, MO, 128
Old River Lake, AR, 47
Old River, LA, 96

Old South, 2, 3, 18, 166, 240
Old Town Creek, MS, 124
Old Town, MD, 110
Oldfields, WV, 228
Olive Branch Church, VA, 199
Olive Branch, LA, 102
Olive Branch, MS, 116
Olley's Creek, GA, 66
Olustee, FL, 60
Opelika, AL, 38
Opelousas, LA, 99
Opequon Creek, VA, 202, 213, 214
Opequon Creek, WV, 229
Opequon, VA, 214
Orange Court House, VA, 196, 204
Orange Grove, LA, 101
Orangeburg, SC, 165
Orchard Knob, TN, 179
Order of Confederate Rose, 29
Oregon, MO, 136
Orton Pond, NC, 155
Osage Branch, AR, 46
Osage Mission, KS, 84
Osage River, MO, 130, 140
Osage, MO, 141
Osago Springs, AR, 41
Osborn's Creek, MS, 115
Osceola, AR, 46, 48
Osceola, MO, 128, 131
Otter Creek, VA, 211
Ouachita River, AR, 47
Overall's Creek, TN, 172
Overland Stage Road, CO, 51, 84
Owen County, KY, 86
Owensboro, KY, 87, 92
Owens' Ford, GA, 64
Owen's Cross-Roads, TN, 185
Ox Ford, VA, 209
Ox Hill, VA, 197
Oxford Bend, AR, 42
Oxford, KS, 84
Oxford, MS, 124
Oyster Point, PA, 159
Ozark Mountains, MO, 134
Ozark, MO, 132
Pack's Ferry, WV, 224
Padre Island, TX, 187
Paducah, KY, 85, 91, 92, 177
Paine's Cross-Roads, VA, 218

Paint Lick Bridge, KY, 91
Paint Rock Bridge, AL, 33, 35
Paint Rock River, 37
Paint Rock River, AL, 37
Paint Rock Station, AL, 36
Paint Rock, AL, 34, 37
Paintsville, KY, 92
Palatka, FL, 60
Palmetto Ranch, TX, 188
Palmyra, MO, 128
Palmyra, TN, 179
Palo Alto, MS, 118
Pamunkey River, VA, 200
Panola, MS, 119, 120
panther, 184
Panther Creek, MO, 132
Panther Gap, WV, 228
Panther Springs, TN, 182, 184
Paola, KS, 83
Papinsville, MO, 128, 135
Paraje, NM, 149
paranormal, 3, 299
Paris, KY, 86, 89, 91
Paris, MO, 140
Paris, TN, 167, 177
Parkersville, MO, 127
Parker's Cross-Roads, GA, 65
Parker's Cross-Roads, TN, 172
Parker's Ford, VA, 212
Parker's Store, VA, 206
Parkins' Mill, VA, 216
Parkville, MO, 138
Park's Gap, TN, 183
Parton, Dolly, 299
party, 13, 14, 17, 18, 192, 236, 297
Pasquotank, NC, 153
Pass Christian, MS, 115
Pass Manchac, LA, 95, 96
patriots, 19
Patterson, MO, 134, 139, 142
Pattersonville, LA, 96
Patterson's Creek Bridge, WV, 228
Patterson's Creek Station, WV, 230
Patterson's Creek, WV, 228, 230
Paw Paw Tunnel, WV, 224
Pawnee Agency, NE, 145
Pawnee Rock, KS, 84
Payne's Farm, VA, 206

Payne's Plantation, MS, 120
Pea Ridge Prairie, MO, 129
Pea Ridge, AR, 41
Pea Ridge, TN, 168
Pea Vine Creek, GA, 63
Pea Vine Ridge, GA, 64
Pea Vine Valley, TN, 180
Peach Grove, VA, 217
Peach Orchard, VA, 195
Peachtree Creek, GA, 66
Pearl River, MS, 120, 123
Pease Creek, FL, 60
Pebbly Run, NC, 151
Peck's House, TN, 181
Peeble's Farm, VA, 214
Pekin, IN, 77
Peletier's Mill, NC, 153
Pelham, TN, 176
Pemberton, John C., 8, 70
Pemiscot Bayou, AR, 46
Pennsylvania, 10, 159
Pensacola, FL, 59, 60
Peralta, NM, 149
Perche Hills, MO, 142
Perkins' Mill, TN, 172
Perry County, AR, 47, 49
Perry, Steve, 62
Perryville, Indian Territory, 80
Perryville, KY, 88
Perry's Ferry, MS, 118
Petersburg Gap, WV, 226
Petersburg Lines, VA, 211
Petersburg, TN, 173
Petersburg, VA, 210, 211, 217
Petersburg, WV, 222, 225, 227-229
Petit Jean, AR, 48
Petite Anse Island, LA, 96
Peytona, WV, 222
Peyton's Mill, MS, 116
Phelps' Bayou, LA, 97
Philadelphia, TN, 177, 178, 180, 186
Philippi, WV, 221, 223
Phillips' Cross-Roads, NC, 155
Phillips' Fork, KY, 90
Philomont, VA, 197, 198
Pickett's Mill, GA, 66
Piedmont Station, VA, 201
Piedmont, VA, 193, 207, 210, 215

Piedmont, WV, 229
Pig Point, VA, 191
Pigeon Hills, TN, 180
Pigeon Mountain, GA, 64
Pigeon's Ranch, NM, 149
Piggot's Mill, WV, 222
Pike County, KY, 90, 92
Pike Creek, MO, 134
Piketon, KY, 85, 88, 89, 93
Pikeville, NC, 156
Pillowville, TN, 179
Pilot Knob, MO, 132, 140
Pin Hook, LA, 97
Pinckney Island, SC, 162
Pine Bluff, AR, 44, 47, 48, 50
Pine Bluff, TN, 183
Pine Hill, GA, 66
Pine Island, SC, 163
Pine Log Creek, GA, 65
Pine Mountain, TN, 169, 170
Pineberry Battery, SC, 162
Pineville, LA, 100
Pineville, MO, 131, 134, 135
Piney Branch Church, VA, 209
Piney Factory, TN, 179
Piney Mountain, AR, 46
Piney River, MO, 137
Pink Hill, MO, 130, 131
Pinos Altos Mines, NM, 150
Pinos Altos, AZ, 39
Pisgah, MO, 139
Pitman's Cross-Roads, KY, 88
Pitman's Ferry, AR, 42
Pittsburg Landing, TN, 167
Pittsburg, TN, 167
Pitt's Cross-Roads, TN, 178
Plains Store Road, LA, 97
Plains Store, LA, 97
plantation, 3, 23, 34-37, 42, 43, 48, 61, 69, 96, 98, 100-103, 116, 118-123, 151, 162, 164, 165, 209, 237, 238
plantations, 96
Plantersville, AL, 38
Plaquemine, LA, 96, 97, 102
Platte Bridge, Dakota Territory, 58
Platte City, MO, 138
Platte County, MO, 132, 138
Platte Valley (steamboat), 129
Plattsburg, MO, 138

Pleasant Hill Landing, LA, 100
Pleasant Hill Landing, TN, 182
Pleasant Hill, GA, 70
Pleasant Hill, LA, 100
Pleasant Hill, MO, 131, 135, 137, 139
Pleasureville, KY, 92
Plentytude, MS, 123
Plum Butte, KS, 84
Plum Creek, NE, 145
Plum Point, TN, 168
Plymouth, NC, 152, 154
Po River, VA, 209
Pocahontas County, WV, 225
Pocahontas, AR, 41
Pocahontas, MO, 137
Pocotah, SC, 164
Pocotaligo Road, SC, 164
Pocotaligo, SC, 162, 164
Pohick Church, VA, 191, 192, 205
Pohick Run, VA, 192
Poindexter's Farm, VA, 195
Point Isabel, TX, 187, 188
Point of Rocks, KS, 84
Point of Rocks, MD, 107-109
Point of Rocks, VA, 195
Point Pleasant, LA, 101
Point Pleasant, MO, 130
Point Pleasant, WV, 224, 225
Point Washington, FL, 60
Poison Creek, Idaho Territory, 73
Poison Spring, AR, 47
Pole Cat Creek, VA, 210
political parties, 13, 14
political party, 17
politically incorrect, 240
politics, 236, 299
Polk's Plantation, AR, 43
Pollard, AL, 37
Pollocksville Road, NC, 152
Pomeroy, OH, 157
Pomme de Terre, MO, 128
Pon Pon River, SC, 162
Ponca (tribe), 231
Ponchatoula, LA, 96, 97
Pond Creek, KY, 90, 92
Pond Spring, AL, 37
Pond Springs, AL, 36
Pontotoc, MS, 118, 122, 123
Pony Mountain, VA, 203

Pooler Station, GA, 69
Poolesville, MD, 107
Pope's Island, SC, 162
Poplar Bluff, MO, 137
Poplar Grove Church, VA, 214
Poplar Spring Church, VA, 214
Poplar Springs Church, VA, 214
Poplar Springs, MD, 108
Port Conway, VA, 203
Port Deposit, AL, 34
Port Gibson, MS, 118, 121, 124, 125
Port Hudson, LA, 95-97, 99-102
Port Republic, VA, 194, 210, 214
Port Royal Ferry, SC, 161, 162
Port Royal, SC, 161
Port Walthall Junction, VA, 208, 209
Porter's Plantation, LA, 96
Portland Harbor, ME, 105
Portland, MO, 134
Portland, WV, 225
Portsmouth, VA, 208
Post Oak Creek, MO, 130
Potecasi Creek, NC, 153
Potomac Creek, VA, 191
Potomac River, WV, 225
Potts' Hill, AR, 41
Pound Gap, KY, 86, 92
Powder River, 26
Powder River, Dakota Territory, 58
Powder River, Montana Territory, 143
Powder River, MT, 26
Powder Springs Gap, TN, 175
Powder Springs, GA, 66, 67
Powell River, TN, 168
Powell Valley, TN, 176
Powell's Big Fort Valley, VA, 195
Powell's Bridge, TN, 182, 207
Powell's River, VA, 206
Powhatan, VA, 216
Prairie Chapel, MO, 133
Prairie Du Rocher, IL, 75
Prairie D'Ane, AR, 46
Prairie Grove, AR, 43, 46
Prairie Station, MS, 122
Prentiss, MS, 116
presentism, 18, 19
preservationist, 299

Presidio del Norte, NM, 150
Presley, Elvis, 299
Presley, Lisa M., 299
Preston, MO, 138
Prestonburg, KY, 86, 89
Price, Sterling, 8
Price's Landing, MO, 129
Prim's Blacksmith Shop, TN, 171
Prince Edward Court House, VA, 218
Prince George Court House, VA, 216
Prince William County, VA, 200
Princeton Court House, WV, 223
Princeton, AR, 44, 47
Princeton, VA, 208
Princeton, WV, 222, 223
Pritchard's Mill, VA, 192
pro-Union, 22
Proctor's Creek, VA, 209
products, 23
propagandizing, main function of mainstream history, 28
Prophet Bridge, MS, 117
prostitution, 3
Providence Church Road, VA, 200
Providence Church, VA, 198, 199, 201
Pryor's Creek, Indian Territory, 80
Pueblo Colorado, NM, 150
Pulaski, TN, 168, 169, 176, 178, 183, 184
Pulliam's, MO, 136
Pungo Landing, NC, 153
Purdy Road, TN, 167
Purgitsville, WV, 225
Putnam, MO, 133
Quaker Road, VA, 217
Quarles Mills, VA, 209
Queen of the West (steamer), 116
Queen's Hill, MS, 120, 122
Quicksand Creek, KY, 92
Quincy, MO, 136, 141
Quinn's Mill, MS, 121
Quinn's Mills, MS, 119
Quitman, AR, 46, 49
Raccoon Ford, VA, 201, 203, 204, 206
Raccourci, LA, 102
Ragland Mills, KY, 91

Raiford's Plantation, MS, 122
Raleigh, NC, 156
Raleigh, TN, 182
rallies, 29
Rally Hill, TN, 185
Ramer's Crossing, MS, 116
Rancho Las Rinas, TX, 188
Randolph County, AR, 49
Randolph, AL, 38
Rankin's Ferry, TN, 168
Rapidan River, VA, 204, 207
Rapidan Station, VA, 193, 196, 201, 203
Rappahannock Bridge, VA, 205
Rappahannock County, VA, 193
Rappahannock River, VA, 191, 193, 196, 198, 202
Rappahannock Station, VA, 193, 196, 198, 205
Ratliff's Landing, LA, 101
Ravenswood, WV, 223, 224, 226, 227
Rawle's Mill, NC, 152
Ray County, MO, 138, 142
Raymond, MS, 118, 119
Raytown, MO, 131
Readsville, MO, 142
Readyville, TN, 168, 178, 183
Reagan, 77
Reagan, John H., 77
Reams Station, VA, 211, 213
rebellion, 236, 237
reconnoissance, 64, 129, 152, 164, 167, 196
Reconstruction, 2, 13, 235, 236, 240
Rectortown, VA, 207, 215
Rector's Farm, AR, 49
Red Bird Creek, KY, 86, 90
Red Bone, MS, 123
Red Chief (C.S. steamer), 97
Red Clay, GA, 65
Red House, WV, 221
Red Mound, AR, 46
Red Mound, TN, 172
Red Oak, GA, 67
Red River, LA, 97, 98, 100, 101
Red River, NM, 150
Redmount Camp, AR, 48
Reed's Bridge, AR, 44
Reed's Bridge, GA, 64

Reed's Ferry, VA, 201
Reed's Mountain, AR, 43
Reeves' Mill, MO, 141
Reeves' Point, NC, 155
Release (U.S. steamer), 191
religion, 299
Rennight's Mills, MO, 128
Republican Party, 13, 14, 18, 236
Resaca, GA, 65, 68
Resolute (steamer), 49
reunion, 17, 19, 62, 237
Revolutionary War, 15, 299
Revolutionary War, American, 299
Reynoldsburg, TN, 182
Reynolds' Station, TN, 169
re-enactments, 29
Rheatown, TN, 177, 178, 183, 184
Rhea's Mill, AR, 43
Rhea's Mills, AR, 46
rice, 57
Rice's Station, VA, 218
Rich Mountain, WV, 221
Richardson, John, 237
Richard's Ford, VA, 204
Richfield, MO, 135
Richland Creek, AR, 46-48
Richland Creek, TN, 169, 170, 184, 185
Richland Plantation, LA, 103
Richland Station, TN, 174
Richland, AR, 49, 50
Richmond Fortifications, VA, 209
Richmond, KY, 86, 91
Richmond, LA, 96, 97
Richmond, MO, 138
Richmond, VA, 76, 110, 194, 207, 211
Richwoods, MO, 140
Riddle's Point, MO, 130
Riddle's Shop, VA, 195, 211
Ridgely, MO, 137, 140
Rienzi, MS, 115, 116, 120
Riggin's Hill, TN, 170
Ringgold Gap, GA, 64, 65
Ringgold, GA, 64, 69
Rio de las Animas, NM, 150
Rio Hondo, NM, 150
Ripley, MS, 116, 117, 120, 121, 123

Ripley, TN, 172
Rising Sun, TN, 168
Ritchie Court House, WV, 226
Rivers' Bridge, SC, 164
Rixeyville Ford, VA, 203
Rixeyville, VA, 205
Rixey's Ford, VA, 203
Roane County, WV, 223, 227
Roanoke Island, NC, 151
Roanoke Station, VA, 211
Roanoke, MO, 133, 139
Roan's Tan-Yard, MO, 129
Roaring Spring, KY, 92
Robertson's Ford, VA, 203
Robertson's River, VA, 204
Robertson's Tavern, VA, 206
Robertsville, SC, 164
Roberts' Ford, LA, 97
Robinson's Mills, MS, 121
Rocheport, MO, 135, 139, 142
Rock Creek Ford, TN, 176
Rock Creek, Dakota Territory, 58
Rock Cut, AL, 34
Rock Spring, GA, 64
Rock Spring, TN, 172
Rockcastle Hills, KY, 85
Rockcastle River, KY, 88
Rockfish Gap, VA, 214
Rockford, TN, 179
Rockingham, NC, 155
Rockport, AR, 46
Rockville, MD, 108, 109
Rockville, OH, 157
Rocky Bluff, MO, 132
Rocky Creek Bridge, GA, 70
Rocky Creek Church, GA, 69
Rocky Creek, MS, 119
Rocky Face Ridge, GA, 65
Rocky Ford, MS, 119
Rocky Gap, KY, 90
Rocky Gap, WV, 226
Rocky Hill, KY, 88
Rocky Hock Creek, NC, 153
Rocky Mount, SC, 165
Rocky Mountains, 299
Rocky Run, NC, 154
Rodgers' Crossing, AR, 49
Rodman's Point, NC, 153
Rodney, MS, 121, 123, 125
Rogersville, KY, 90
Rogersville, TN, 179, 183, 185

Rogers' Gap, TN, 168, 169, 175
Rolla, MO, 139, 141, 142
Rolling Fork, MS, 124
Rolling Prairie, AR, 45
Rome, 62, 68
Rome, GA, 62, 65, 68
Rome, TN, 171
Romney, WV, 222, 225
Roosevelt, Theodore, 52
Rosedale, LA, 102
Roseville Creek, AR, 45
Roseville, AR, 46
Ross Landing, AR, 45
Rossville, GA, 64
Roswell, GA, 67
Rottenwood Creek, GA, 66
Rough and Ready Station, GA, 67
Rough and Ready, GA, 68
Rough Riders, 52
Round Grove, Indian Territory, 79
Round Hill, AR, 42
Round Mountain, AL, 36
Round Mountain, Indian Territory, 79
Round Mountain, TN, 169
Round Ponds, MO, 135
Rover, TN, 173, 175, 176
Rowan County, KY, 90
Rowanty Creek, VA, 216
Rowell's Run, WV, 222
Rowlesburg, WV, 225
Rowlett's Station, KY, 85
Rucker, Edmund W., 299
Ruckersville, MS, 116
Rude's Hill, VA, 193, 209, 216, 217
Ruff's Mill, GA, 66
Ruff's Station, GA, 68
ruins, 110
Rural Hill, TN, 171
Rush Creek, NE, 147
Russellville, AL, 33, 37
Russellville, KY, 86, 87, 90
Russellville, MO, 140
Russellville, TN, 180, 184
Russell's Ford, VA, 204
Russell's house, MS, 115
Rutherford Creek, TN, 174
Rutherford's Creek, TN, 185
Rutherford's Farm, VA, 212

Rutherford's Station, TN, 171
Rutledge, MO, 139
Rutledge, TN, 180
Sabine Cross-Roads, LA, 100
Sabine Pass, TX, 187, 188
Sacramento Mountains, NM, 150
Sacramento, KY, 85
Sage Creek, CO, 54
Sailor's Creek, VA, 218
Saint Andrew's Bay, FL, 59
Saint Augustine, FL, 59, 60
Saint Charles Court House, LA, 96
Saint Charles, AR, 42, 49, 50
Saint Charles, LA, 102
Saint Francis Road, AR, 43
Saint Francisville, LA, 102
Saint Francisville, MO, 129
Saint George, WV, 225
Saint Helena Island, SC, 162
Saint James, MO, 137
Saint John's Bluff, FL, 59
Saint John's Mill, FL, 60
Saint John's River, FL, 61
Saint Joseph's Island, TX, 187
Saint Martinsville, LA, 99
Saint Mary's Church, VA, 211
Saint Mary's Station, Dakota Territory, 57
Saint Mary's Steamer, 98
Saint Peter's Church, VA, 211
Saint Stephen's Church, VA, 205
Salem Church, VA, 201, 210
Salem Heights, VA, 201
Salem, IN, 77
Salem, KY, 92
Salem, MO, 129, 131, 132, 136
Salem, MS, 121, 123
Salem, TN, 174, 175
Salem, VA, 193, 198, 211
Salient, the, VA, 209
Saline Bottom, AR, 47
Saline River, AR, 45
Salineville, OH, 157
Salisbury, NC, 156
Salkehatchie River, SC, 164
Salt Lick Bridge, WV, 227
Salt River, MO, 131
Salt Springs, GA, 67
salt works, 216
Saltville, VA, 215
Salyersville, KY, 91, 92
Samuel Orr (steamboat), 85
San Andres Mountains, NM, 150
San Bois Creek, Indian Territory, 80
San Luis Pass, TX, 187
Sand Creek, CO, 53
Sand Mountain, 34
Sand Mountain, AL, 34, 35
Sand Mountain, GA, 67
Sandersville, GA, 68
Sandtown, GA, 67
Sandusky, OH, 82
Sandy Hook, MD, 107, 109
Sandy Ridge, NC, 152, 153
Sandy River, WV, 227
Sandy Swamp, NC, 154
Sangster Station, VA, 192
Sangster's Station, VA, 206
Santa Fe Road, MO, 130
Santa Fe Road, NM, 150
Santa Fe, MO, 131
Santa Rosa Island, FL, 59
Sappony Church, VA, 211
Saratoga, KY, 85
Satartia, MS, 121, 122
Sauk Centre, MN, 113
Saulsbury, TN, 169
Saunders, FL, 60, 61
Saunders' Farm, NC, 156
Savage's Station, VA, 195
Savannah Creek, SC, 165
Savannah, GA, 69
Sayler's Creek, VA, 218
Scary Creek, WV, 221
Scatterville, AR, 42, 48
scholars, 7, 28
school, 195, 236
Schultz's Mill, TN, 181
Schuyler County, MO, 131
science, 22, 235, 299
Scotland, 134
Scotland County, MO, 134
Scott County, VA, 215
Scott, George C., 299
Scottsville Road, KY, 86
Scottsville, AL, 38
Scottsville, KY, 90, 91
Scott's Cross-Roads, VA, 217
Scott's Ford, MO, 136
Scullyville, Indian Territory, 80
sculptures, 29

Scupperton, NC, 153
SCV, 5, 29
Sea Raven Press, 3, 5, 6, 17, 20, 218, 238-240, 301
Seabrook, Lochlainn, 6, 29, 299, 301
Searcy County, AR, 48
Searcy Landing, AR, 41
Searcy, AR, 47-49
Sears' Ford, MO, 132
Sears' House, MO, 131
Sebago (U.S. steamer), 36
secession, 2, 15, 236, 237, 239, 301
Secessionville, SC, 162, 163
Second Co. Stuart Horse Virginia Light Artillery Battery, 190
Second Creek, WV, 227
Second Virginia Infantry Regiment, 190
Sedalia and Marshall Road, MO, 138
Sedalia, MO, 131, 140
Seivers' Ford, VA, 214
Selma, AL, 38
Seminoles (tribe), 231
Senatobia, MS, 119, 122
Seneca Creek, MD, 107
Seneca Mills, MD, 107, 108
Seneca Trace Crossing, WV, 227
Seneca, MD, 108
Sequatchie Valley, TN, 178, 182
servant, 62
servants, 62
Seven Pines, VA, 194
Sevierville Road, TN, 182
Sevierville, TN, 181, 182
Sewell's Point, VA, 191, 193
Sexton's Station, VA, 210
Shady Grove, GA, 69
Shady Grove, VA, 210
Shallow Creek, VA, 210
Shallow Ford Gap, TN, 177
Shallow Ford, AR, 44
Shallow Ford, NC, 156
Shanghai, MO, 129, 137
Shanghai, WV, 226
Shannon County, MO, 136
Shannon's Cross-Roads, VA, 201
Sharon, MS, 123
Sharpsburg, KY, 93

Sharpsburg, MD, 108
Shaver Mountain, WV, 227
Sheffield, TX, 80
Shelbina, MO, 138
Shelby County, KY, 93
Shelbyville Pike, TN, 172, 173, 175
Shelbyville Road, TN, 168
Shelbyville, KY, 86
Shelbyville, TN, 176, 178, 185
Sheldon's Place, Indian Territory, 80
Shellmound, TN, 177
Shell's Mill, MO, 134
Shenandoah (C.S.S. cruiser), 56
Shenandoah River, VA, 193
Shepherdstown Ford, WV, 224
Shepherdstown, WV, 222, 224-226, 228, 229
Shepherdsville Road, KY, 87
Shepherdsville, KY, 87, 90
Sherwood, MO, 134, 135
Shiloh, MO, 130
Shiloh, TN, 167
Ship Island, MS, 115
shipping, 192, 196
Shipping Point, VA, 192
Ship's Gap, GA, 68
Shirley, VA, 195
Shirley's Ford, MO, 133
Shoal Creek, AL, 35, 37
Shoal Creek, TN, 180
Short Mountain Cross-Roads, TN, 169
shrines, 29
Shut-in Gap, MO, 140
Sibley County, KY, 93
Sibley, MO, 133, 135
siege, 23, 25, 36, 38, 95, 115, 130, 153, 167, 179, 193, 200, 211, 224
siege of Spanish Fort, 23
Signal (U.S.S. steamship), 101
Sikeston, MO, 130, 137, 140, 141
Silver Creek, MO, 129
Silver Springs, TN, 171
Simkins Battery, SC, 163
Simmon's Bluff, SC, 162
Simpsonville, KY, 93
Simpson's Creek, WV, 226
Simsport, LA, 97, 101

Sims' Cove, MO, 133
Sims' Farm, TN, 178
Sinking Creek, MO, 132
Sipsey Creek, AL, 38
Sir John's Run, WV, 223, 228
Sister's Ferry, GA, 69
Six-Mile Creek, AL, 38
Sixteenth South Carolina Infantry Regiment, 220
Sixth Virginia Infantry Regiment, 298
Skaggs, Ricky, 299
skirmish, 22, 23, 25, 33-39, 41-51, 53-55, 57-61, 63-71, 73, 77, 79, 80, 83-93, 95-103, 107-110, 113, 115-125, 127-142, 145, 147, 149-157, 159-165, 167-186, 188, 191-218, 221-231
Slane's Cross-Roads, WV, 223
Slate Creek, KY, 89
Slatersville, VA, 193
Slaughter's Gap, MD, 108
Slaughter's House, VA, 196
Slaughter's Mountain, VA, 196
slavery, 2, 17, 62, 235, 237, 239, 301
slaves, 236
Smith, Edmund K., 8
Smithfield Crossing, WV, 229
Smithfield, NC, 156
Smithfield, VA, 196, 203
Smithfield, WV, 225, 227, 229
Smithsburg, MD, 109
Smithville, AR, 42, 46
Smithville, NC, 155
Smithville, TN, 175
Smith's Bridge, MS, 119, 121
Smith's Creek, NC, 155
Smith's Cross-Roads, TN, 178
Smith's Ford, TN, 174
Smith's Mills, KY, 92
Smith's Mills, NC, 155
Smith's Plantation, LA, 101
Smith's Shoals, KY, 91
Smith's Station, NE, 145
Smith's Store, VA, 211
Smith's, KY, 87
Smoky Hill Crossing, KS, 84
Smoky Hill, KS, 84
Smyrna, FL, 59

Snake Creek Gap, GA, 65, 67, 68
Snake Creek, AR, 50
Snapfinger Creek, GA, 66
Sneedville, TN, 184
Snickersville, VA, 197, 208
Snicker's Ferry, VA, 200, 212
Snicker's Gap, VA, 198, 202, 214, 216
Snow Hill, NC, 156
Snow Hill, TN, 174, 175
Snow's Pond, KY, 87
Snyder's Bluff, MS, 118, 123
Snyder's Mill, MS, 117, 118
socialism, 14, 17, 236, 237
socialist, 13, 17, 18, 236, 237, 297
socialists, 15
Socorro, NM, 149
soldiers, 2, 3, 7, 8, 22, 40, 62, 75, 78, 81, 144, 158, 189, 239, 240, 299
Solomon's Gap, MD, 109
Somerset, KY, 89
Somerton Road, VA, 200
Somerville Ford, VA, 203
Somerville Heights, VA, 193
Somerville Road, AL, 36
Somerville, TN, 171, 172, 174, 181
Somerville, VA, 199
Sons of Confederate Veterans, 17, 22, 29, 114
Sons of Union Veterans, 29
South, 2, 3, 5, 10, 15, 16, 18, 19, 22, 26-29, 62, 108, 110, 146, 147, 151, 154, 161, 164-166, 183, 189, 193, 217, 220, 236, 237, 239, 240, 299
South Anna Bridge, VA, 201, 202, 217
South Branch Bridge, WV, 222, 228
South Carolina, 10, 26, 161, 220
South Edisto River, SC, 164
South Mills, NC, 151, 153
South Mountain, MD, 108
South Newport, GA, 67
South Quay Bridge, VA, 201
South Quay Road, VA, 200
South Quay, VA, 217
South River, GA, 68

South River, NC, 155
South Side Railroad, VA, 217
South Union, KY, 90
Southerland's Farm, KY, 87
Southern battle names, 24
Southern Cause, 3, 239
Southern Confederacy, 2, 3, 81, 239, 240
Southern point of view, 22
Southern states, 27, 236
Southerners, 2, 3, 13, 15, 16, 18, 24-26, 166, 240
Southwest Creek, NC, 152, 154, 155
South's perspective, 19
Spangler's Mill, AL, 33
Spanish Fort, AL, 23, 37
Sparta, NC, 153
Sparta, TN, 169, 176, 179
Spaulding's, GA, 63
Spavinaw, AR, 47
Spencer's Ranch, NM, 150
Spirit Lake, MN, 113
Sporting Hill, PA, 159
Spotsylvania Court House, VA, 23, 208
Spottsylvania Court House, VA, 201
Spring Creek, AR, 45
Spring Creek, GA, 64
Spring Creek, MO, 133
Spring Creek, TN, 171
Spring Dale Bridge, MS, 117
Spring Hill, GA, 70
Spring Hill, MO, 128
Spring Hill, TN, 23, 174, 182, 185
Spring Island, SC, 163
Spring Place, GA, 69
Spring River Mills, MO, 135
Spring River, AR, 41, 45, 46
Spring River, MO, 133
Spring Valley, MO, 142
Springfield Landing, LA, 98
Springfield Road, LA, 97
Springfield Station, VA, 192
Springfield, GA, 69
Springfield, KY, 88, 89
Springfield, LA, 97
Springfield, MO, 49, 128, 129, 134

Springfield, OH, 157
Springfield, WV, 222, 228
Spurgeon's Mill, TN, 178
squirrel, 209
Squirrel Creek Crossing, CO, 51
St. Albans raid, 189
St. Albans, VT, 189
Stafford Court House, VA, 203
Stanardsville, VA, 207, 208
Stanard's Mill, VA, 209
Standing Stone, WV, 224
Stanford, KY, 88, 91
Star House, MO, 142
Starlight (C.S. steamer), 97
Stars and Bars, 29
State Line, MO, 141
Statesboro, GA, 69
Statesburg, SC, 165
states' rights, 13, 14
Station Four, FL, 61
Station No. 5, Georgia Central Railroad, GA, 69
Statuary Hall, 114
statues, 29
Staunton River Bridge, VA, 211
Staunton, VA, 58
steamboat, 85, 129
Steele's Bayou, MS, 124
Steelville, MO, 139
Stephens, Alexander H., 13, 16, 77, 299
Stephenson Station, VA, 192
Stephenson's Depot, VA, 212, 213
Steubenville, OH, 157
Stevensburg, VA, 196, 200, 202-205
Stevenson, AL, 33, 35
Stevenson's Gap, AL, 37
Stevens' Furnace, PA, 160
Stevens' Gap, GA, 63, 64
Stewartsboro, TN, 174
Stewart's Creek Bridge, TN, 172
Stewart's Creek, TN, 172
Stewart's Ferry, TN, 171
Stewart's Plantation, AR, 42
Stickleyville, VA, 206
Stilesboro, GA, 65, 66
Stirling's Plantation, LA, 98
Stock Creek, TN, 179
stockade, 82, 89, 101, 185
Stockbridge, GA, 68

Stockton, MO, 132, 135, 136
Stone Chapel, VA, 213
Stone Church, GA, 65
Stone County, MO, 135
Stoner Bridge, KY, 89
Stone's Mill, TN, 180
Stone's River, 25, 171, 172, 178
Stone's River Railroad Bridge, TN, 178
Stone's River, TN, 171, 172, 176
Stono River, SC, 163
Stony Creek Depot, VA, 211
Stony Creek Station, VA, 208, 216
Stony Creek, VA, 193, 211
Stony Lake, ND, 55
Stony Point, AR, 47
Strasburg, VA, 192, 194, 199, 201, 204, 206, 207, 209, 213-215
Strawberry Hill, VA, 209
Strawberry Plains, TN, 175, 181, 182, 184
Strawberry Plains, VA, 212
Street's Ferry, NC, 153
Strother Fork, MO, 133
Stroud's Mill, SC, 165
Stroud's Store, AR, 44
Stuart, Jeb, 8
Stuart's, VA, 205
Stubbs, William, 13
students, 28
Stumptown, MO, 135
Sturgeon, MO, 142
Subligna, GA, 64
Suffolk, VA, 199, 200, 202, 208
sugar, 41, 103, 131, 155
Sugar Creek, 41, 131
Sugar Creek, AR, 41, 42
Sugar Creek, MO, 131
Sugar Creek, TN, 178, 185
Sugar Loaf Hill, NC, 155
Sugar Loaf Mountain, MD, 108
Sugar Loaf Prairie, AR, 50
Sugar Loaf, NC, 155
Sugar Valley, GA, 65
Sullivan's Island Batteries, SC, 163
Sulphur Branch Trestle, AL, 36
Sulphur Springs Road, AL, 35
Sulphur Springs, AR, 45
Sulphur Springs, TN, 178, 182
Sulphur Springs, VA, 196, 198, 204, 205
Summerfield, AL, 38
Summertown, TN, 177
Summerville, GA, 63, 68, 70
Summerville, WV, 224, 226
Summit Point, WV, 227, 229
Sumterville, SC, 165
Sunnyside Landing, AR, 48
Sunshine Sisters, the, 299
Sutherland's Station, VA, 217
Sutton, WV, 226, 227, 229
SUV (Sons of Union Veterans), 29
Swallow Bluffs, TN, 178
Swan Lake, AR, 47
Swan Quarter, NC, 152
Swann's Island, TN, 182
Sweeden's Cove, TN, 168
Sweet Sulphur Springs, WV, 228
Sweet Water, TN, 177, 178, 186
Sweetwater Station, Dakota Territory, 57
Swift Creek Village, NC, 153
Swift Creek, NC, 156
Swift Creek, VA, 209
Switzler's Mill, MO, 132, 135, 142
Swoope's Depot, VA, 216
Sycamore Church, VA, 196, 212, 213
Sycamore Springs, AZ, 39
Sylamore, AR, 41, 45
Sylvan Grove, GA, 68
Syracuse, MO, 136
Tabernacle Church, VA, 218
Taberville, MO, 131, 132
Tahkahokuty Mountain, 57
Tahkahokuty Mountain, ND, 57
Tait's Ferry, KY, 86
Talbott's Station, TN, 181
Talbot's Ferry, AR, 41, 50
Tallahatchie River, 119
Tallahatchie River, MS, 117, 119, 122, 124
Tallahatchie, MS, 123
Tallulah, LA, 95
Tampa, FL, 52, 59, 60
Tap's Gap, AL, 35
Tarboro, NC, 153
Taylor, Richard, 8, 16, 94
Taylorsville, KY, 93
Taylorsville, VA, 207

Taylortown, VA, 216
Taylor's Bayou, TX, 187
Taylor's Creek, AR, 43
Taylor's Farm, MO, 135
Taylor's Hole Creek, NC, 155
Taylor's Ridge, GA, 64, 65
Tazewell, TN, 168, 169, 177, 181, 186
Teche Bayou, LA, 96, 98
Telford's Station, TN, 177
Ten Island Ford, AL, 36
Ten-Mile Run, FL, 60
Tennessee, 3, 10, 167, 168, 171, 177, 179, 180, 182-184, 238, 299
Tennessee River, 177, 179, 184
Tennessee River, TN, 177, 179, 184
Terman's Ferry, KY, 91
Terre Noir Creek, AR, 46
Texas, 10, 102, 141, 187
Texas County, MO, 141
Texas Prairie, MO, 135
The Bittersweet Bond (Seabrook), 18, 166
the Left, 18, 19, 62
the North, 2, 146, 147, 212, 239
The Orchard, VA, 195
The Park, LA, 103
The Ponds, MS, 124
The Rise and Fall of the Confederate Government (Davis), 17, 218
The South, 15, 16, 19, 22, 27, 29, 62, 146, 154, 189, 236, 237, 240
The Unholy Crusade (Seabrook), 110
the West, 116
Thibodeaux, LA, 98
Third Virginia Cavalry Regiment, 106
Thomasville, MO, 139
Thomas' Station, GA, 69
Thompson's Bridge, NC, 152
Thompson's Creek, LA, 97
Thompson's Creek, SC, 165
Thompson's Cross-Roads, VA, 201
Thompson's Plantation, LA, 103
Thompson's Station, TN, 173-175, 185
Thorn Hill, AL, 37
Thorn Hill, TN, 184
Thornburg, VA, 196
Thoroughfare Gap, VA, 197, 202
Thoroughfare Mountain, VA, 207
Tickfaw Bridge, LA, 97
Tickfaw River, LA, 97
Tilton, GA, 65
Timberville, VA, 214
Tippah River, MS, 123
Tipton, MO, 136, 139
Tobesolkee Creek, GA, 70
Todd's Tavern, VA, 208
Tomahawk Gap, AR, 45
Tomahawk, AR, 45
Tompkinsville, KY, 86, 89
Tom's Brook, VA, 194, 215
Tongue River, Dakota Territory, 58
Toombs, Robert A., 77
Toone's Station, TN, 169
Totopotomoy Creek, VA, 210
Totopotomoy River, VA, 210
Totten's Plantation, MS, 116
Towaliga Bridge, GA, 68
Town Creek, AL, 34
Town Creek, NC, 155
Township, FL, 59
Tracy Battery, AL, 38
Tracy City, TN, 181, 183
trade shows, 29
traditionalism, 14
Tranter's Creek, NC, 152
Travisville, TN, 167
Treadwell's Plantation, MS, 121
Treadwell's, MS, 121
Trent River, NC, 154
Trent Road, NC, 152, 154
Trenton and Pollocksville Cross-Roads, NC, 152
Trenton Road, NC, 151
Trenton, AR, 42
Trenton, GA, 64
Trenton, NC, 153
Trenton, TN, 175
Trent's Reach, VA, 216
Trevilian Raid, VA, 210
Trevilian Station, VA, 210
Trevilian's Depot, VA, 193
Trinity, AL, 33

Trinity, LA, 98, 99
Trion Factory, GA, 64
Trion, AL, 38
Triplett's Bridge, KY, 90
Triune, TN, 172, 174, 175, 183, 186
Troublesome Creek, KY, 92
Trout Creek, FL, 60
Tullahoma, TN, 176
Tunica Bend, LA, 99, 100
Tunica County, MS, 116
Tunnel Hill, GA, 64, 65, 69
Tunnel Hill, KY, 88
Tunstall's Station, VA, 195, 201, 211
Tupelo, MS, 118, 124
Turkey Creek, VA, 212
Turkeytown, AL, 36
Turnback Creek, MO, 130
Turner's Farm, VA, 210
Turner's Ferry, GA, 68
Turner's Mills, VA, 199
Turner's Pass, MD, 108
Tuscaloosa, AL, 38
Tuscumbia, AL, 33-35, 37
Tuscumbia, MO, 141
Tuskegee, AL, 38
Twelve Years in Hell (Seabrook), 13
Twelve-Mile Ordinary, VA, 208
Twenty-Sixth South Carolina Infantry Regiment, 220
Two League Cross-Roads, SC, 165
Tyler (U.S.S. steamer/gunboat), 48
Tyler's Mills, MO, 140
Tyree Springs, TN, 170
Tyson's Cross-Roads, VA, 206
U.C.V. (United Confederate Veterans), 62
U.S. Capitol, 114
U.S. Capitol, Washington, D.C., 114
U.S. forces, 230
U.S. National Park Service, 22
U.S.A., 15, 16, 21
UDC, 29
UDC (United Daughters of the Confederacy), 29
unconstitutional acts, 28
Underwood's Farm, MO, 128

Undine (gunboat), 93
Union, 2, 6, 13, 14, 17, 22, 24, 29, 33, 34, 49, 65, 89-91, 95, 98, 101, 119, 138, 146, 171, 175, 177, 179, 189, 192, 196, 224, 226, 227, 235-237, 239, 240, 297
Union Church, MO, 138
Union Church, MS, 118
Union City, KY, 92
Union City, TN, 176, 177, 179, 182
Union forces, 22, 89, 95, 98, 171, 224
Union gunboats, 34, 101, 119
Union Mill, MO, 138
Union Mills, MO, 129
Union Mills, VA, 199
Union pickets, 33, 65, 91
Union Station, TN, 184
Union transports, 49, 175
Union, MO, 140
Union, MS, 122
Union, VA, 198
Union, WV, 227
Uniontown, KY, 86
Uniontown, MO, 134
Uniontown, TN, 176
Unionville, TN, 173
United Confederate Veterans, 16, 17, 19, 62, 237
United Daughters of the Confederacy, 29
United States, 2, 6, 14, 187, 235-237, 240
United States Ford, VA, 198
United States of America, 2, 6, 237, 240
University Depot, TN, 176
Upperville, VA, 201, 202, 204, 206, 207, 215
Upshaw's Farm, MO, 141
Upton's Hill, KY, 85
Urbana, MD, 109
Utica, MS, 118, 123
Utoy Creek, GA, 67
Utz's Ford, VA, 204
Vache Grass, AR, 49
Valley Bridge, SC, 164
Valley Mines, MO, 142
Valley Road, TN, 178

Valley Station, CO, 53, 54
Valley Woods, KY, 88
Valverde, NM, 149
Van Buren County, AR, 46
Van Buren, AR, 43, 46, 48, 50
Van Buren, MO, 132, 134
Van Buren, TN, 170
Van Wert, GA, 67
Vanceburg, KY, 93
Vanderburgh's House, VA, 192
Varnell's Station Road, GA, 65
Varnell's Station, GA, 65
Vaughan Road, VA, 213, 214, 217
Vaughn Road, VA, 214, 216
Vaught's Hill, TN, 174
Velasco, TX, 188
Venus Point, GA, 63
Vera Cruz, MO, 141
Vermillion Bayou, LA, 96, 98-100
Vermillionville, LA, 99
Vermont, 10, 189
Vernon Cross-Roads, MS, 121
Vernon River, GA, 69
Verona, MS, 124
Versailles, MO, 138
Via's House, VA, 210
Vicksburg, MS, 116, 119, 123
Victorian terminology, 23
Vidalia, LA, 98, 99, 101
Vienna, AL, 36
Vienna, VA, 191, 192
Village Creek, AR, 41, 42
Vincent's Creek, SC, 163
Vincent's Cross-Roads, MS, 121
Vine Prairie, AR, 43
Vinegar Hill, KY, 87
Virginia, 8, 10, 106, 190, 191, 218, 221, 232, 235, 298, 299
Voche, Mrs., 50
Volney, KY, 91
W. B. Terry (steamboat), 85
Waccamaw Neck, SC, 163
Waccomo Neck, NC, 154
Waddell's Farm, AR, 42
Wadesburg, MO, 129, 131
Wagner Battery, SC, 162, 163
Waitsboro, KY, 90
Walden's Ridge, TN, 168
Waldron, AR, 44, 45, 48
Walker, Leroy P., 77
Walkersville, MO, 130
Walkerton, VA, 208
Walker's Bridge, SC, 164
Walker's Ford, TN, 180
Wall Hill, MS, 122
Wallace's Cross-Roads, TN, 168
Wallace's Ferry, AR, 48
Walls Bridge, LA, 97
Walnut Creek, GA, 68
Walnut Creek, KS, 84
Walnut Creek, MO, 132
Walnut Hill, MS, 118
Wapping Heights, VA, 202
war, 2, 3, 5-7, 13-19, 21, 23, 24, 28, 29, 40, 62, 77, 114, 146, 189, 236-240, 297, 299, 301
War Against Northern Aggression, 16
War Between the States, 2, 5-7, 17, 21, 29, 240
war crimes, 28
War for Southern Independence, 6, 14, 16
War for the Constitution, 16, 21, 28
Wardensville, WV, 223, 225
Warder's Church, MO, 138
Ware Bottom Church, VA, 209
Ware's Point, VA, 199
Warfield's, TN, 185
Warm Springs, NC, 153, 154
Warm Springs, WV, 226
Warner (steamship), 101
Warrensburg Road, MO, 139
Warrensburg, MO, 128, 130, 131, 137-139, 142
Warrenton batteries, MS, 117
Warrenton Junction, VA, 197, 201
Warrenton Springs, VA, 198
Warrenton, MO, 141
Warrenton, VA, 199, 201, 204, 205, 207
Warsaw, MO, 130, 136
Warsaw, NC, 153
Warsaw, VA, 217
Wartburg, TN, 175
Wartrace, TN, 168, 177
Warwick Road, VA, 193
Warwick Swamp, VA, 212
Washington County, AR, 50
Washington County, MO, 138

Washington Louisiana Light
  Artillery Battery, 148
Washington, AR, 47, 50
Washington, D.C., 6, 10, 14, 27,
  114, 219, 235, 236, 240
Washington, George, 15
Washington, LA, 96, 97, 99
Washington, NC, 152, 153
Washington, OH, 157
Washington, TN, 182
Washita Cove, AR, 45
Water Valley, MS, 117
Wateree River, SC, 165
Waterford, VA, 197, 199, 203,
  209
Waterhouse's Mill, TN, 183
Waterloo Bridge, VA, 196
Waterloo, AL, 37
Waterloo, LA, 97, 102
Waterloo, VA, 198
Waterproof, LA, 100
Watkins House, VA, 217
Watkins' Ferry, GA, 63
Watkins' Plantation, AL, 36
Wauhatchie, TN, 179
Waverly, MO, 131, 135
Waverly, TN, 170, 173
Wayland Springs, TN, 180
Wayman's Mill, MO, 133
Wayne County, MO, 137
Wayne Court House, WV, 222
Waynesboro, GA, 68
Waynesboro, VA, 210, 214
Waynesville, MO, 131, 135, 136,
  140-142
wealth, 3
Weaverville, VA, 203, 205
Webber's Falls, Indian Territory,
  80
Webster County, WV, 223
Webster, MO, 138, 139
Weems' Springs, TN, 176
Welaka, FL, 60, 61
Welch's Spring, WV, 229
Weldon Railroad, VA, 211
Welford's Ford, VA, 203
Wellington, MO, 135
Wells' Hill, TN, 184
Wells' Plantation, LA, 101
Wentzville, MO, 127
West Branch, VA, 200

West Bridge, AL, 33
West Chickamauga Creek, GA, 64
West Creek, WV, 226
West Fork, WV, 224
West Harpeth River, TN, 185
West Liberty, KY, 87, 91
West Plains, MO, 129
West Point, AR, 44, 48
West Point, VA, 193, 200
West Union, WV, 226
West Virginia, 10, 221, 299
Westbrook's, GA, 67
Westminster, MD, 109
Weston, KY, 93
Weston, WV, 224
Westport, MO, 135, 141
West's Cross-Roads, SC, 165
Wet Glaze, MO, 128
Wetumpka, AL, 38
Weyer's Cave, VA, 214
Whaley's Mill, MO, 133
Wheeler, Joseph, 8, 52
Whig party, 14
Whippoorwill Creek, KY, 85
Whippy Swamp Creek, SC, 164
Whippy Swamp, SC, 164
Whistler Bridge, AL, 38
Whistler, William G. M., 75
White Cloud (steamer), 102, 124
White County, AR, 45
White County, TN, 181
White Hall Bridge, NC, 152
White Hall, NC, 152
White Hare, MO, 138
White House, 13
White House, SC, 162
White House, VA, 195, 211
White Oak Bayou, MS, 116
White Oak Creek, AR, 46, 48, 49
White Oak Creek, NC, 152
White Oak Creek, TN, 186
White Oak Ridge, MO, 132
White Oak Ridge, VA, 217
White Oak Road, VA, 217
White Oak Springs, KY, 92
White Oak Springs, TN, 170
White Oak Swamp Bridge, VA,
  196
White Oak Swamp, VA, 195, 211
White Plains, VA, 203, 215
White Point, SC, 162, 163

White Pond, SC, 164
White Post, VA, 202, 213
White Range, TN, 171
White River Station, AR, 48
White River, AR, 42, 43, 46, 49
White River, MO, 132, 134
White Springs, AR, 43
White Stone Hill, ND, 55
White Sulphur Springs, WV, 226
White Water Bridge, MO, 135
Whiteley's Mills, AR, 46
Whitemarsh Island, GA, 63, 64
Whitesburg, AL, 33
Whiteside, FL, 60
Whitesville, FL, 60
White's Bridge, VA, 208
White's Farm, KY, 86
White's Ford, MD, 108
White's Ford, VA, 204
White's Ranch, TX, 188
White's Station, TN, 183, 185
White's Tavern, VA, 213
Whitmore's Mill, AR, 47
Widow Wheeler's, MO, 136
Wiggenton's Mills, VA, 199
Wilcox's Landing, VA, 212
Wild Cat Camp, KY, 88
Wild Cat Mountain, KY, 88
Wild Cat, KY, 85
Wilderness, VA, 208
Wilkesboro, NC, 156
Wilkinson's Cross-Roads, TN, 171, 172
Williamsburg Road, VA, 195
Williamsburg, KY, 90
Williamsburg, VA, 193, 197, 200
Williamsport, LA, 102
Williamsport, MD, 108-110
Williamsport, TN, 169
Williams' Bridge, LA, 97
Willich, August von, 17, 297
Willis Church, VA, 195
Williston, SC, 165
Willow Springs, MS, 118
Willstown Bluff, SC, 162
Willstown, SC, 162
Will's Valley, AL, 34
Wilmington Island, GA, 63
Wilmington, NC, 155
Wilson, Woodrow, 299
Wilson's Creek Pike, TN, 171

Wilson's Creek, MO, 127
Wilson's Gap, TN, 168
Wilson's Landing, LA, 101
Wilson's Plantation, LA, 100
Wilson's Store, SC, 165
Wilson's Wharf, VA, 209
Winchester, KY, 91
Winchester, TN, 168, 176, 177, 179, 183
Winchester, VA, 192, 194, 196, 198, 200, 202, 206-208, 213, 214, 216
Windsor, NC, 154
Windsor, VA, 199, 200
Winfield, NC, 153
Winfield, WV, 229
Winston's Gap, AL, 35
Winter's Gap, TN, 177
Winton, NC, 151
Wire Bridge, WV, 228
Wisconsin Ranch, CO, 54
Wise's Cross-Roads, NC, 153
Witherspoon, Reese, 299
Wolf Creek Bridge, TN, 170
Wolf Creek, AR, 46
Wolf Creek, WV, 223
Wolf River Bridge, TN, 180
Wolf River, KY, 92
Wolf River, TN, 168
Wolftown, VA, 196
Wolf's Creek, MS, 115
Wolf's Plantation, SC, 165
Womack, Lee Ann, 299
women, 2, 3, 239
Wood Grove, VA, 212
Wood Lake, MN, 113
Wood Springs, TN, 169
Wood, Leonard, 52
Woodall's Bridge, AL, 35
Woodburn, KY, 87, 90
Woodbury Pike, TN, 174, 183
Woodbury, KY, 85
Woodbury, TN, 169, 173-175, 183
Woodsonville, KY, 87
Woodstock, VA, 194, 206, 214, 217
Woodville, AL, 33
Woodville, MS, 124
Woodville, TN, 170
Woodville, VA, 204, 206

Worsham's Creek, MS, 117
Worthington, WV, 222
Worthington's Landing, AR, 47
wounding, 186
Wright County, MO, 138
Wrightsville, PA, 159
writing, 3, 17, 21, 299
Wyatt, MS, 121, 122
Wyerman's Mills, VA, 207
Wyoming, 5, 6, 29
Wyoming Court House, WV, 224
Wyse Fork, NC, 155
Wytheville, VA, 209, 216, 218
Yankee (U.S.S. tugboat), 191
Yankee myth, 2, 239
Yankees, 23, 189
Yankeetown, TN, 179, 180
Yazoo City, MS, 121, 123
Yazoo Pass, MS, 117
Yazoo River, MS, 117, 122, 123
Yellow Bayou, LA, 101
Yellow Creek, MO, 132
Yellow Creek, TN, 175, 176
Yellow House, VA, 213
Yellow Medicine, MN, 113
Yellow Tavern, VA, 209
Yellville, AR, 42, 49
Yocknapatalfa River, MS, 117
Yocum Creek, MO, 134
Yorktown Road, VA, 193
Yorktown, VA, 193, 202
Yorkville, TN, 173
Young, Bennett H., 19
Young's Cross-Roads, NC, 152
Young's Point, LA, 97
Zoar Church, VA, 200
Zollicoffer, TN, 177, 178
Zuni, VA, 194, 197, 198

Confederate Colonel Ambrosio Jose Gonzales, Confederate States Infantry Regiment, one of the 60,000 Latin-Americans who served in the C.S. military.

Second Battle of Fort Fisher.

Union prisoners at Libby Prison, Richmond, VA., 1863. The man reading in bed at far right is Union General August von Willich, a student of Karl Marx, head of a radical labor party, a communist who fought in the European socialist revolution of 1848, and a supporter of Abraham Lincoln. During Lincoln's War he was present on the fields of Shiloh, Perryville, Chickamauga, and Murfreesboro.

Battle of Baton Rouge.

Confederate General William Mahone, Sixth Virginia Infantry Regiment and Confederate States Infantry Regiment, 1866.

MEET THE AUTHOR

NEO-VICTORIAN SCHOLAR LOCHLAINN SEABROOK, a descendant of the families of Alexander Hamilton Stephens, John Singleton Mosby, Edmund Winchester Rucker, and William Giles Harding, is a 7th generation Kentuckian and one of the most prolific and widely read writers in the world today. Known by literary critics as the "new Shelby Foote," the "American Robert Graves," the "Southern Joseph Campbell," and by his fans as the "Voice of the Traditional South," he is a recipient of the United Daughters of the Confederacy's prestigious Jefferson Davis Historical Gold Medal. A lifelong writer, the Sons of Confederate Veterans member has authored and edited books ranging in topics from history, politics, science, religion, astronomy, military, and biography, to nature, music, humor, gastronomy, alternative health, genealogy, and the paranormal; books that his readers describe as "game changers," "transformative," and "life altering."

One of the world's most popular living historians, he is a 17th generation Southerner of Appalachian heritage who descends from dozens of patriotic Revolutionary War soldiers and Confederate soldiers from Kentucky, Tennessee, North Carolina, and Virginia. Also a history, wildlife, and nature preservationist, the well-respected polymath began life as a child prodigy, later transforming into an archetypal Renaissance Man. Besides being an accomplished and esteemed author, historian, biographer, creative, and Bible authority, the influential litterateur is also a Kentucky Colonel, eagle scout, screenwriter, nature, wildlife, and landscape photographer and videographer, artist, graphic designer, genealogist, former history museum docent, and a former ranch hand, zookeeper, and wrangler. A songwriter (of some 3,000 songs in a dozen genres), he is also a film composer, multi-instrument musician, vocalist, session player, and music producer who has worked and performed with some of Nashville's top musicians and singers.

Currently Seabrook is the author and editor of nearly 100 adult and children's books (totaling some 29,000 pages and 15,000,000 words) that have earned him accolades from around the globe. His works, which have sold on every continent except Antarctica, have introduced hundreds of thousands to vital facts that have been left out of our mainstream books. He has been endorsed internationally by leading experts, museum curators, award-winning historians, bestselling authors, celebrities, filmmakers, noted scientists, well regarded educators, TV show hosts and producers, renowned military artists, venerable heritage organizations, and distinguished academicians of all races, creeds, and colors.

Of northern, western, and central European ancestry, he is the 6th great-grandson of the Earl of Oxford and a descendant of European royalty through his Kentucky father and West Virginia mother. His modern day cousins include: Johnny Cash, Elvis Presley, Lisa Marie Presley, Billy Ray and Miley Cyrus, Patty Loveless, Tim McGraw, Lee Ann Womack, Dolly Parton, Pat Boone, Naomi, Wynonna, and Ashley Judd, Ricky Skaggs, the Sunshine Sisters, Martha Carson, Chet Atkins, Patrick J. Buchanan, Cindy Crawford, Bertram Thomas Combs (Kentucky's 50th governor), Edith Bolling (second wife of President Woodrow Wilson), Andy Griffith, Riley Keough, George C. Scott, Robert Duvall, Reese Witherspoon, Lee Marvin, Rebecca Gayheart, and Tom Cruise.

A constitutionalist, avid outdoorsman, and gun rights advocate, Seabrook is the author of the international blockbuster, *Everything You Were Taught About the Civil War is Wrong, Ask a Southerner!* He lives with his wife and family in the magnificent Rocky Mountains, heart of the American West, where you will find him hiking, filming, and writing.

For more information on author Mr. Seabrook visit
LochlainnSeabrook.com

Second Battle of Corinth.

Battle of Savage's Station.

C.S. President Jefferson Davis, along with 49 Confederate generals. How many can you identify?

If you enjoyed this book you will be interested in Colonel Seabrook's popular related titles:

- ABRAHAM LINCOLN WAS A LIBERAL, JEFFERSON DAVIS WAS A CONSERVATIVE
- EVERYTHING YOU WERE TAUGHT ABOUT THE CIVIL WAR IS WRONG, ASK A SOUTHERNER!
- ALL WE ASK IS TO BE LET ALONE: THE SOUTHERN SECESSION FACT BOOK
- EVERYTHING YOU WERE TAUGHT ABOUT AMERICAN SLAVERY IS WRONG, ASK A SOUTHERNER!
- CONFEDERATE FLAG FACTS: WHAT EVERY AMERICAN SHOULD KNOW ABOUT DIXIE'S SOUTHERN CROSS
- LINCOLN'S WAR: THE REAL CAUSE, THE REAL WINNER, THE REAL LOSER

Available from Sea Raven Press and wherever fine books are sold

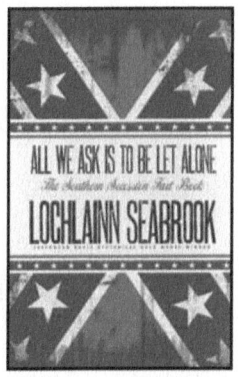

ALL OF OUR BOOK COVERS ARE AVAILABLE AS 11" X 17" COLOR POSTERS, SUITABLE FOR FRAMING

SeaRavenPress.com

www.ingramcontent.com/pod-product-compliance
Lightning Source LLC
Chambersburg PA
CBHW030231170426
43201CB00006B/174